10

Takuma Morishige

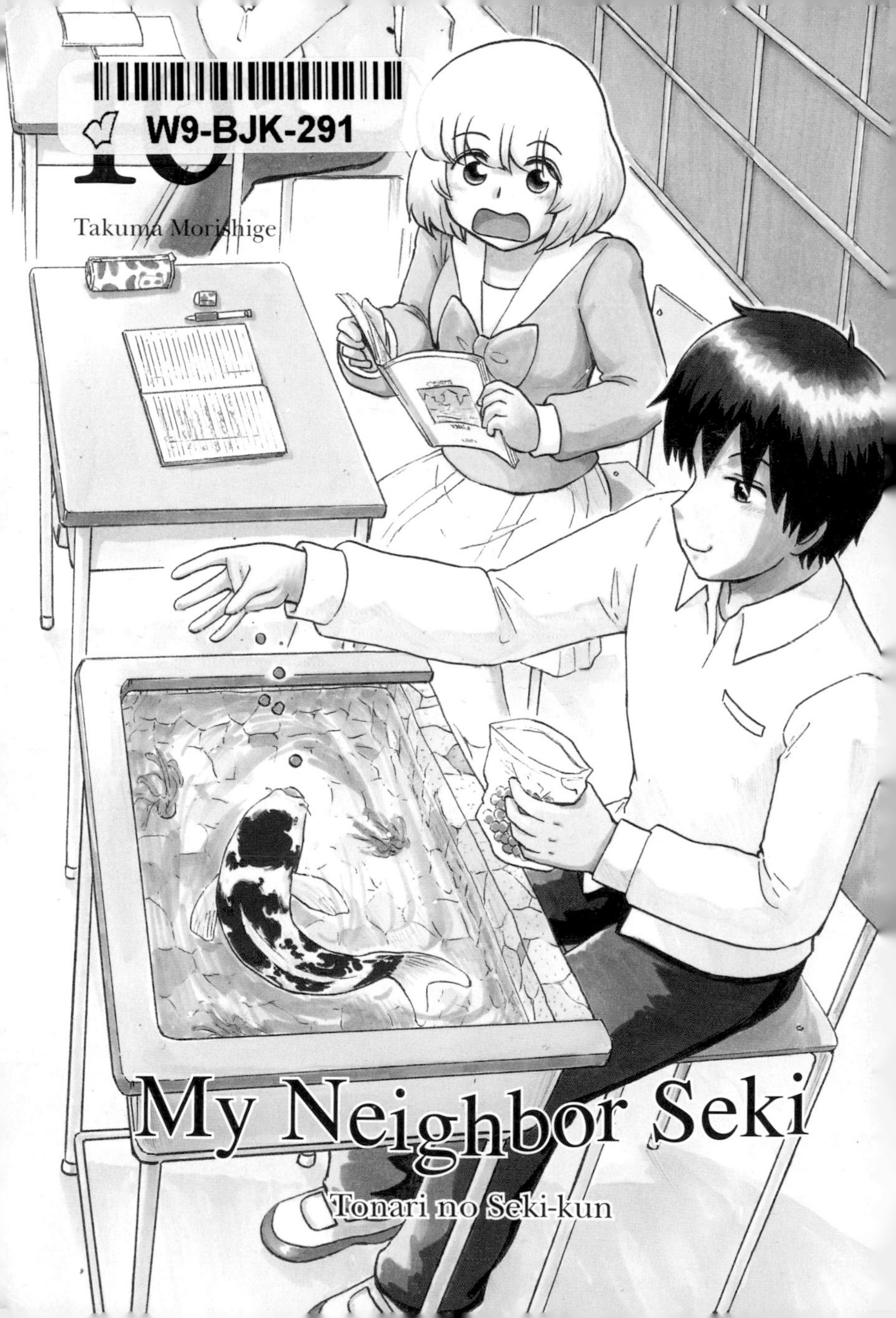

My Neighbor Seki

Tonari no Seki-kun

Schedule

My
Neighbor
Seki

10

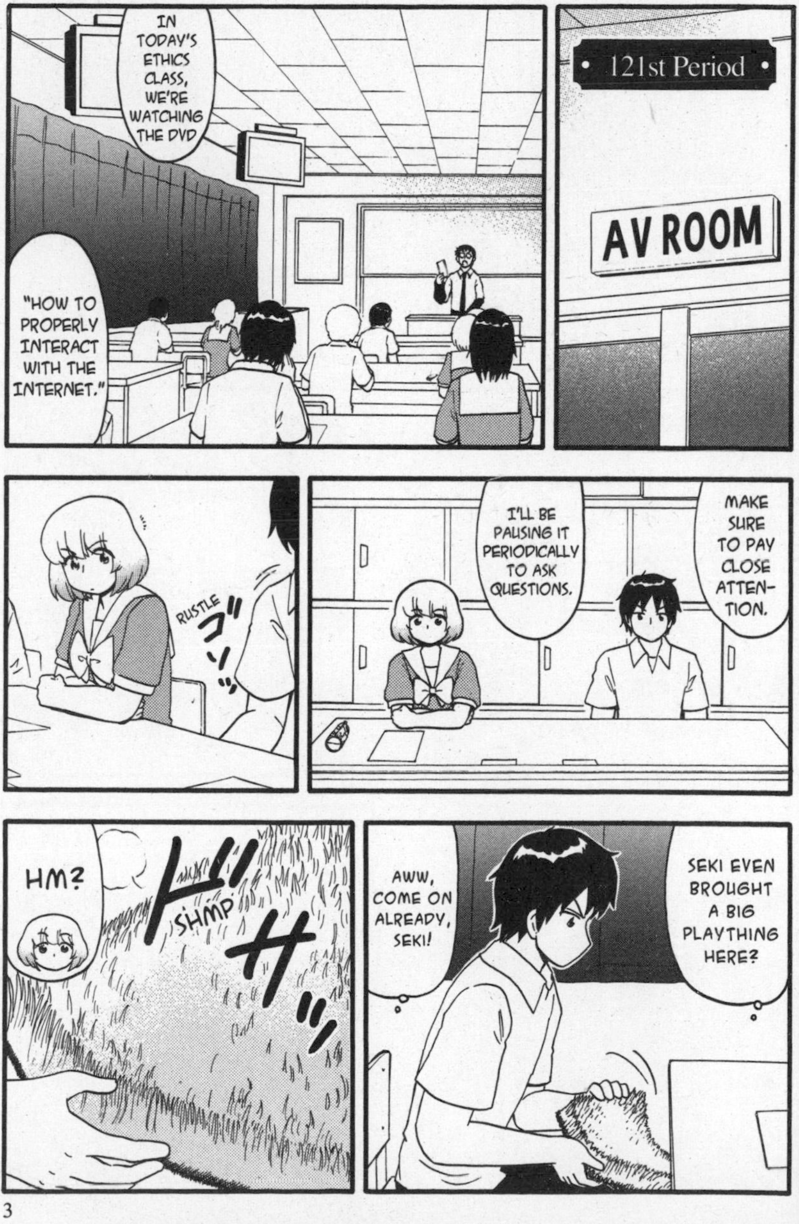
121st Period
AV ROOM
IN TODAY'S ETHICS CLASS, WE'RE WATCHING THE DVD
"HOW TO PROPERLY INTERACT WITH THE INTERNET."
MAKE SURE TO PAY CLOSE ATTENTION.
I'LL BE PAUSING IT PERIODICALLY TO ASK QUESTIONS.
RUSTLE
SEKI EVEN BROUGHT A BIG PLAYTHING HERE?
AWW, COME ON ALREADY, SEKI!
SHMP
HM?

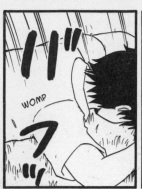

GRASS?
IS THAT REAL GRASS? AND WHAT IS HE GONNA USE IT FOR?
WOMP
ゴロン
ROLL
HUH?
IT'S JUST TO SPRAWL OUT ON?!
ROLL
ゴロンッ
I MEAN, SURE, IT FEELS GOOD TO LIE ON GRASS, BUT...
IT SEEMS A BIT DULL FOR ONE OF SEKI'S GAMES.
OKAY, LET'S GET TO IT.
パッ
PCHK
OH!

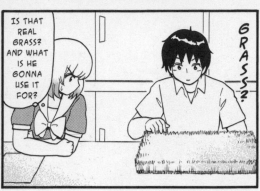

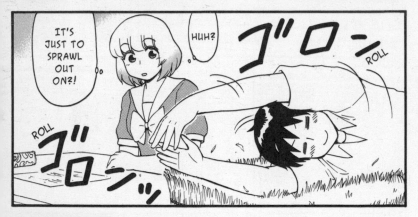

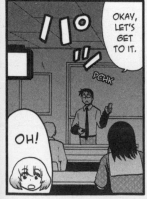

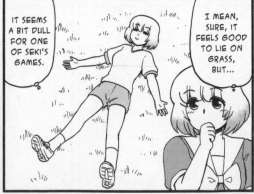

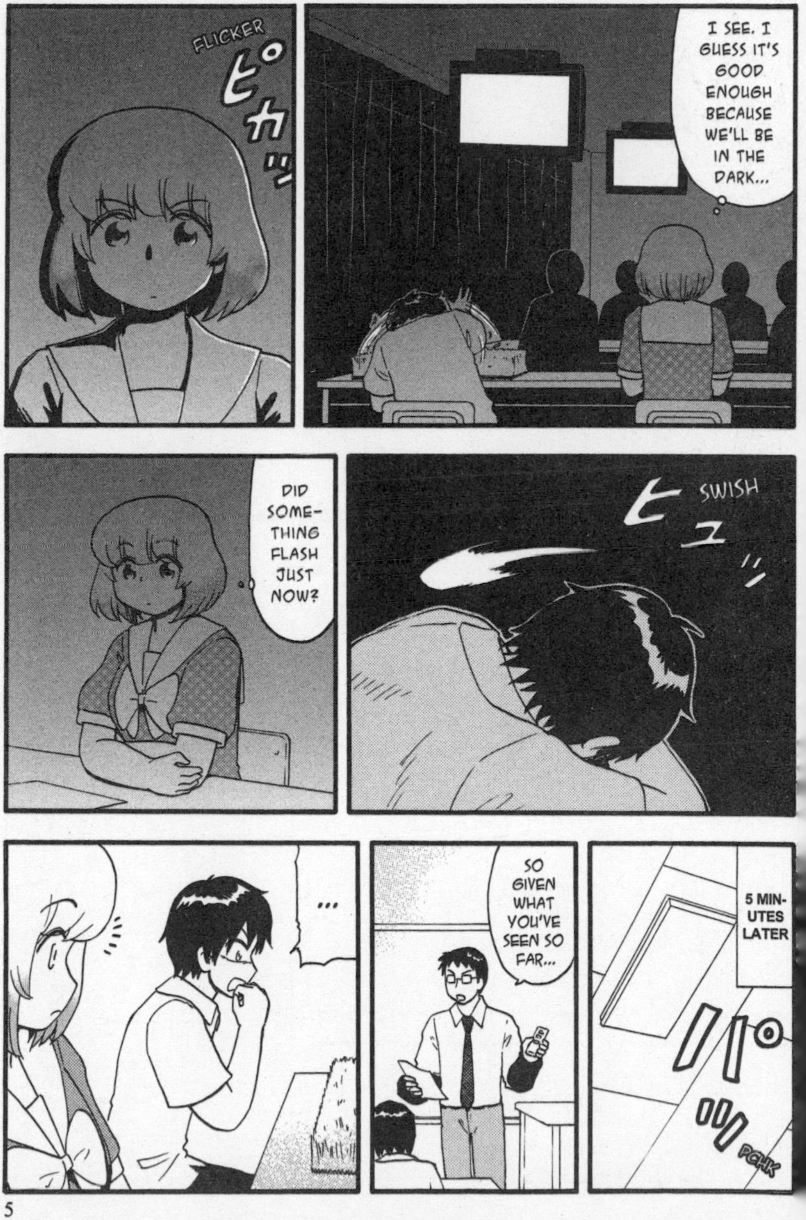
I SEE. I GUESS IT'S GOOD ENOUGH BECAUSE WE'LL BE IN THE DARK...
FLICKER
SWISH
DID SOMETHING FLASH JUST NOW?
5 MINUTES LATER
PCHK
SO GIVEN WHAT YOU'VE SEEN SO FAR...
...

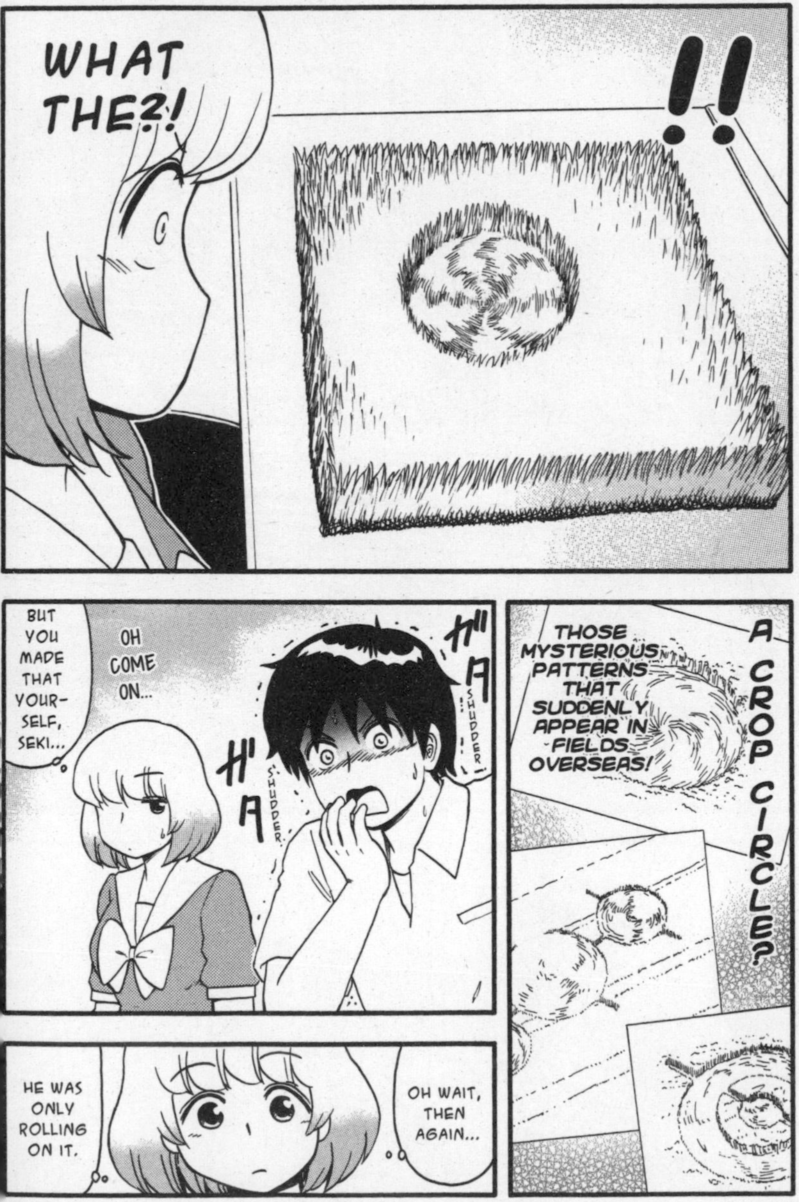
!!
WHAT THE?!
A CROP CIRCLE?
THOSE MYSTERIOUS PATTERNS THAT SUDDENLY APPEAR IN FIELDS OVERSEAS!
SHUDDER
SHUDDER
OH COME ON...
BUT YOU MADE THAT YOURSELF, SEKI...
OH WAIT, THEN AGAIN...
HE WAS ONLY ROLLING ON IT.

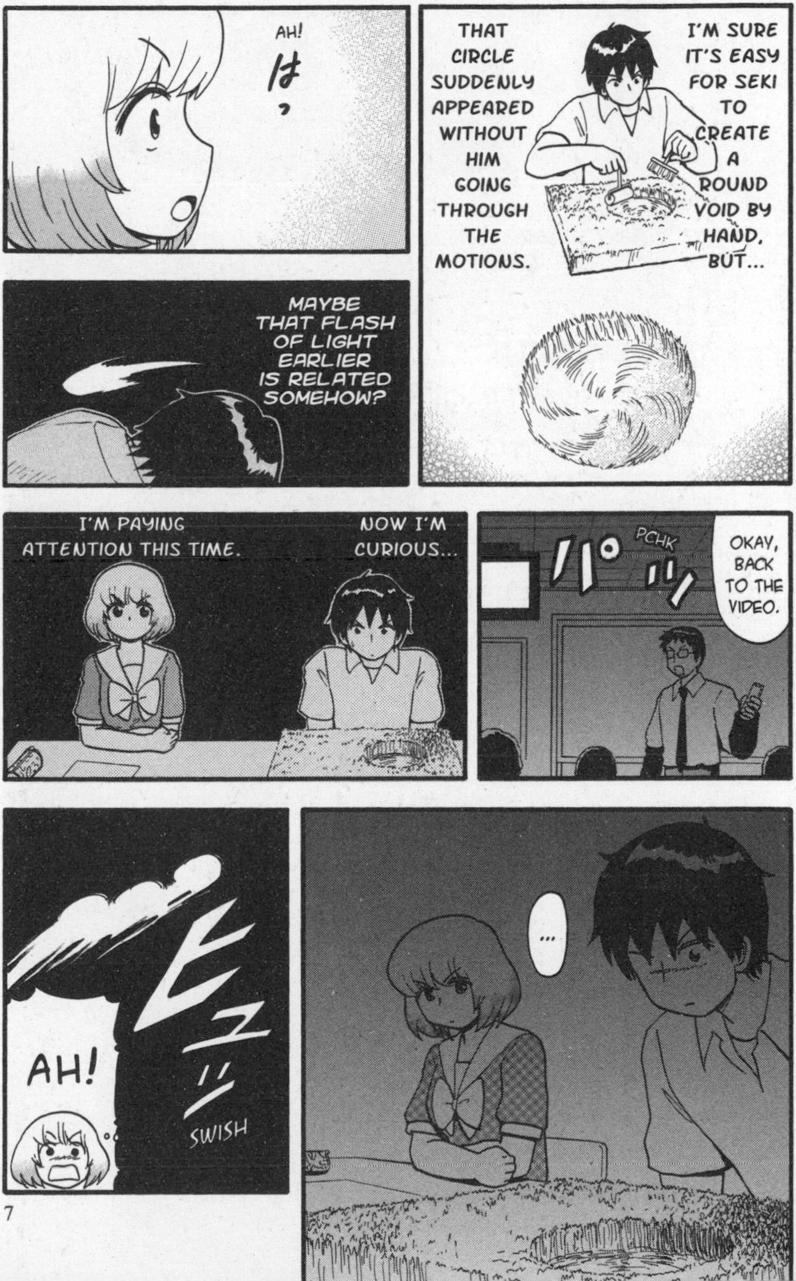
I'M SURE IT'S EASY FOR SEKI TO CREATE A ROUND VOID BY HAND, BUT...
THAT CIRCLE SUDDENLY APPEARED WITHOUT HIM GOING THROUGH THE MOTIONS.
AH!
はっ
MAYBE THAT FLASH OF LIGHT EARLIER IS RELATED SOMEHOW?
OKAY, BACK TO THE VIDEO.
PCHK
NOW I'M CURIOUS...
I'M PAYING ATTENTION THIS TIME.
...
ヒュッ
SWISH
AH!

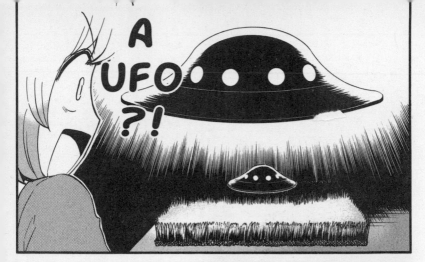

A UFO ?!
THAT LIGHT WAS A UFO?
WHY IS A UFO SHOWING UP DURING CLASS?!
YOU KNOW, I'VE HEARD THAT CROP CIRCLES ARE IMPRESSIONS MADE BY UFO LANDINGS.
SO WAS THAT CROP CIRCLE MADE BY THIS UFO?!
O-OF COURSE IT'S NOT A REAL UFO!
I'M SURE SEKI'S JUST DANGLING A TOY FROM A POLE OR SOMETHING.
I'LL EXPOSE YOUR SCAM!
SHFF
!
SWIP

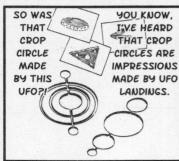

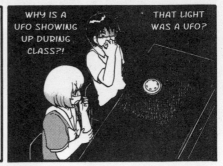

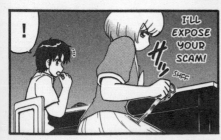

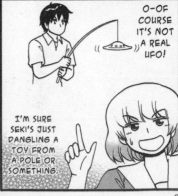

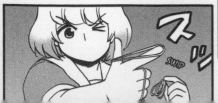

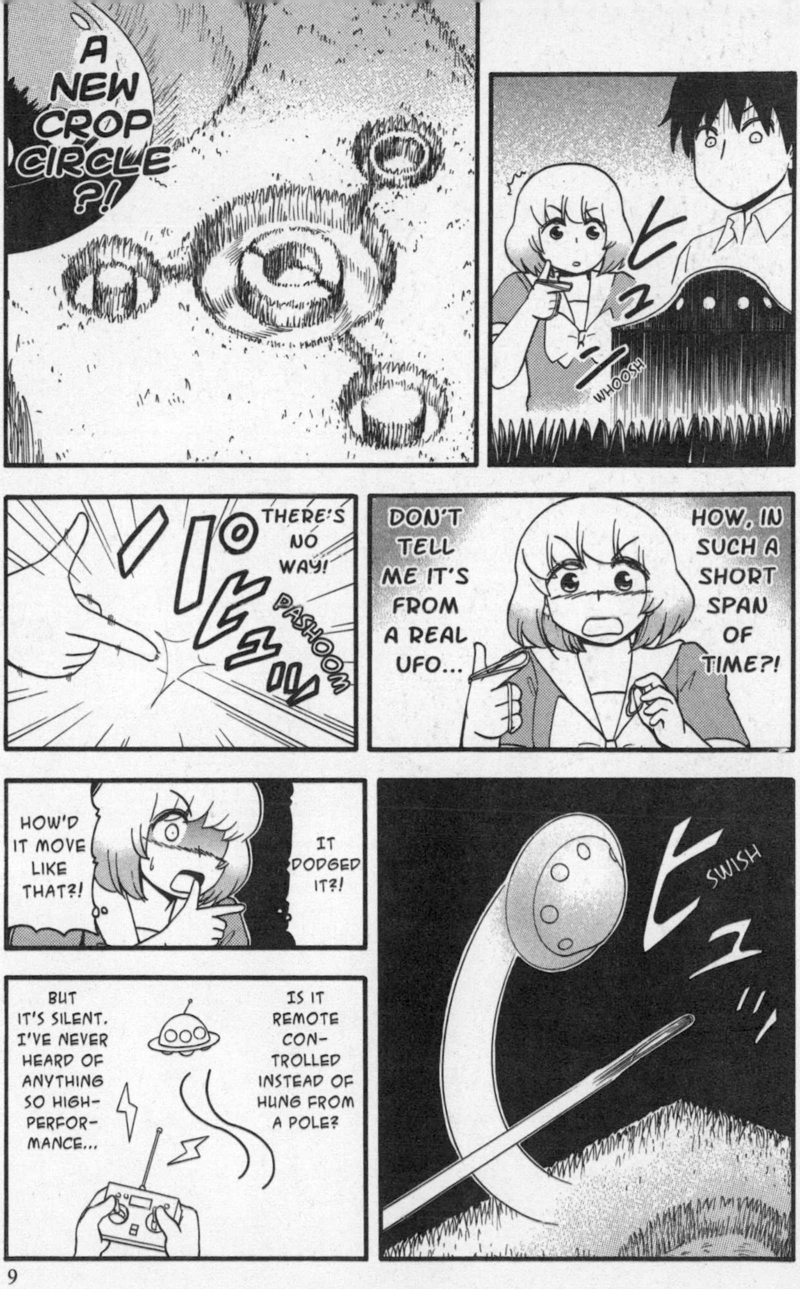
WHOOSH
A NEW CROP CIRCLE ?!
HOW, IN SUCH A SHORT SPAN OF TIME?!
DON'T TELL ME IT'S FROM A REAL UFO...
THERE'S NO WAY!
PASHOOM
SWISH
IT DODGED IT?!
HOW'D IT MOVE LIKE THAT?!
IS IT REMOTE CON-TROLLED INSTEAD OF HUNG FROM A POLE?
BUT IT'S SILENT. I'VE NEVER HEARD OF ANYTHING SO HIGH-PERFOR-MANCE...

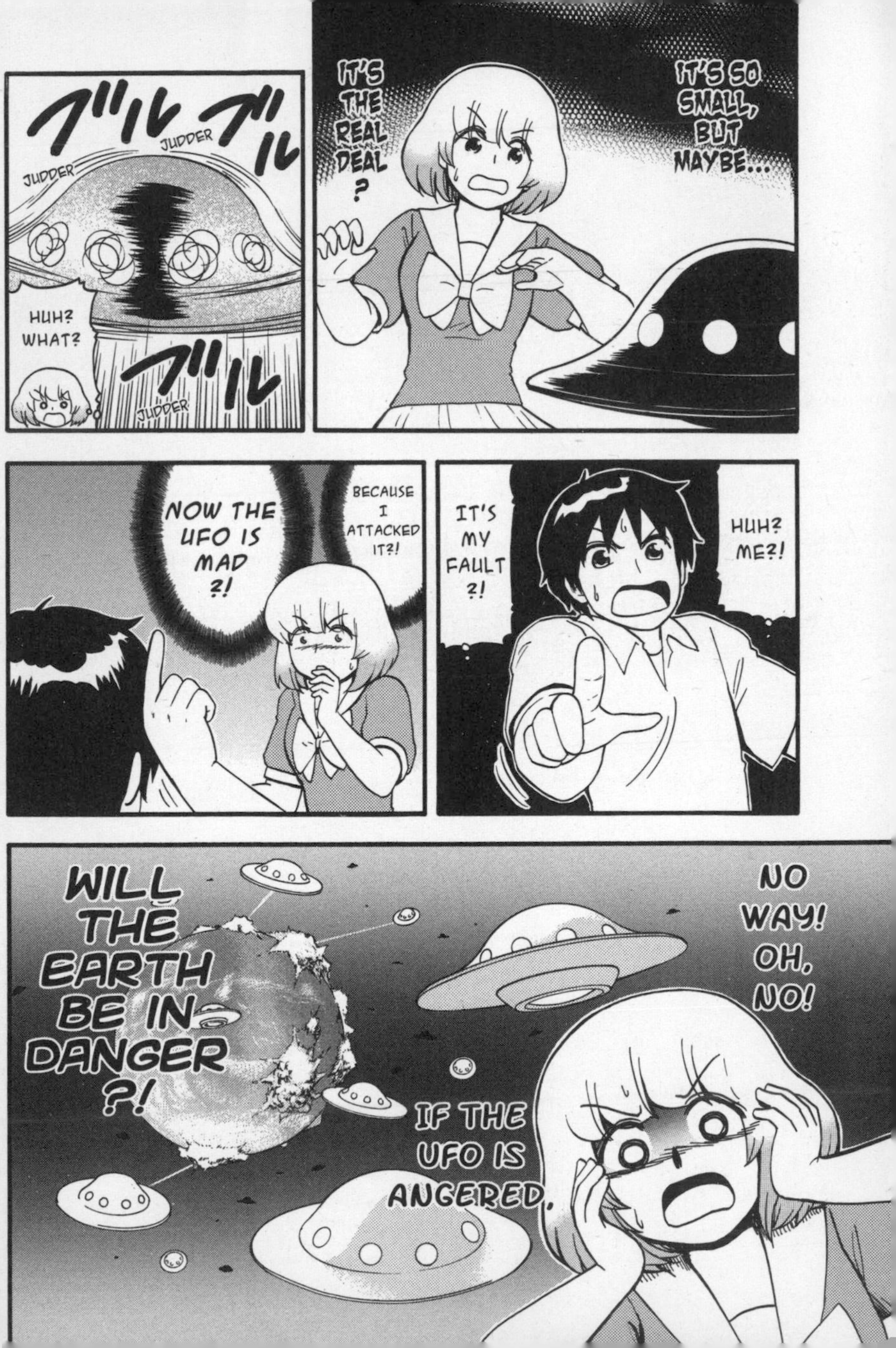
IT'S SO SMALL, BUT MAYBE...
IT'S THE REAL DEAL?
ブルブル
JUDDER
JUDDER
HUH? WHAT?
ブル
JUDDER
HUH? ME?!
IT'S MY FAULT?!
BECAUSE I ATTACKED IT?!
NOW THE UFO IS MAD?!
NO WAY! OH, NO!
IF THE UFO IS ANGERED,
WILL THE EARTH BE IN DANGER?!

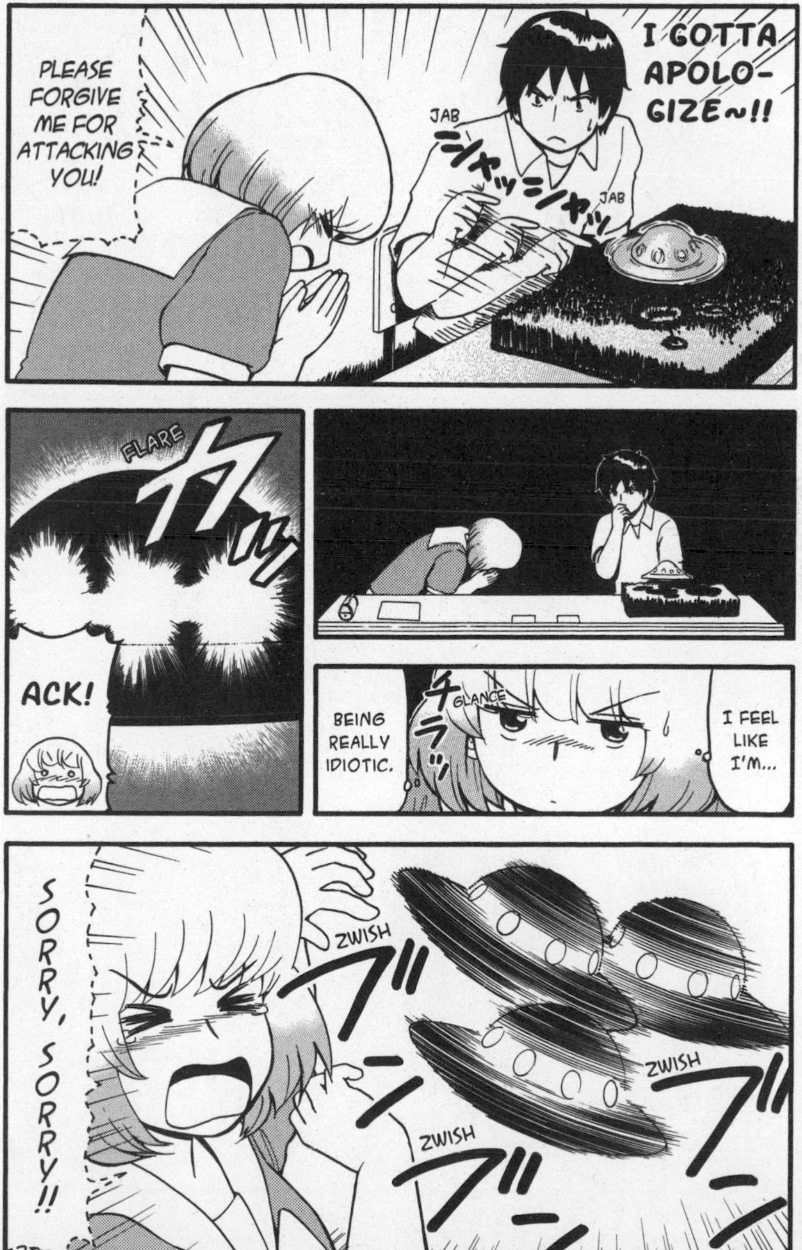
I GOTTA APOLO-GIZE~!!
JAB
JAB
PLEASE FORGIVE ME FOR ATTACKING YOU!
I FEEL LIKE I'M...
GLANCE
BEING REALLY IDIOTIC.
FLARE
ACK!
ZWISH
ZWISH
ZWISH
SORRY, SORRY!!

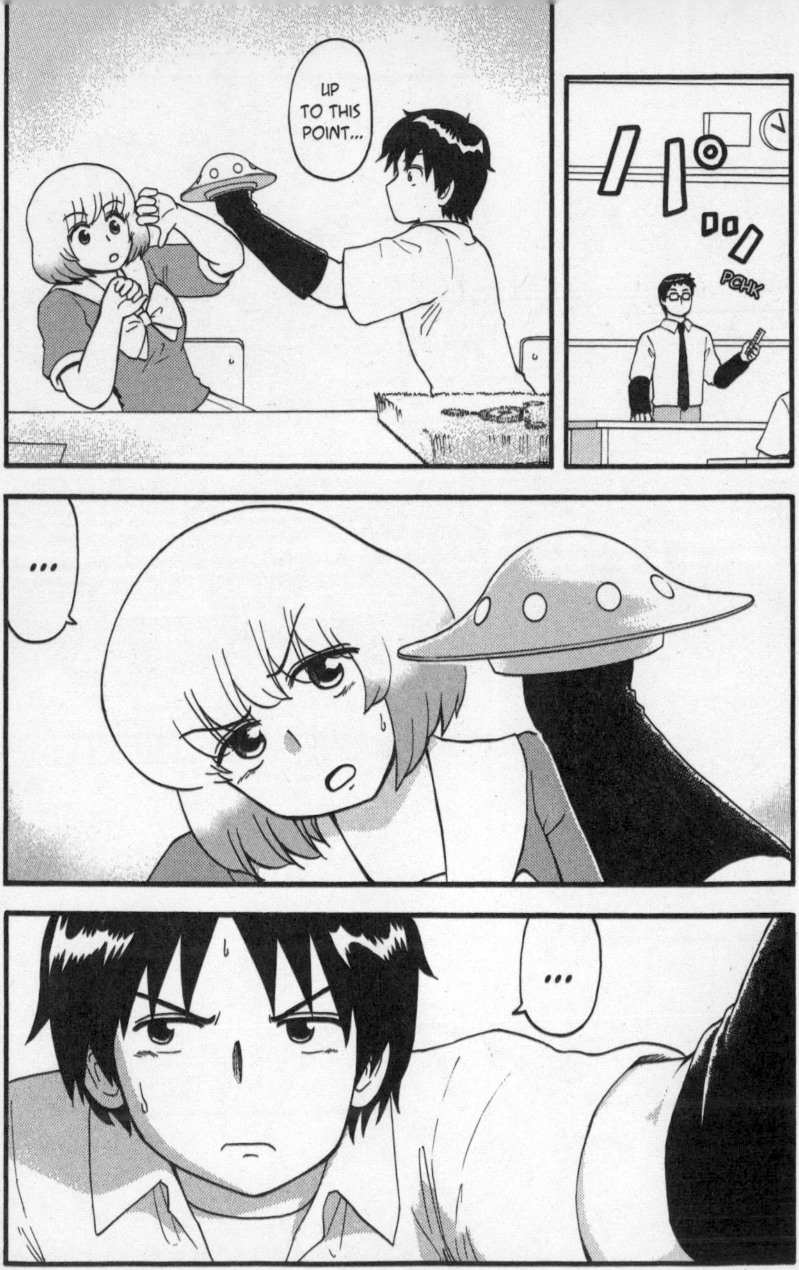
PCHK
UP TO THIS POINT...
...
...

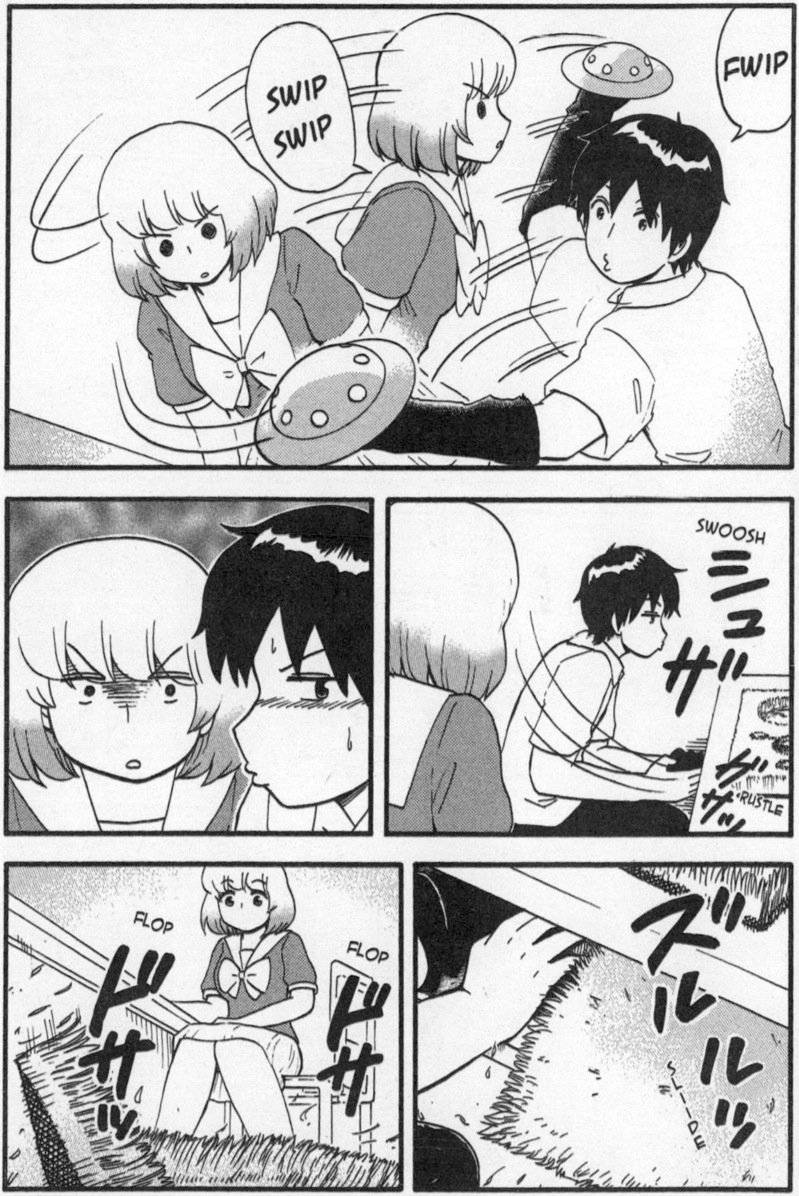
FWIP
SWIP SWIP
SWOOSH
シュザ
ガサッ
RUSTLE
ズルルッ
SLIDE
FLOP
ドサッ
FLOP
ドサッ

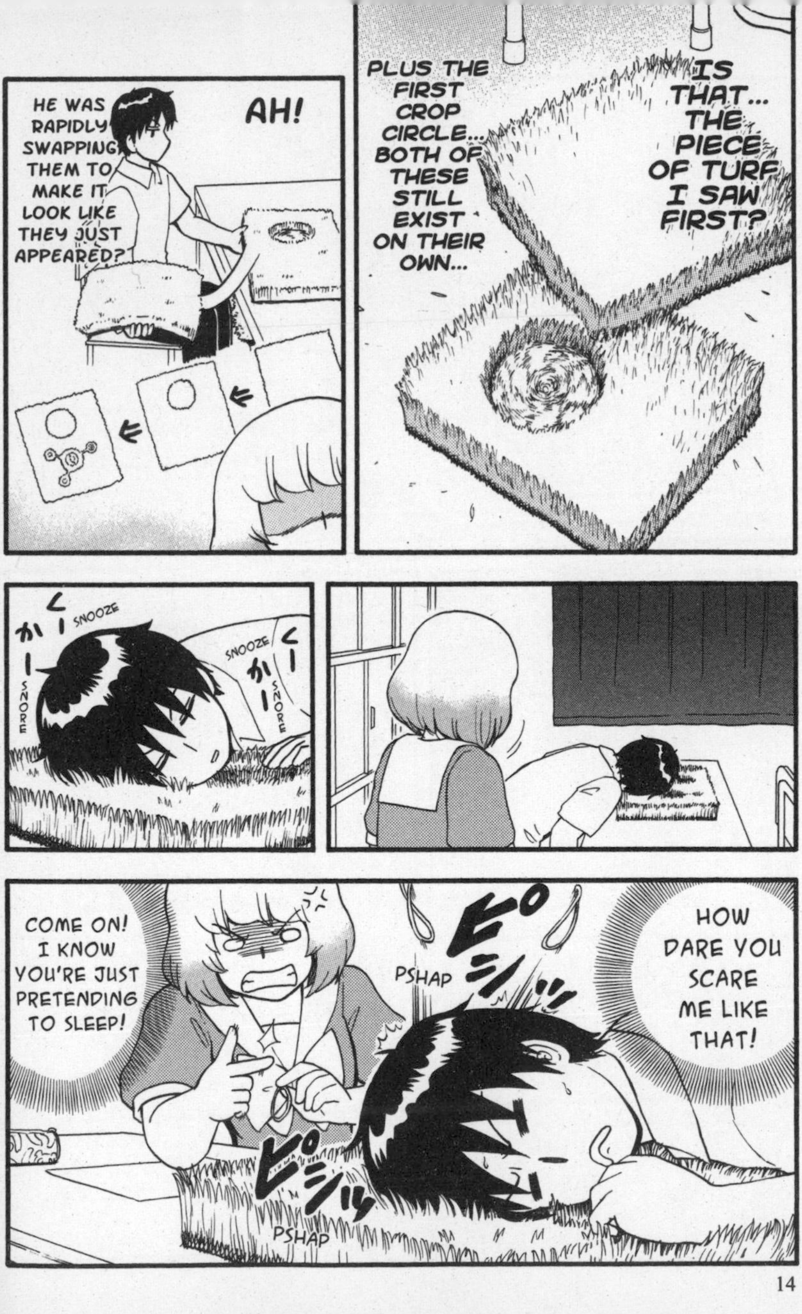
IS THAT... THE PIECE OF TURF I SAW FIRST?
PLUS THE FIRST CROP CIRCLE... BOTH OF THESE STILL EXIST ON THEIR OWN...
AH!
HE WAS RAPIDLY SWAPPING THEM TO MAKE IT LOOK LIKE THEY JUST APPEARED?
くー SNOOZE
かー SNORE
くー SNOOZE
かー SNORE
HOW DARE YOU SCARE ME LIKE THAT!
ピシッ PSHAP
COME ON! I KNOW YOU'RE JUST PRETENDING TO SLEEP!
ピシッ PSHAP

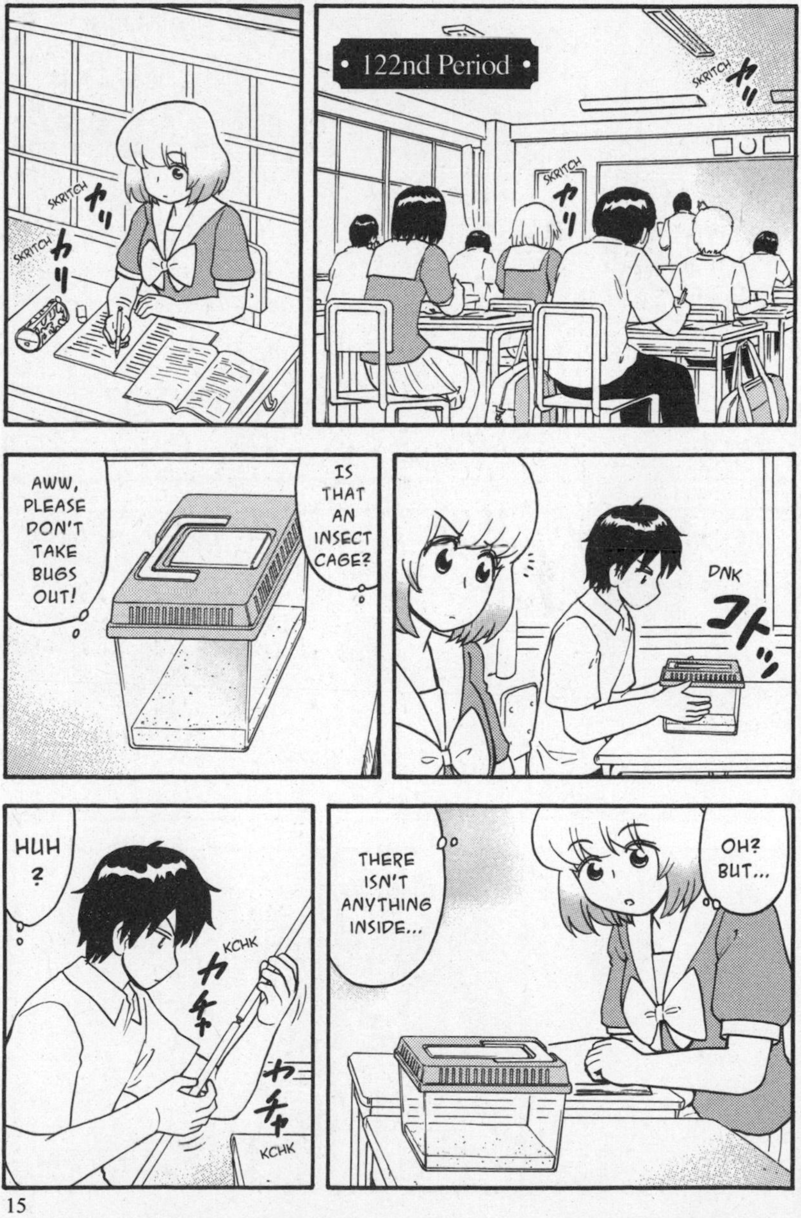
• 122nd Period •
SKRITCH
SKRITCH
SKRITCH
SKRITCH
DNK
IS THAT AN INSECT CAGE?
AWW, PLEASE DON'T TAKE BUGS OUT!
OH? BUT...
THERE ISN'T ANYTHING INSIDE...
HUH?
KCHK
KCHK

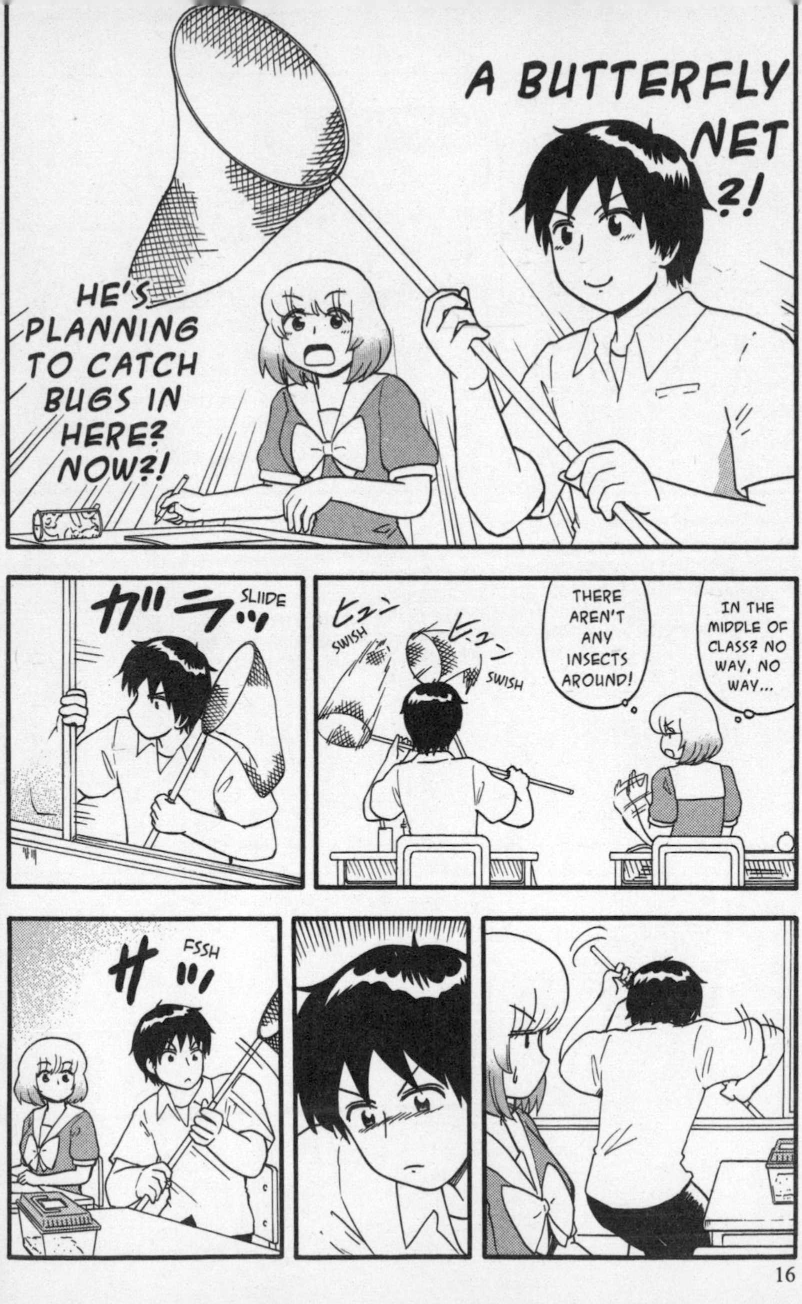
A BUTTERFLY NET ?!
HE'S PLANNING TO CATCH BUGS IN HERE? NOW?!
IN THE MIDDLE OF CLASS? NO WAY, NO WAY...
THERE AREN'T ANY INSECTS AROUND!
ヒュン
SWISH
ヒュン
SWISH
ガラッ
SLIIDE
サッ
FSSH

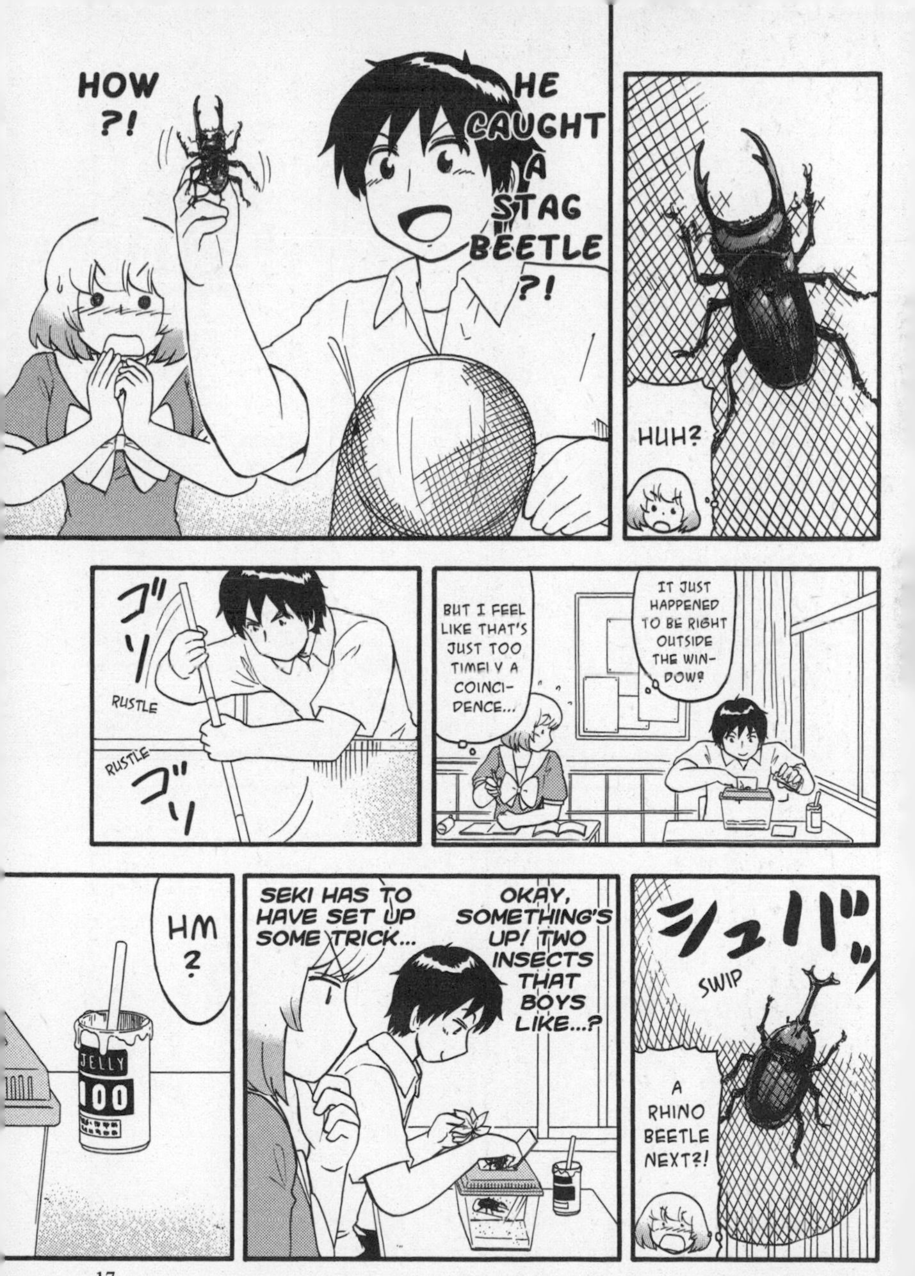
HUH?
HE CAUGHT A STAG BEETLE ?!
HOW ?!
IT JUST HAPPENED TO BE RIGHT OUTSIDE THE WIN-DOW!
BUT I FEEL LIKE THAT'S JUST TOO TIMELY A COINCI-DENCE...
ゴソ
RUSTLE
ゴソ
RUSTLE
シュバッ
SWIP
A RHINO BEETLE NEXT?!
OKAY, SOMETHING'S UP! TWO INSECTS THAT BOYS LIKE...?
SEKI HAS TO HAVE SET UP SOME TRICK...
HM ?
JELLY
100

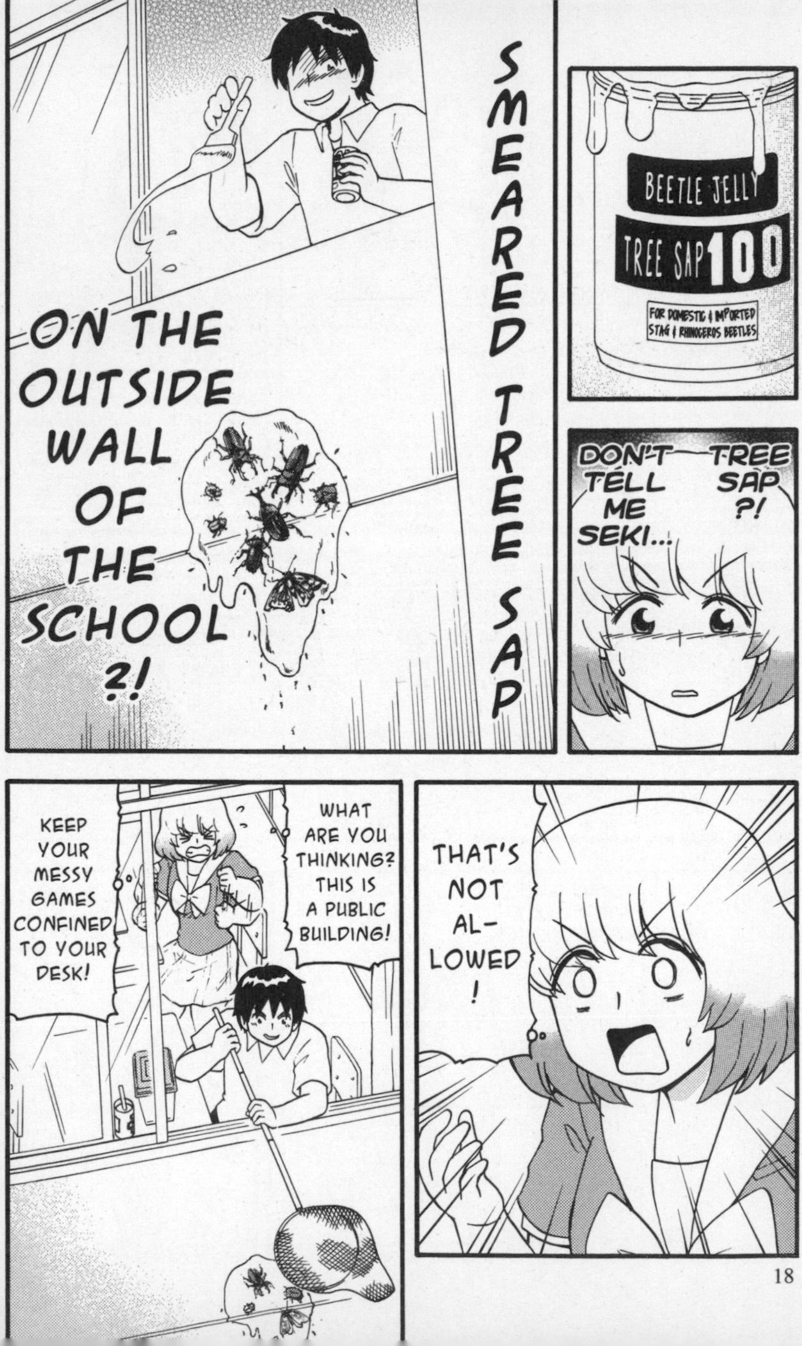
BEETLE JELLY
TREE SAP 100
FOR DOMESTIC & IMPORTED STAG & RHINOCEROS BEETLES
TREE SAP ?!
DON'T TELL ME SEKI...
SMEARED TREE SAP
ON THE OUTSIDE WALL OF THE SCHOOL ?!
THAT'S NOT AL-LOWED!
WHAT ARE YOU THINKING? THIS IS A PUBLIC BUILDING!
KEEP YOUR MESSY GAMES CONFINED TO YOUR DESK!

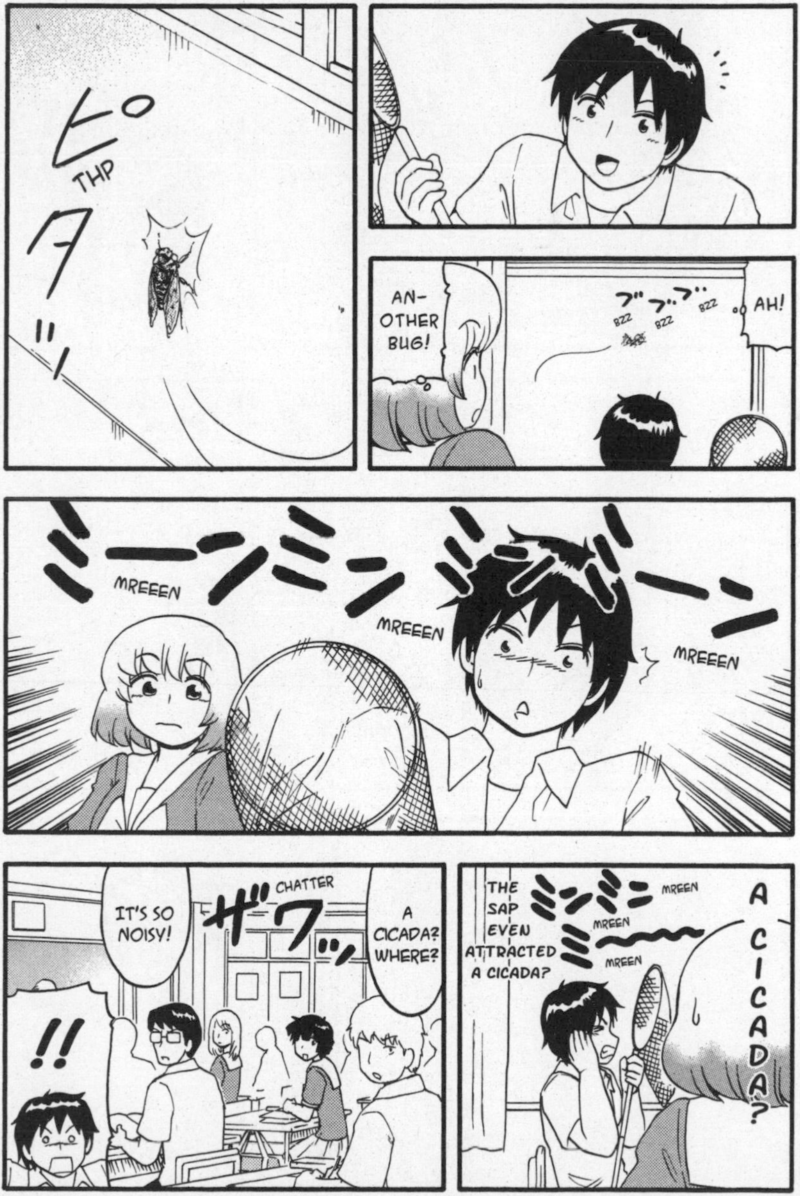
AH!
ブブブ
BZZ BZZ BZZ
AN-OTHER BUG!
ピタッ
THP
ミーンミンミーン
MREEEN
MREEEN
MREEEN
A CICADA?
ミンミンミ〜
MREEN
MREEN
MREEN
THE SAP EVEN ATTRACTED A CICADA?
A CICADA? WHERE?
ザワッ
CHATTER
IT'S SO NOISY!
!!

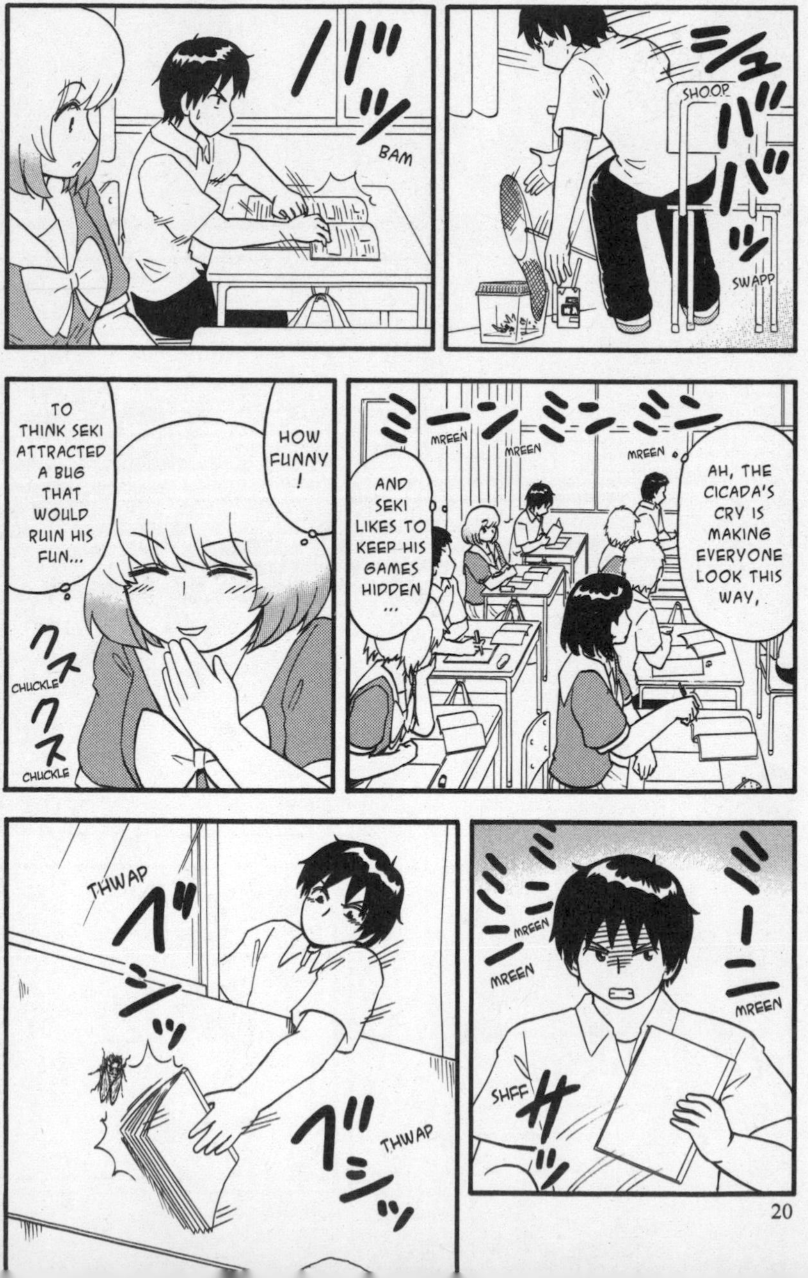
SHOOP
SWAPP
BAM
MREEN
MREEN
MREEN
AH, THE CICADA'S CRY IS MAKING EVERYONE LOOK THIS WAY,
AND SEKI LIKES TO KEEP HIS GAMES HIDDEN ...
HOW FUNNY !
TO THINK SEKI ATTRACTED A BUG THAT WOULD RUIN HIS FUN...
CHUCKLE
CHUCKLE
MREEN
MREEN
MREEN
SHFF
THWAP
THWAP

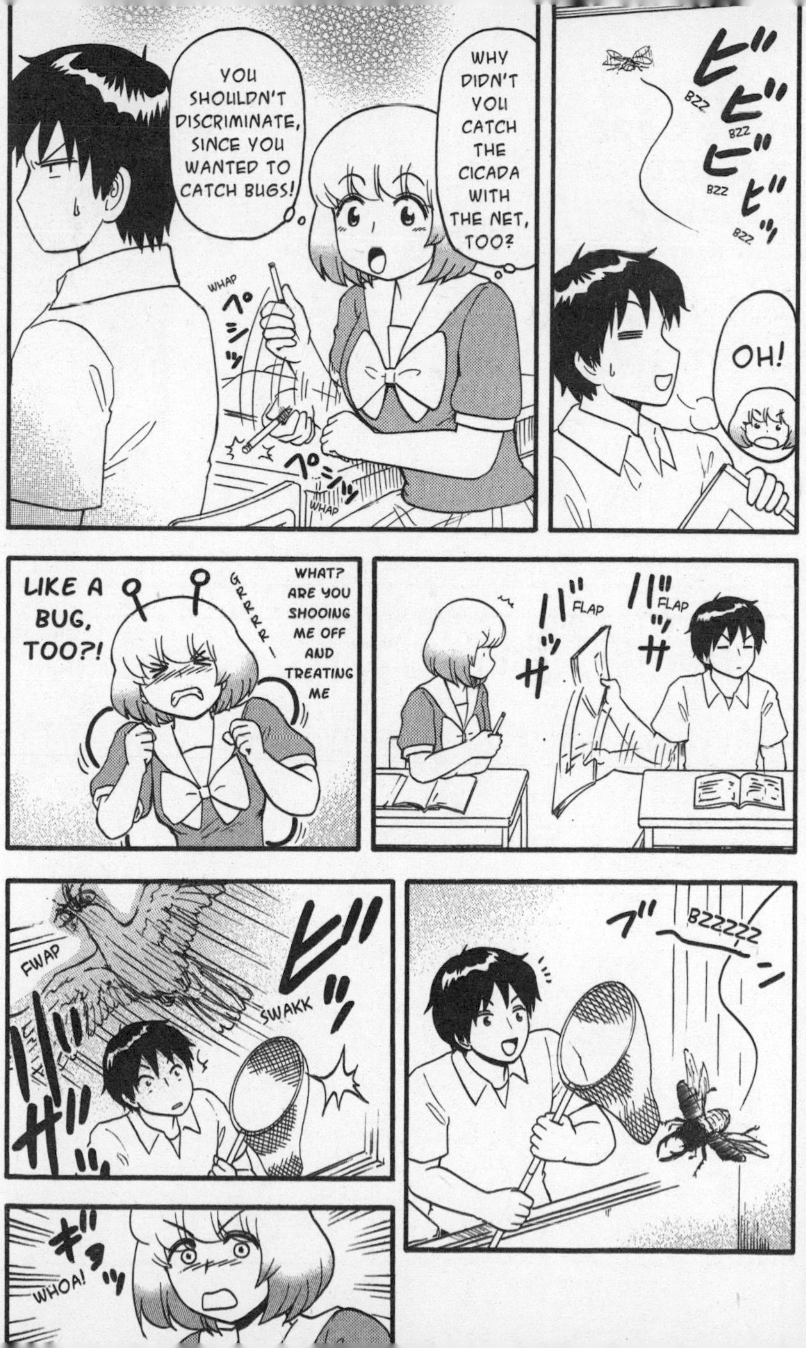
BZZ
BZZ
BZZ
BZZ
OH!
WHY DIDN'T YOU CATCH THE CICADA WITH THE NET, TOO?
YOU SHOULDN'T DISCRIMINATE, SINCE YOU WANTED TO CATCH BUGS!
WHAP
WHAP
FLAP
FLAP
WHAT? ARE YOU SHOOING ME OFF AND TREATING ME
GRRRR!
LIKE A BUG, TOO?!
BZZZZZZ
SWAKK
FWAP
WHOA!

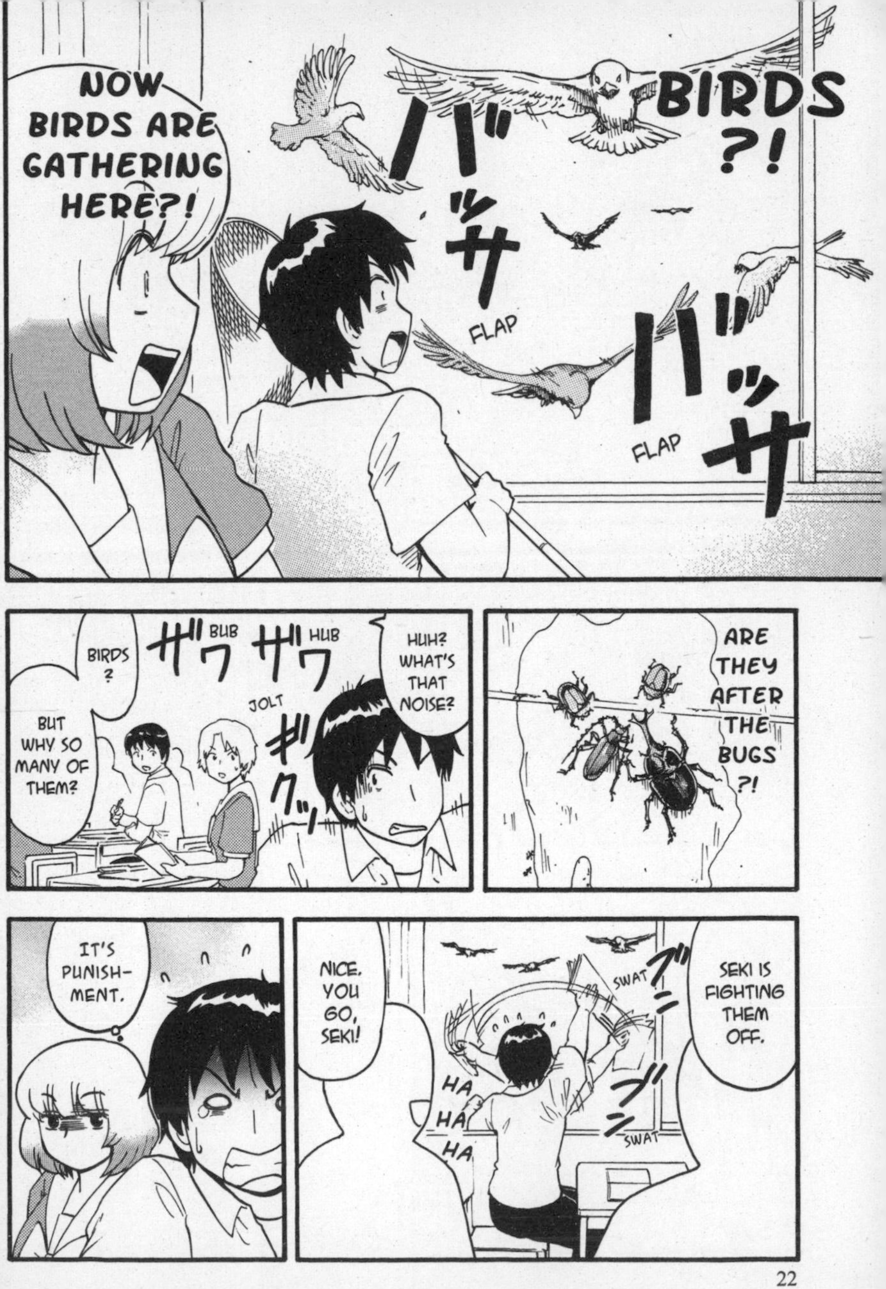
BIRDS ?!
バッサ
FLAP
バッサ
FLAP
NOW BIRDS ARE GATHERING HERE?!
ARE THEY AFTER THE BUGS ?!
HUH? WHAT'S THAT NOISE?
ザワ ザワ
BUB HUB
JOLT
ギクッ
BIRDS ?
BUT WHY SO MANY OF THEM?
SEKI IS FIGHTING THEM OFF.
ブン
SWAT
ブン
SWAT
NICE. YOU GO, SEKI!
HA HA HA
IT'S PUNISH-MENT.

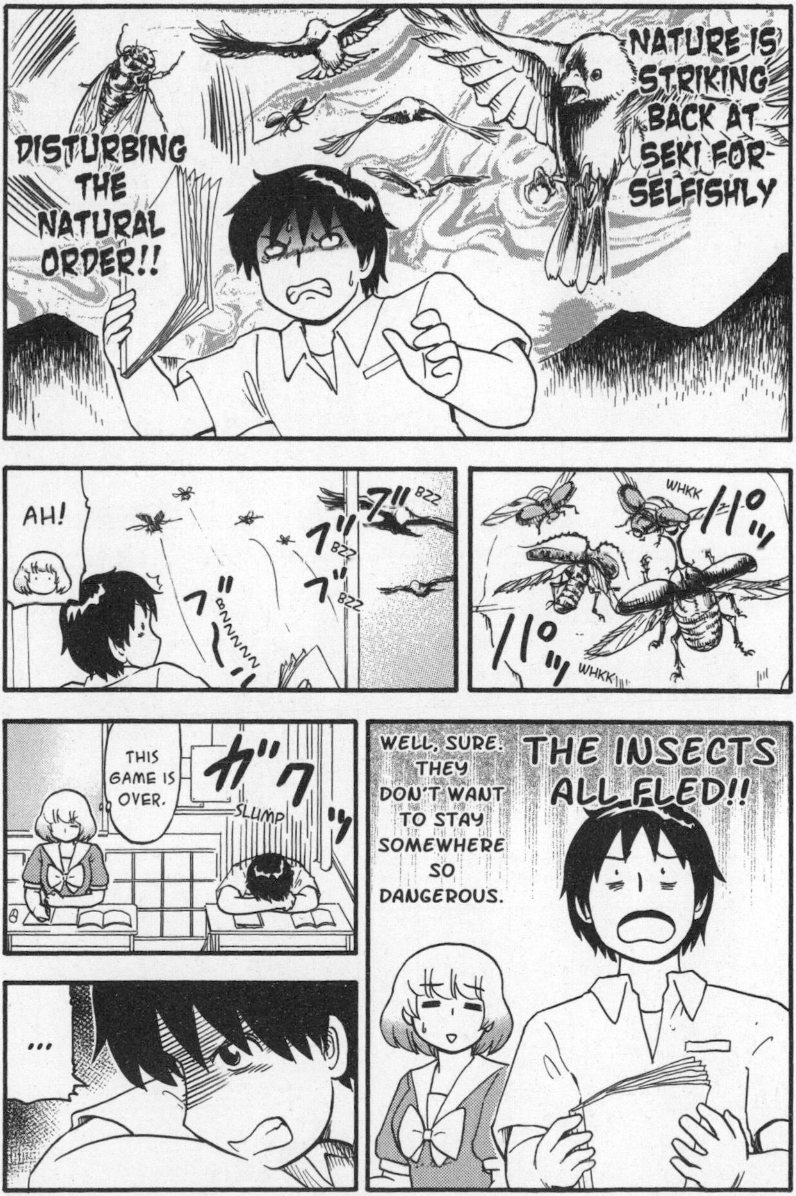
NATURE IS STRIKING BACK AT SEKI FOR SELFISHLY
DISTURBING THE NATURAL ORDER!!
パッ
WHKK
パッ
WHKK
ブブ
BZZ
ブ
BZZ
ブ
BZZ
AH!
ブーン
BNNNNN
THE INSECTS ALL FLED!!
WELL, SURE. THEY DON'T WANT TO STAY SOMEWHERE SO DANGEROUS.
THIS GAME IS OVER.
ガクッ
SLUMP
...

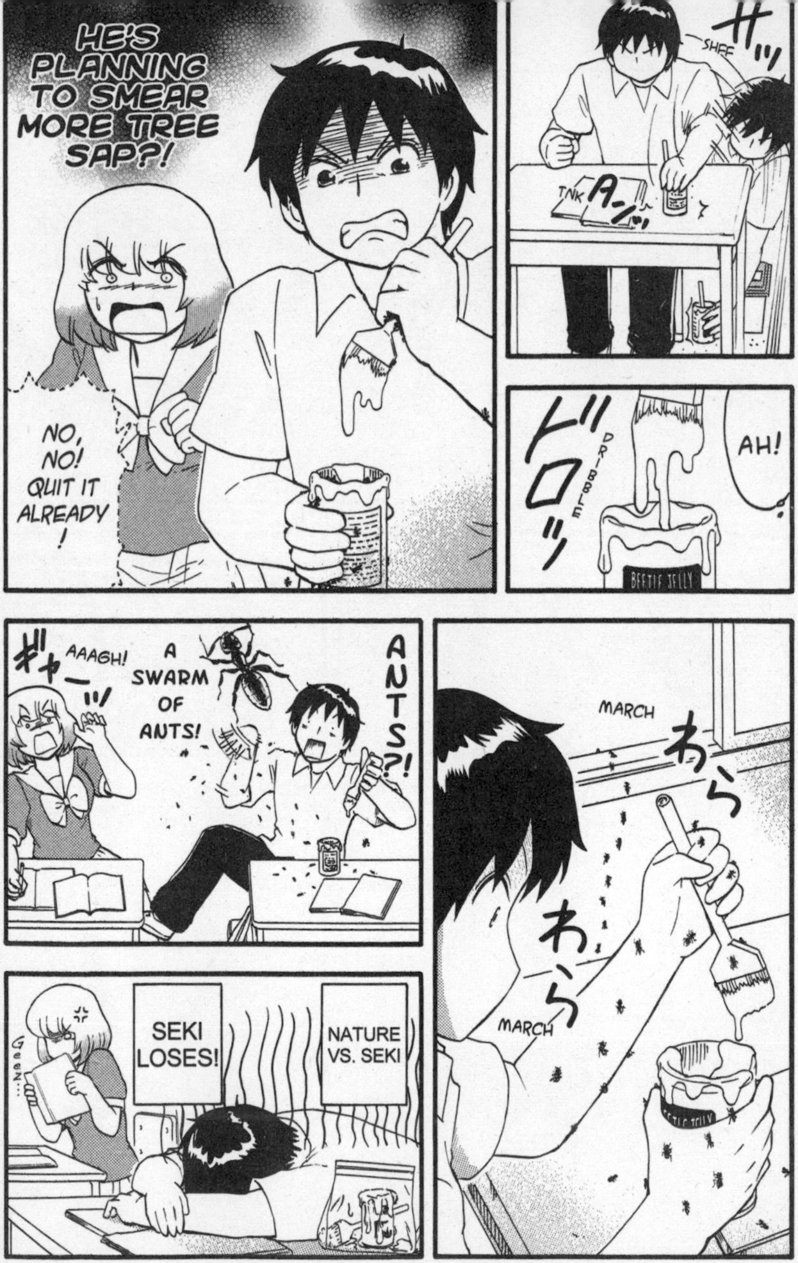
ザッ
SHFF
TNK
ドロッ
DRIBBLE
AH!
HE'S PLANNING TO SMEAR MORE TREE SAP?!
NO, NO! QUIT IT ALREADY!
MARCH
わら
わら
MARCH
ANTS?!
A SWARM OF ANTS!
ギャー
AAAGH!
NATURE VS. SEKI
SEKI LOSES!
Geez...

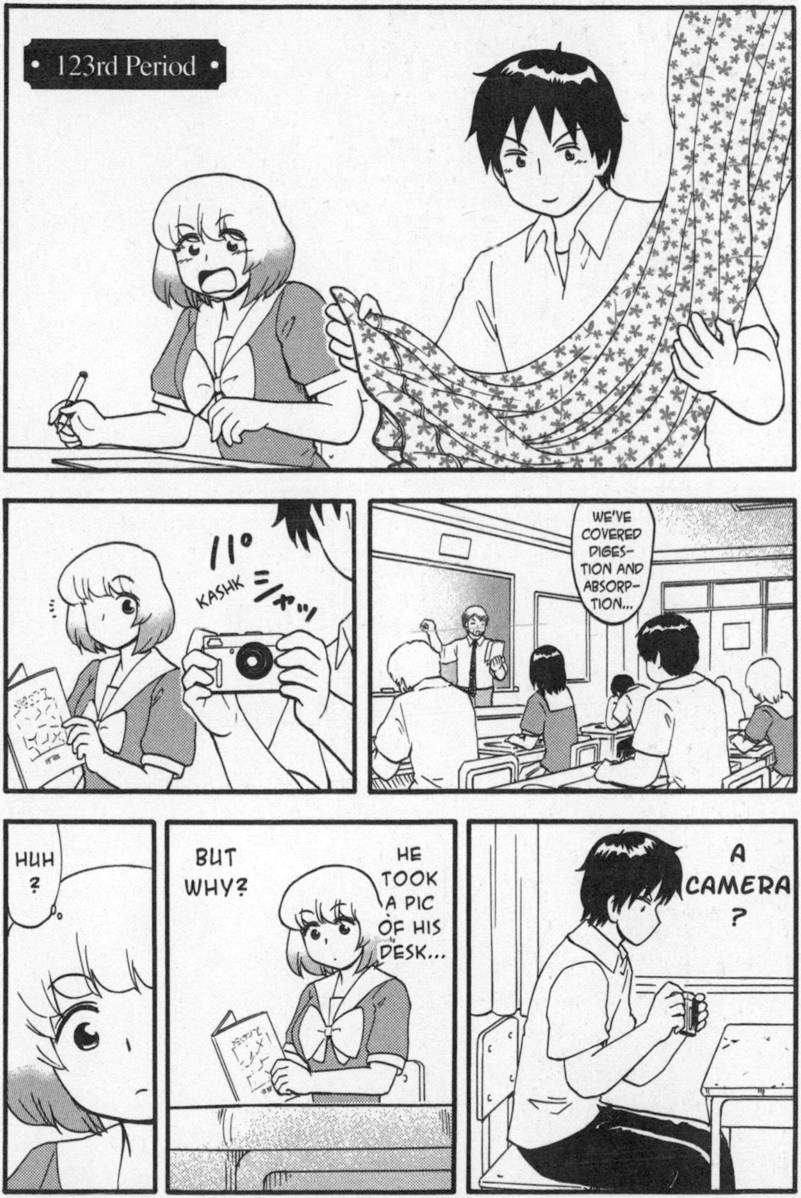
• 123rd Period •
WE'VE COVERED DIGESTION AND ABSORPTION...
パシャッ
KASHK
A CAMERA?
HE TOOK A PIC OF HIS DESK...
BUT WHY?
HUH?

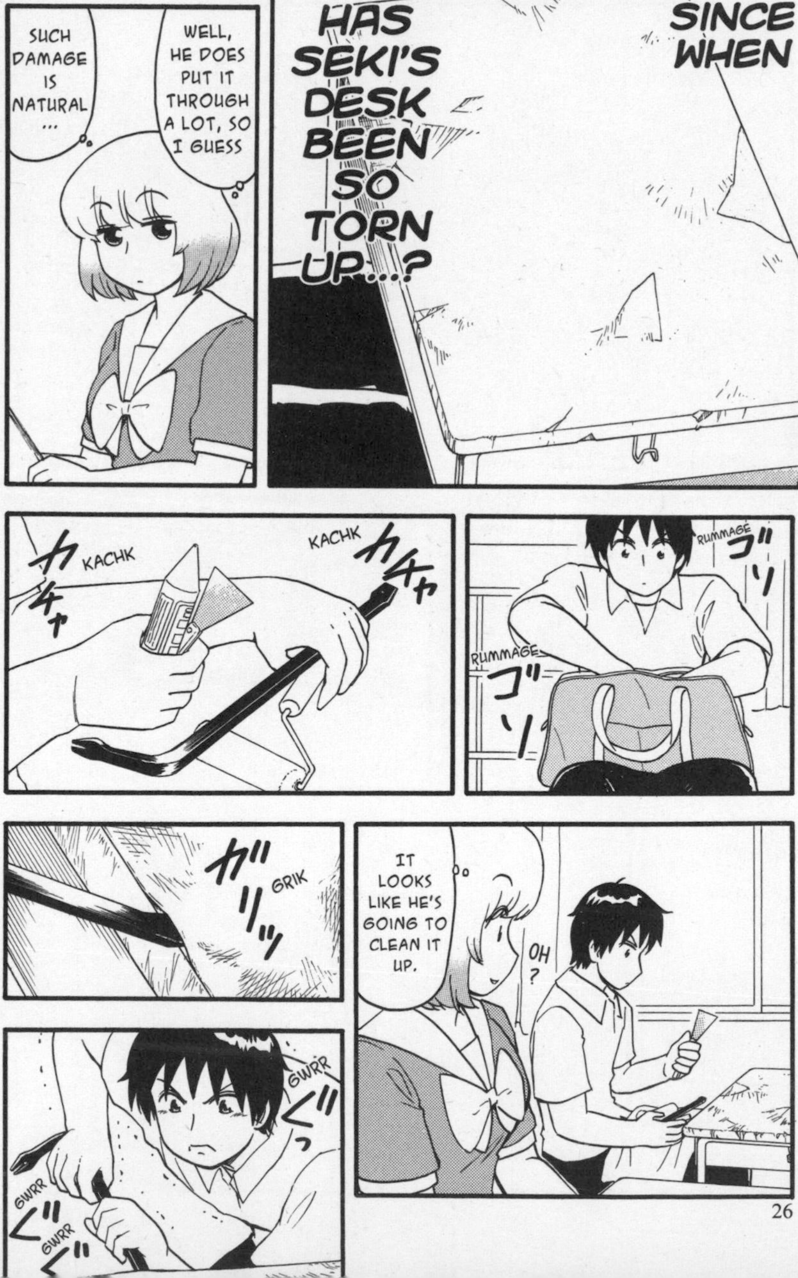
SINCE WHEN
HAS SEKI'S DESK BEEN SO TORN UP...?
WELL, HE DOES PUT IT THROUGH A LOT, SO I GUESS
SUCH DAMAGE IS NATURAL...
RUMMAGE ゴソ
RUMMAGE ゴソ
KACHK カチャ
KACHK カチャ
OH?
IT LOOKS LIKE HE'S GOING TO CLEAN IT UP.
GRIK ガリッ
GWRR ぐぐっ
GWRR ぐ
GWRR ぐ

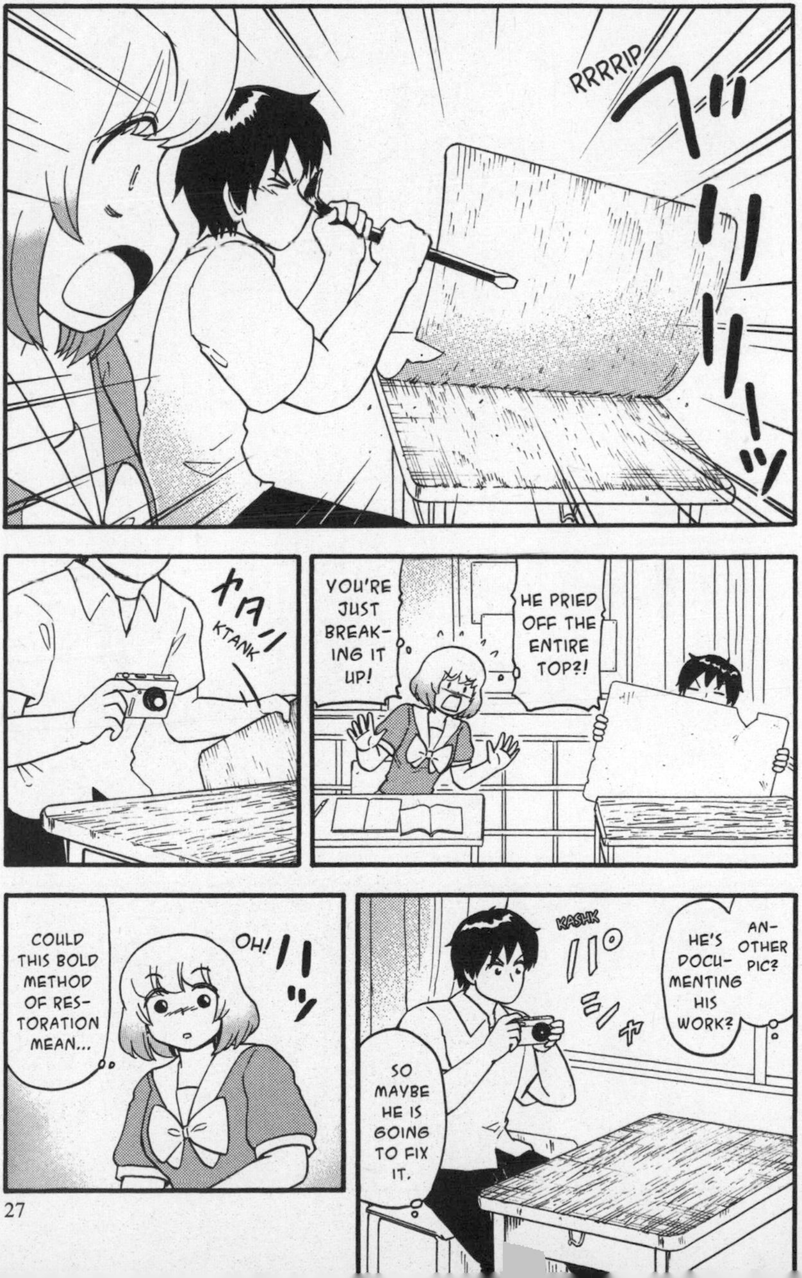
RRRRIP
HE PRIED OFF THE ENTIRE TOP?!
YOU'RE JUST BREAKING IT UP!
KTANK
ANOTHER PIC?
HE'S DOCUMENTING HIS WORK?
KASHK
SO MAYBE HE IS GOING TO FIX IT.
OH!
COULD THIS BOLD METHOD OF RESTORATION MEAN...

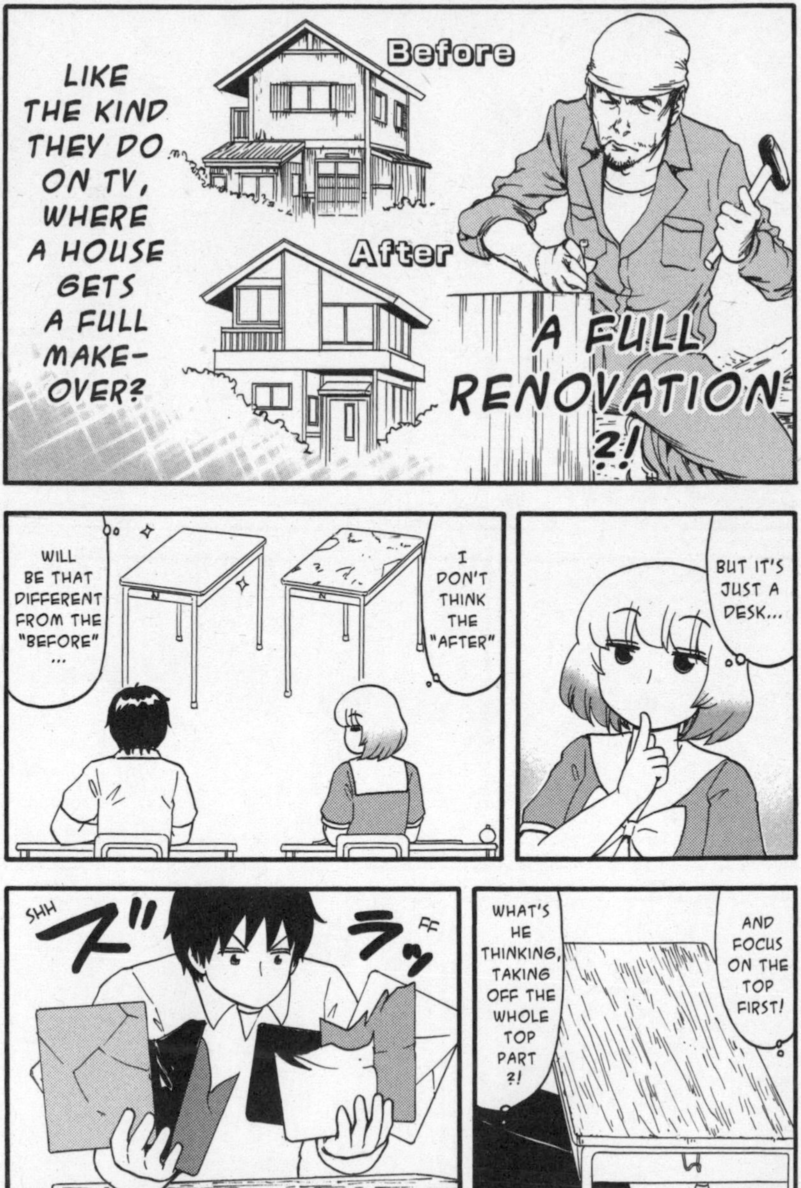
Before
LIKE THE KIND THEY DO ON TV, WHERE A HOUSE GETS A FULL MAKE-OVER?
After
A FULL RENOVATION ?!
BUT IT'S JUST A DESK...
I DON'T THINK THE "AFTER"
WILL BE THAT DIFFERENT FROM THE "BEFORE" ...
AND FOCUS ON THE TOP FIRST!
WHAT'S HE THINKING, TAKING OFF THE WHOLE TOP PART ?!
ズ
SHH
ラッ
FF

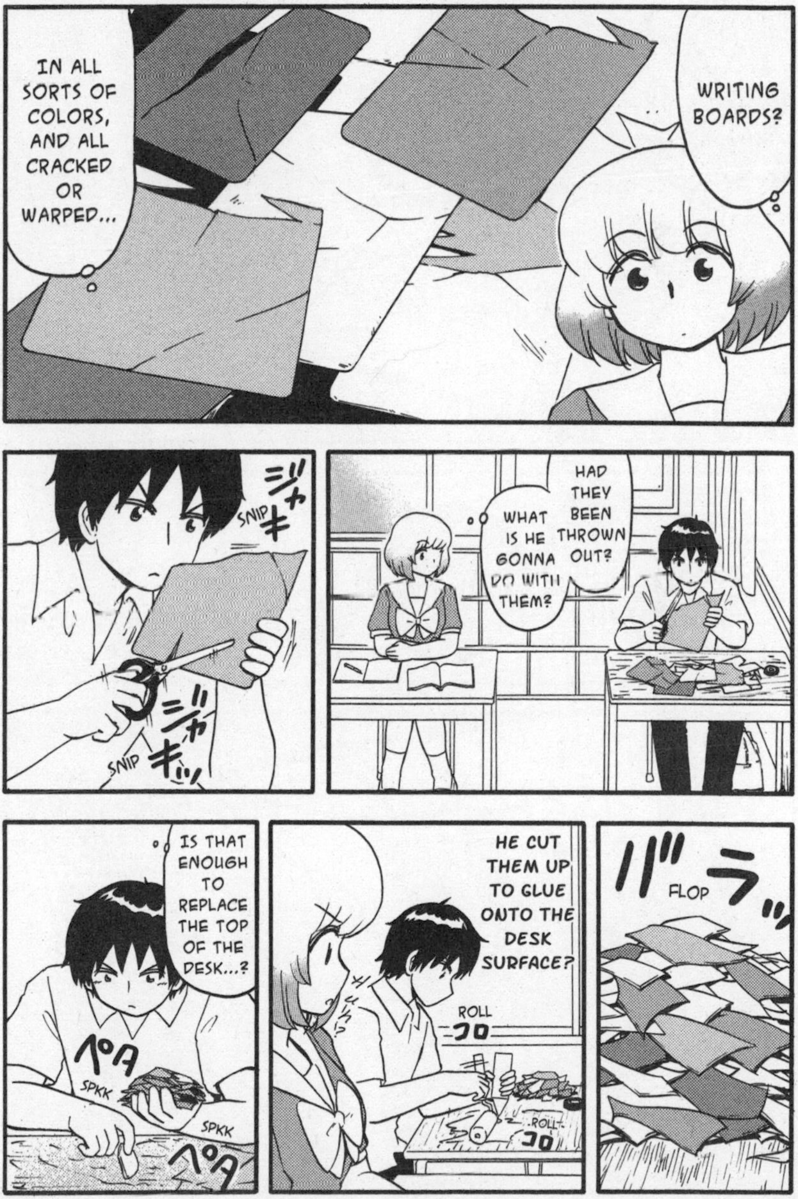
WRITING BOARDS?
IN ALL SORTS OF COLORS, AND ALL CRACKED OR WARPED...
HAD THEY BEEN THROWN OUT?
WHAT IS HE GONNA DO WITH THEM?
ジャキ
SNIP
ジャキッ
SNIP
バラッ
FLOP
HE CUT THEM UP TO GLUE ONTO THE DESK SURFACE?
!?
ROLL
コロ
ROLL
コロ
IS THAT ENOUGH TO REPLACE THE TOP OF THE DESK...?
ペタ
SPKK
SPKK
ペタ

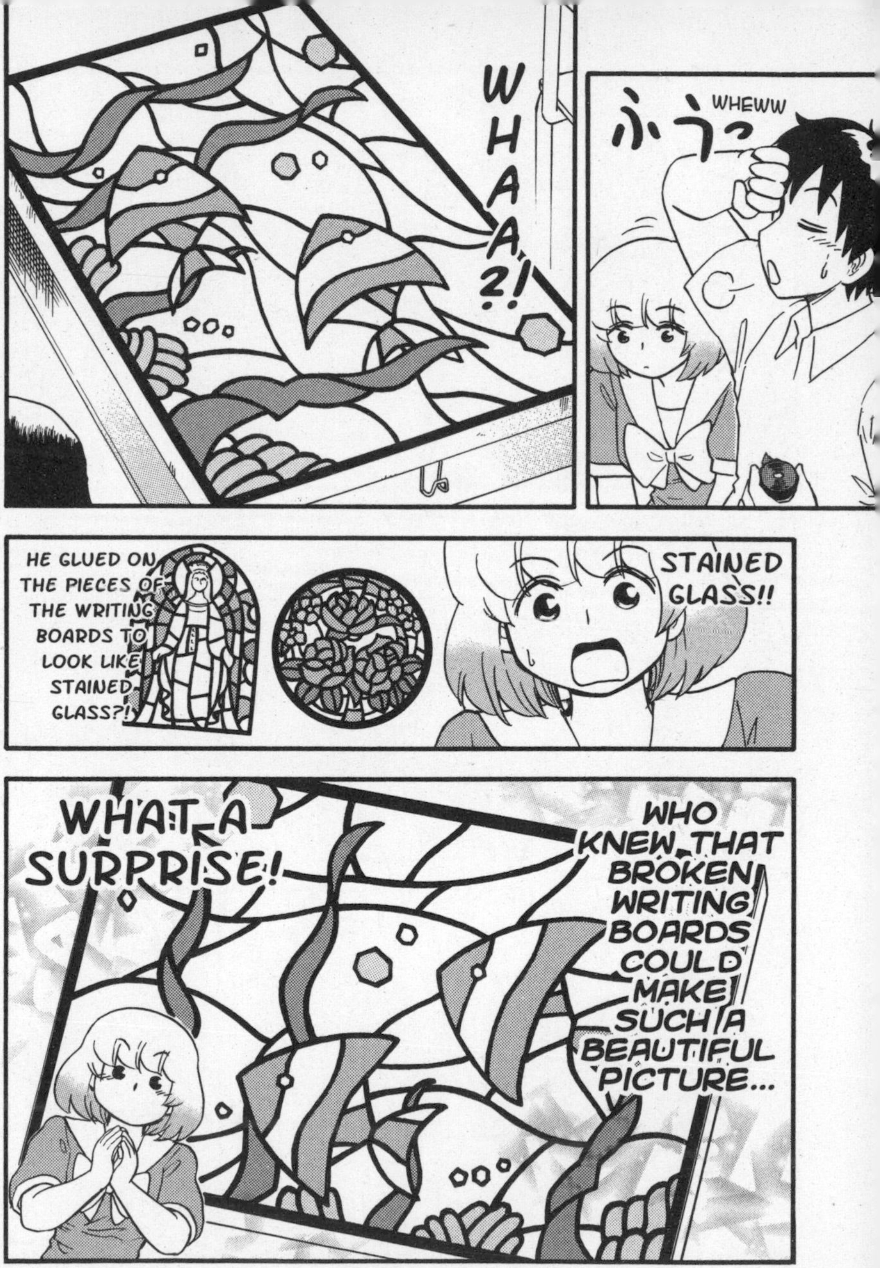
ふうっ
WHEWW
WHAAA?!
STAINED GLASS!!
HE GLUED ON THE PIECES OF THE WRITING BOARDS TO LOOK LIKE STAINED GLASS?!
WHO KNEW THAT BROKEN WRITING BOARDS COULD MAKE SUCH A BEAUTIFUL PICTURE...
WHAT A SURPRISE!

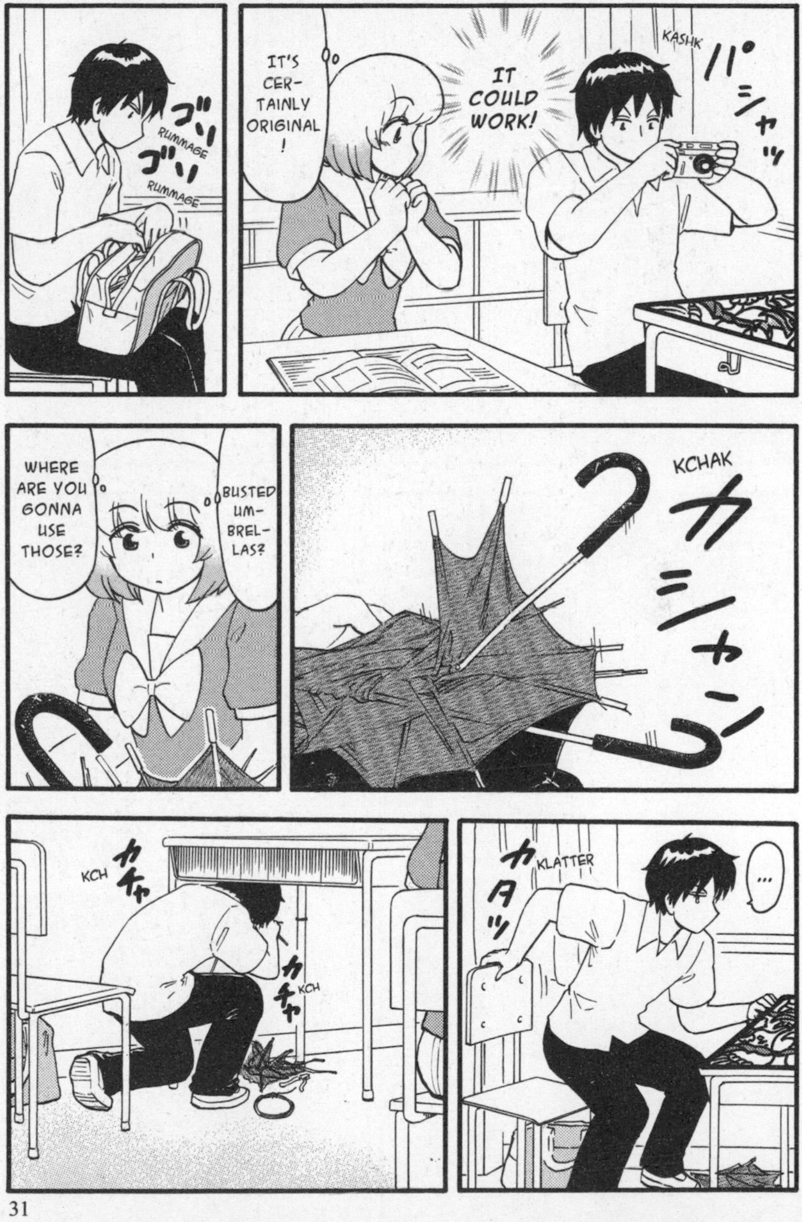
KASHK
パシャッ
IT COULD WORK!
IT'S CER-TAINLY ORIGINAL!
ゴソ
RUMMAGE
ゴソ
RUMMAGE
KCHAK
カシャーン
BUSTED UM-BREL-LAS?
WHERE ARE YOU GONNA USE THOSE?
...
カタッ
KLATTER
KCH
カチャ
カチャ
KCH

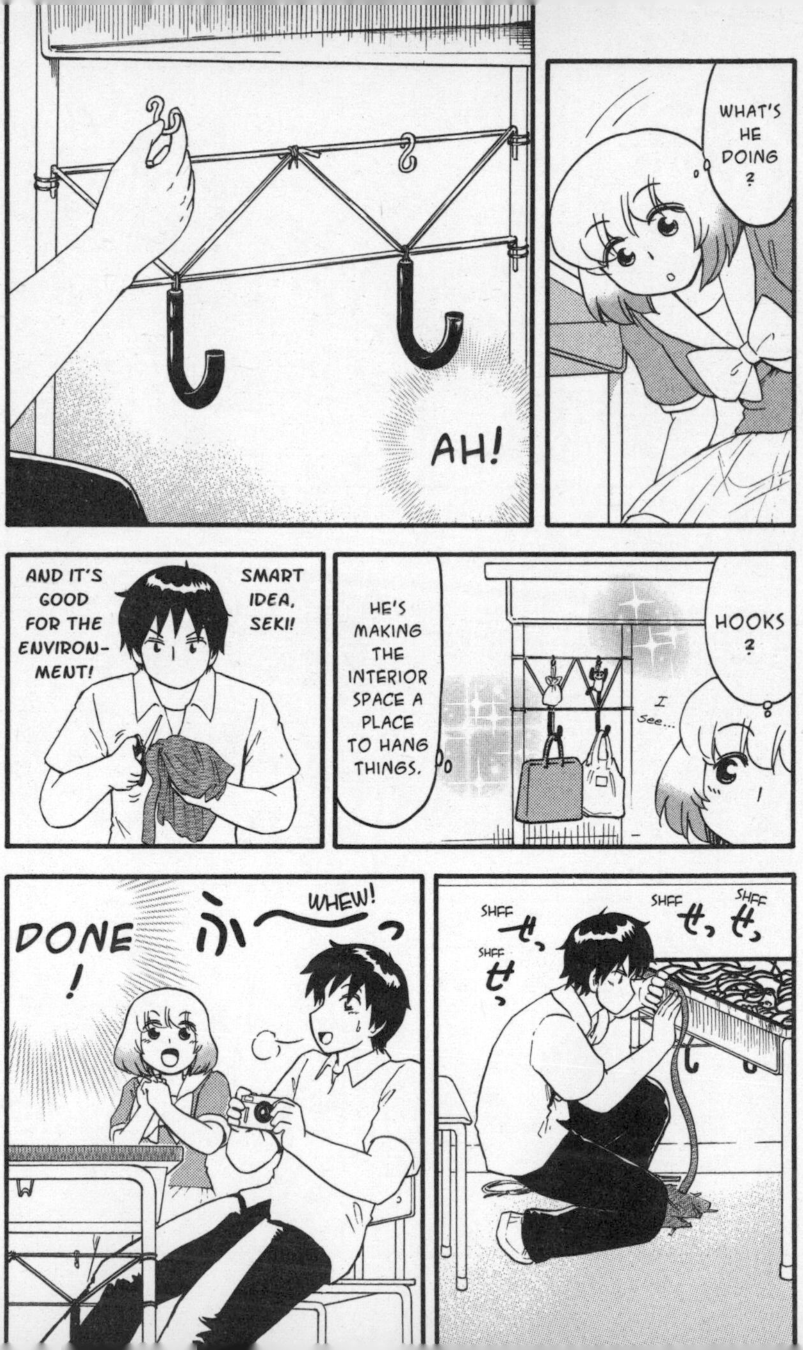
WHAT'S HE DOING?
AH!
HOOKS?
HE'S MAKING THE INTERIOR SPACE A PLACE TO HANG THINGS.
I see...
!
SMART IDEA, SEKI!
AND IT'S GOOD FOR THE ENVIRONMENT!
SHFF せっ
SHFF せっ
SHFF せっ
SHFF せっ
ふ〜っ
WHEW!
DONE!

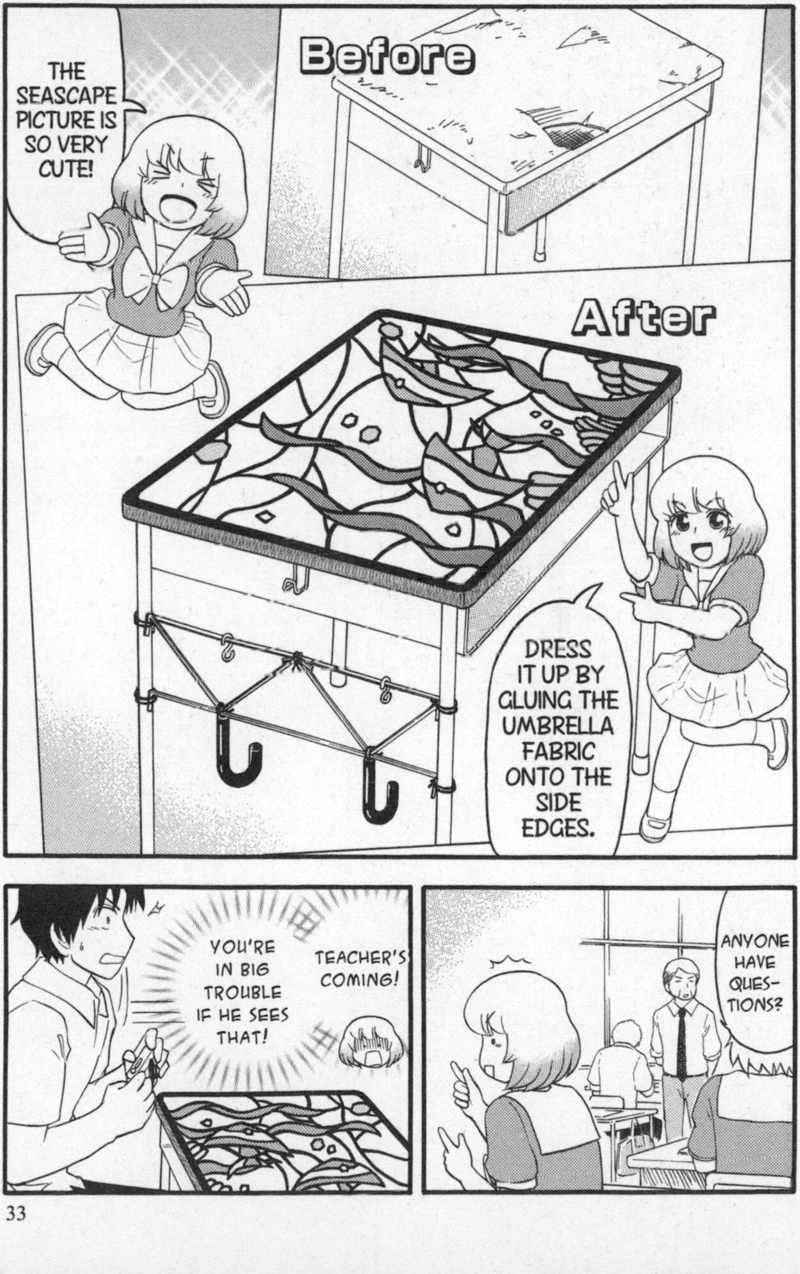
Before
THE SEASCAPE PICTURE IS SO VERY CUTE!
After
DRESS IT UP BY GLUING THE UMBRELLA FABRIC ONTO THE SIDE EDGES.
ANYONE HAVE QUES-TIONS?
TEACHER'S COMING!
YOU'RE IN BIG TROUBLE IF HE SEES THAT!

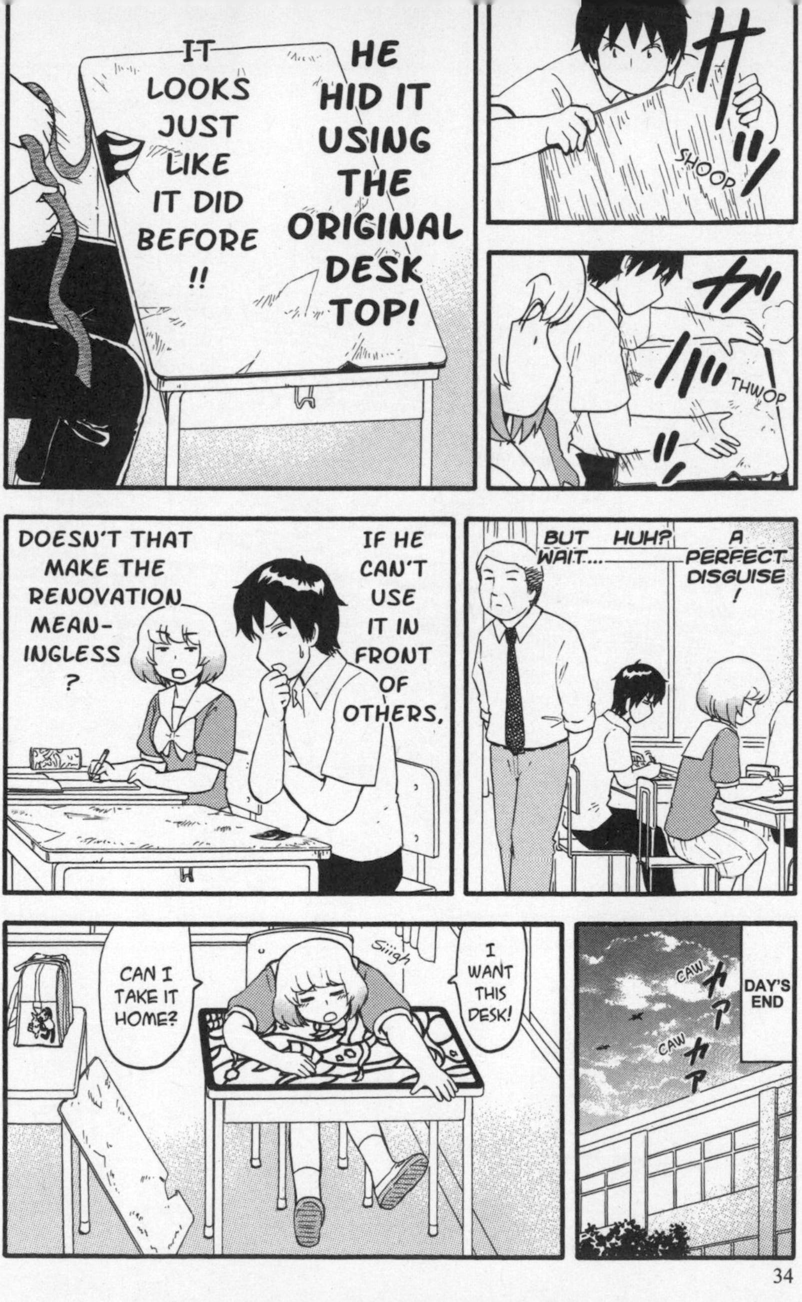
SHOOP
THWOP
HE HID IT USING THE ORIGINAL DESK TOP!
IT LOOKS JUST LIKE IT DID BEFORE !!
A PERFECT DISGUISE!
HUH?
BUT WAIT...
IF HE CAN'T USE IT IN FRONT OF OTHERS,
DOESN'T THAT MAKE THE RENOVATION MEAN-INGLESS?
DAY'S END
CAW
CAW
I WANT THIS DESK!
Siiigh
CAN I TAKE IT HOME?

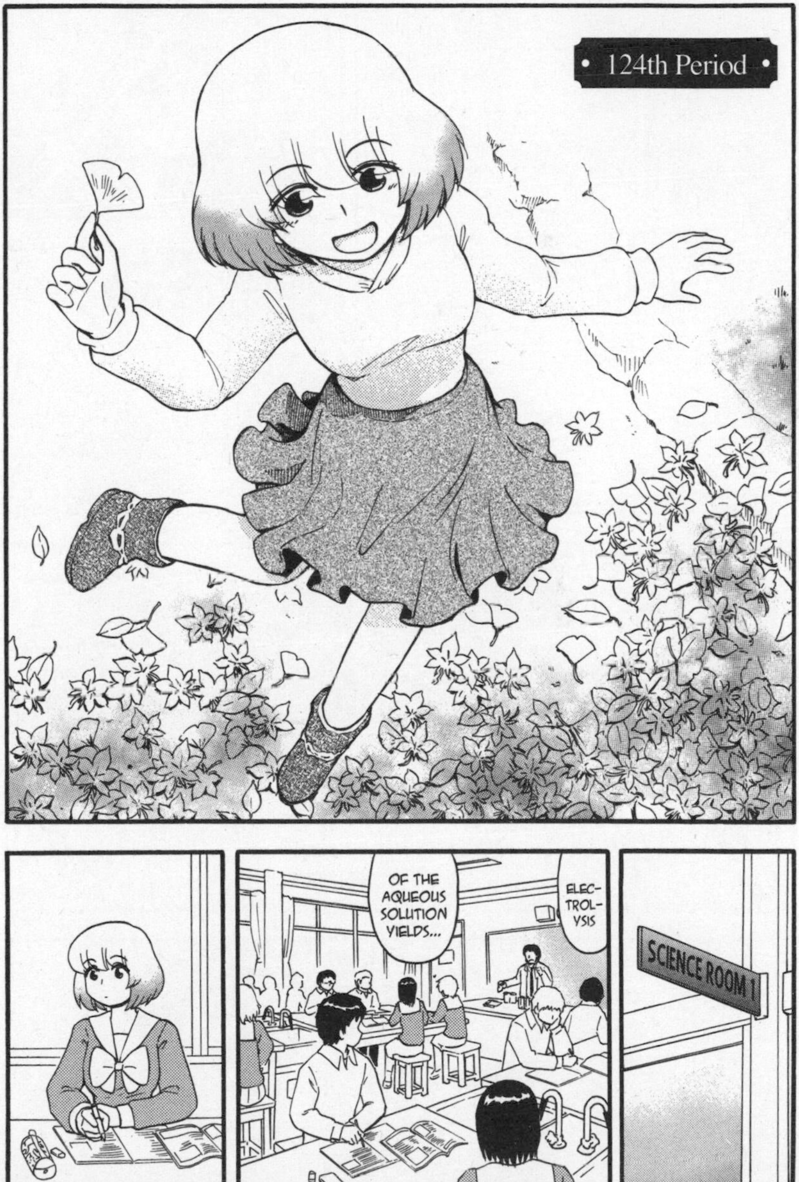
• 124th Period •
SCIENCE ROOM 1
ELEC-TROL-YSIS
OF THE AQUEOUS SOLUTION YIELDS...

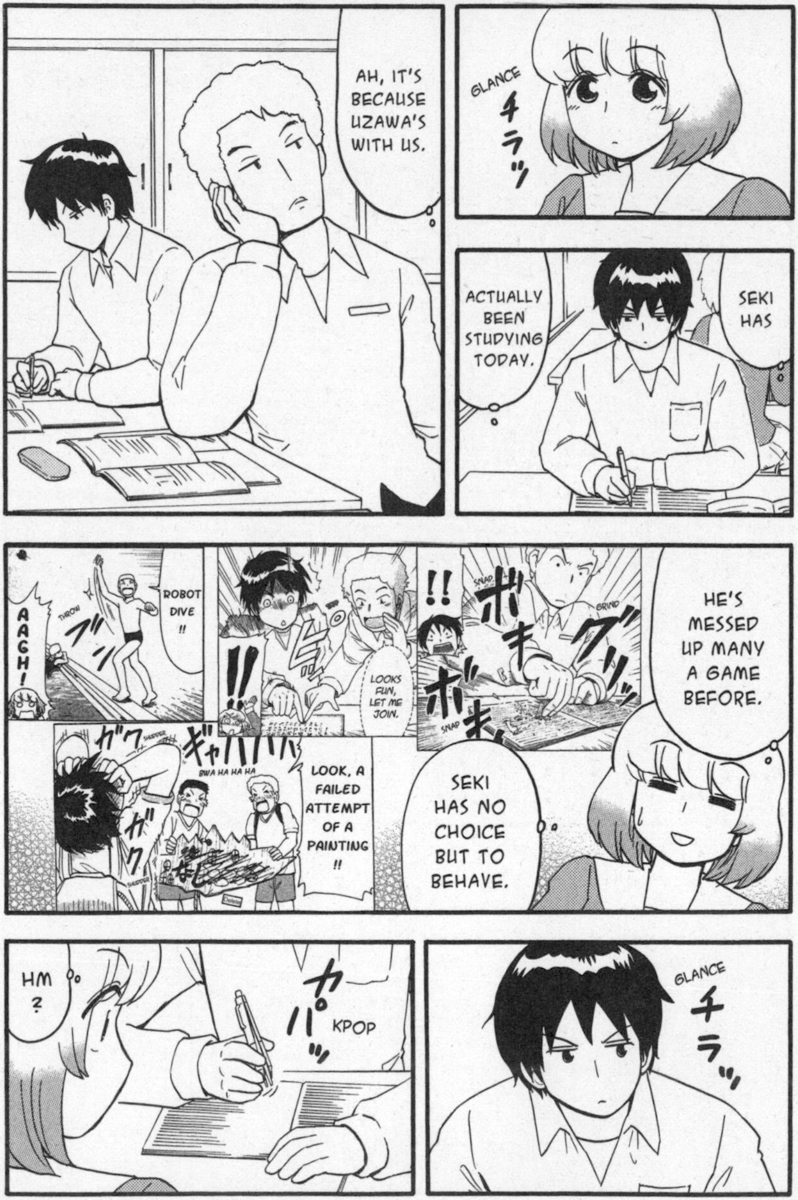
GLANCE
チラッ
SEKI HAS
ACTUALLY BEEN STUDYING TODAY.
AH, IT'S BECAUSE UZAWA'S WITH US.
HE'S MESSED UP MANY A GAME BEFORE.
SNAP
ボキ
GRIND
グリッ
ボキ
SNAP
!!
LOOKS FUN, LET ME JOIN.
!!
ROBOT DIVE!!
THROW
ブンッ
AAGH!
LOOK, A FAILED ATTEMPT OF A PAINTING!!
ギャハハハ
BWA HA HA HA
ガク
SHUDDER
ガク
SHUDDER
SEKI HAS NO CHOICE BUT TO BEHAVE.
GLANCE
チラッ
カパッ
KPOP
HM?

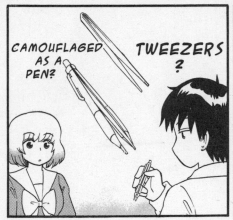

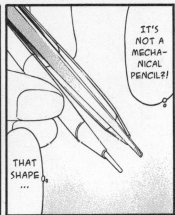

IT'S NOT A MECHANICAL PENCIL?!
THAT SHAPE ...
TWEEZERS ?
CAMOUFLAGED AS A PEN?
HE'S MAKING SOME-THING ?
BUT I DON'T SEE ANY STUFF TO PLAY WITH ANY-WHERE...
?

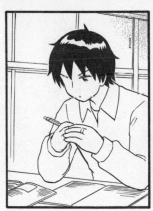

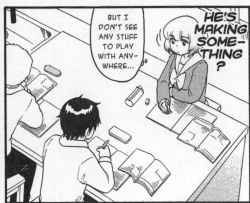

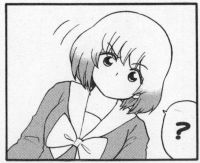

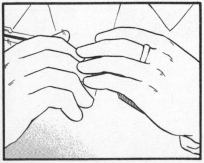

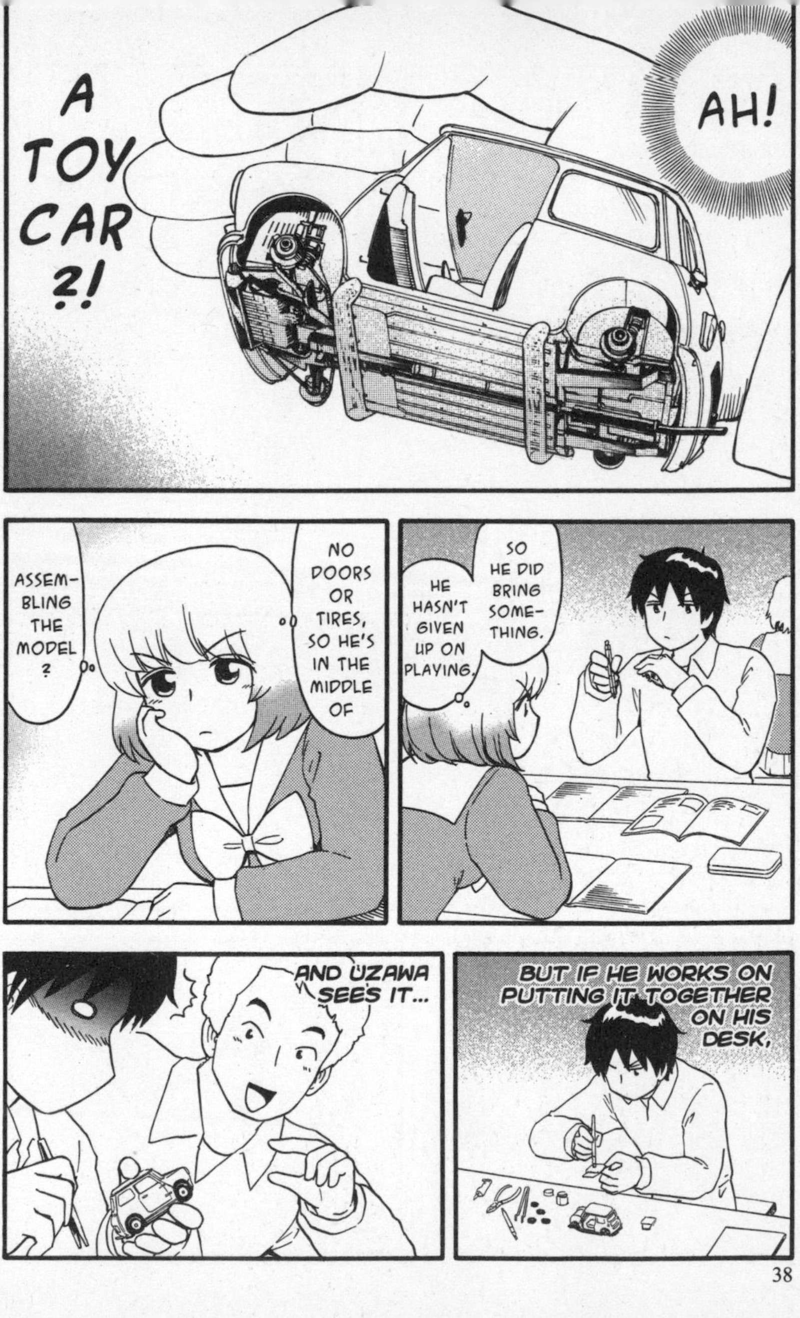
AH!
A TOY CAR ?!
SO HE DID BRING SOMETHING.
HE HASN'T GIVEN UP ON PLAYING.
NO DOORS OR TIRES, SO HE'S IN THE MIDDLE OF
ASSEMBLING THE MODEL?
BUT IF HE WORKS ON PUTTING IT TOGETHER ON HIS DESK,
AND UZAWA SEES IT...

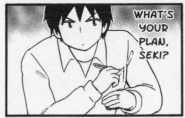

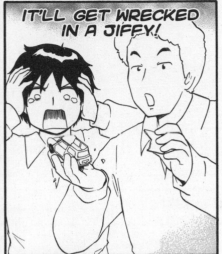

IT'LL GET WRECKED IN A JIFFY!
WHAT'S YOUR PLAN, SEKI?
SHFF
スッ
SWIP
サッ
...
AH!
IT'S GOT A DOOR NOW!
KACHIK
カチャッ

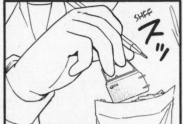

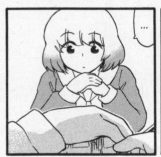

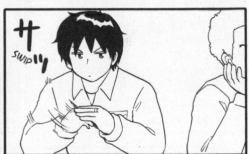

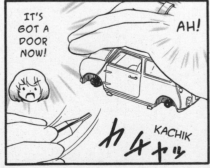

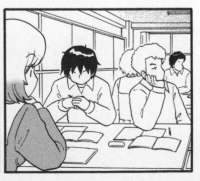

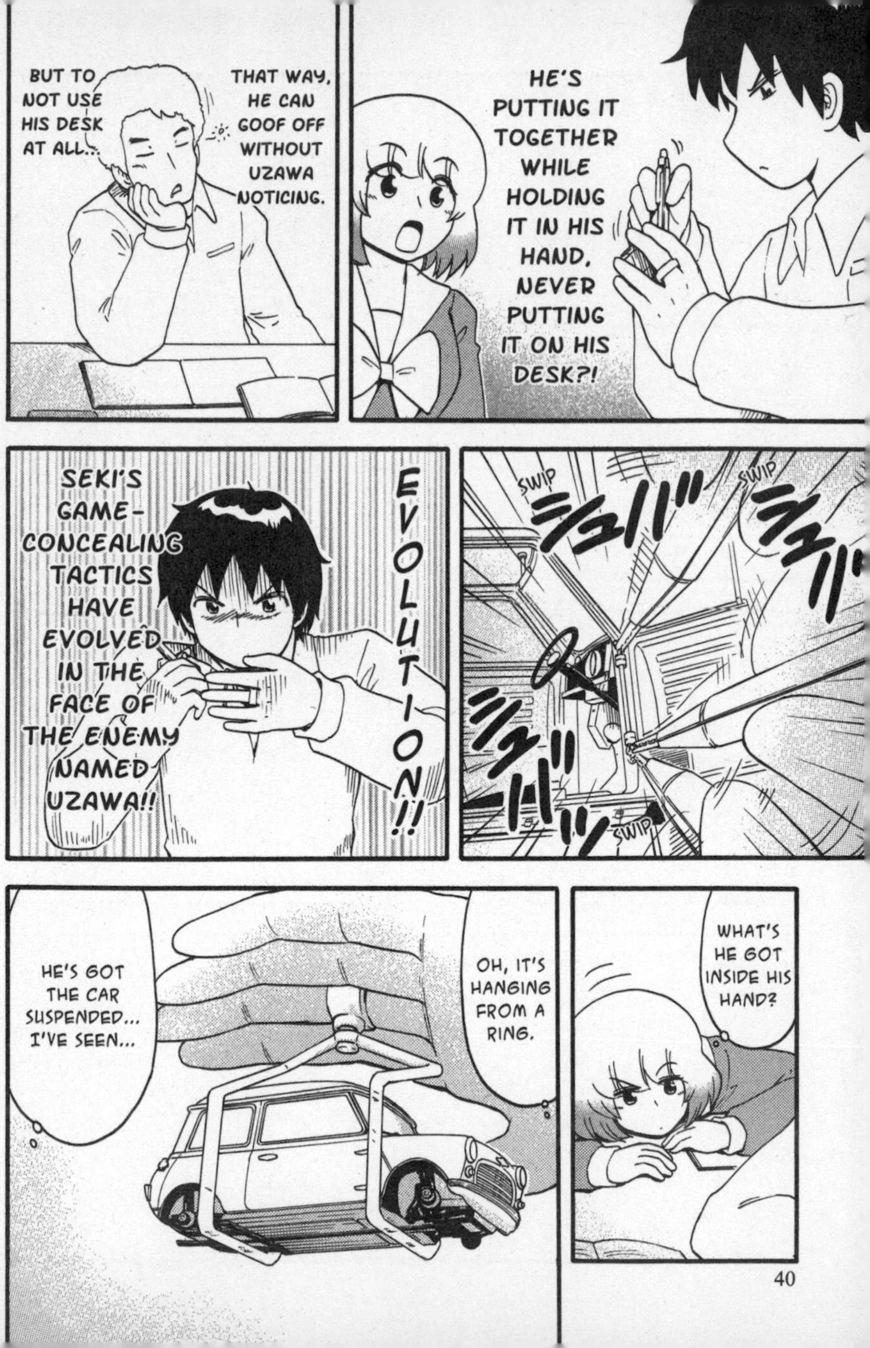
HE'S PUTTING IT TOGETHER WHILE HOLDING IT IN HIS HAND, NEVER PUTTING IT ON HIS DESK?!
THAT WAY, HE CAN GOOF OFF WITHOUT UZAWA NOTICING.
BUT TO NOT USE HIS DESK AT ALL...
SWIP
SWIP
SWIP
EVOLUTION!!
SEKI'S GAME-CONCEALING TACTICS HAVE EVOLVED IN THE FACE OF THE ENEMY NAMED UZAWA!!
WHAT'S HE GOT INSIDE HIS HAND?
OH, IT'S HANGING FROM A RING.
HE'S GOT THE CAR SUSPENDED... I'VE SEEN...

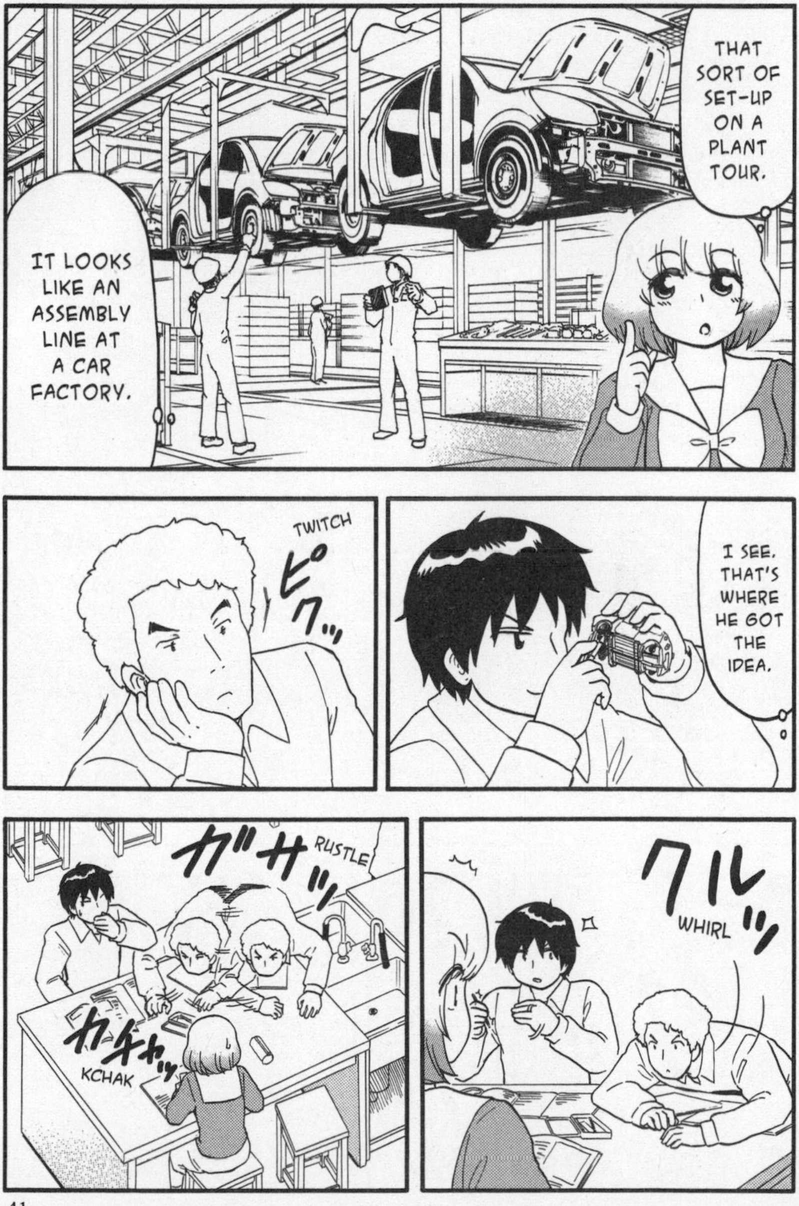
THAT SORT OF SET-UP ON A PLANT TOUR.
IT LOOKS LIKE AN ASSEMBLY LINE AT A CAR FACTORY.
I SEE. THAT'S WHERE HE GOT THE IDEA.
ピクッ
TWITCH
クルッ
WHIRL
ガサッ
RUSTLE
カチャッ
KCHAK

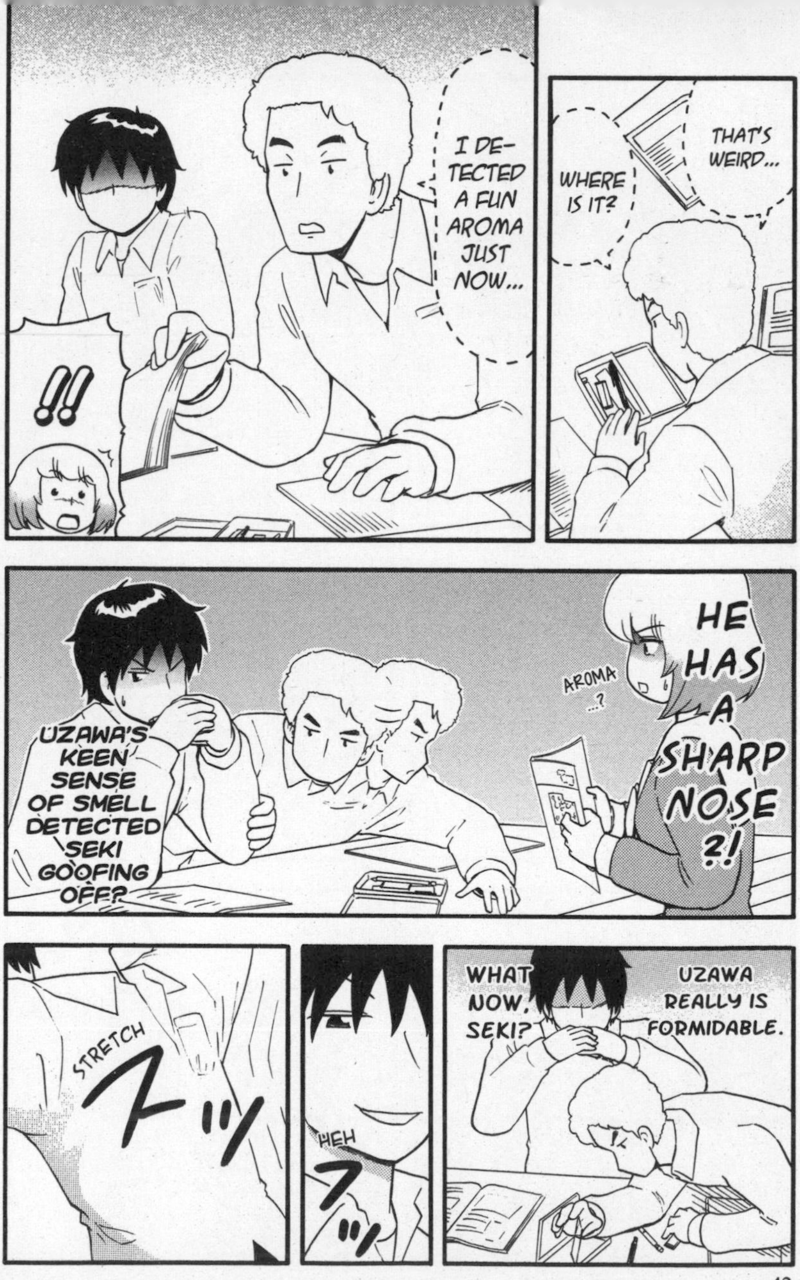
THAT'S WEIRD...
WHERE IS IT?
I DE-TECTED A FUN AROMA JUST NOW...
!!
HE HAS A SHARP NOSE ?!
AROMA ...?
UZAWA'S KEEN SENSE OF SMELL DETECTED SEKI GOOFING OFF?
UZAWA REALLY IS FORMIDABLE.
WHAT NOW, SEKI?
HEH
STRETCH

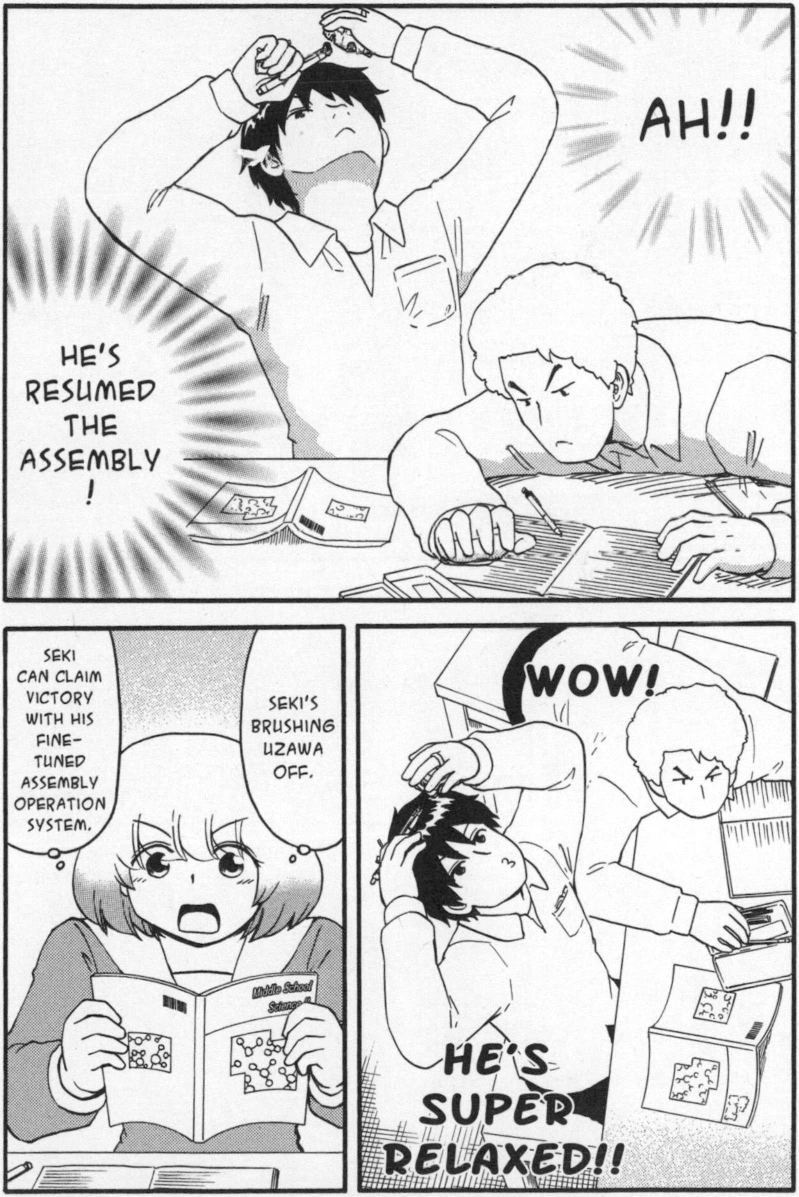
AH!!
HE'S RESUMED THE ASSEMBLY!
WOW!
HE'S SUPER RELAXED!!
SEKI'S BRUSHING UZAWA OFF.
SEKI CAN CLAIM VICTORY WITH HIS FINE-TUNED ASSEMBLY OPERATION SYSTEM.
Middle School Science II

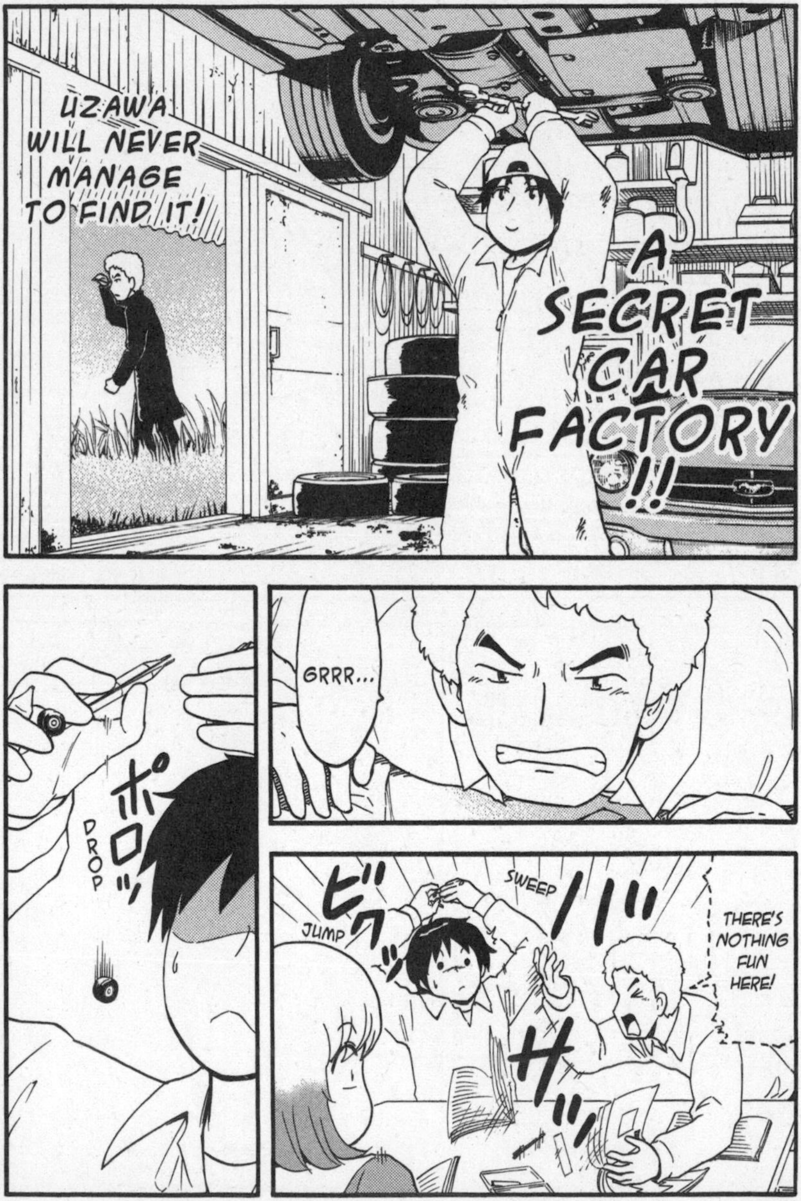
A SECRET CAR FACTORY!!
UZAWA WILL NEVER MANAGE TO FIND IT!
GRRR...
THERE'S NOTHING FUN HERE!
バッ
SWEEP
ビクッ
JUMP
ザッ
ポロッ
DROP

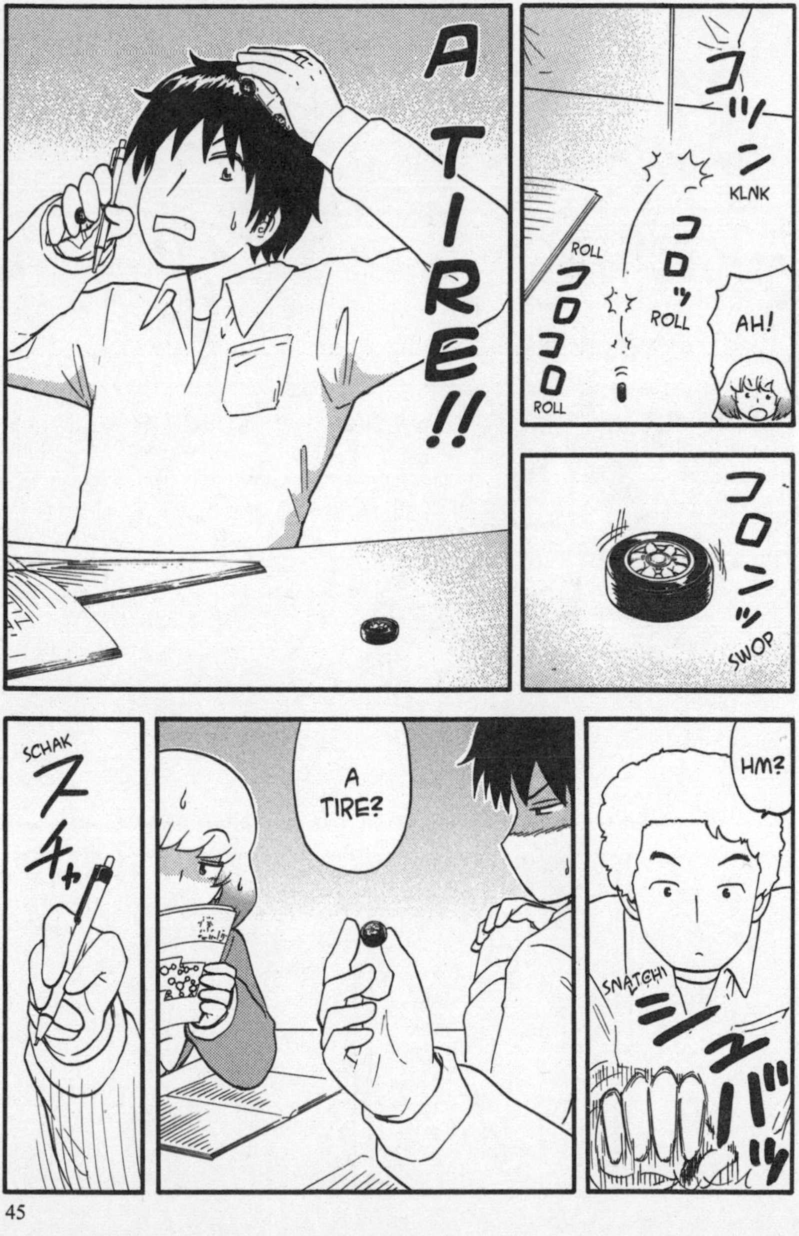
コツン
KLNK
コロッ
ROLL
AH!
ROLL
コロコロ
ROLL
コロンッ
SWOP
A TIRE!!
HM?
SNATCH!
シュバッ
A TIRE?
SCHAK
スチャ

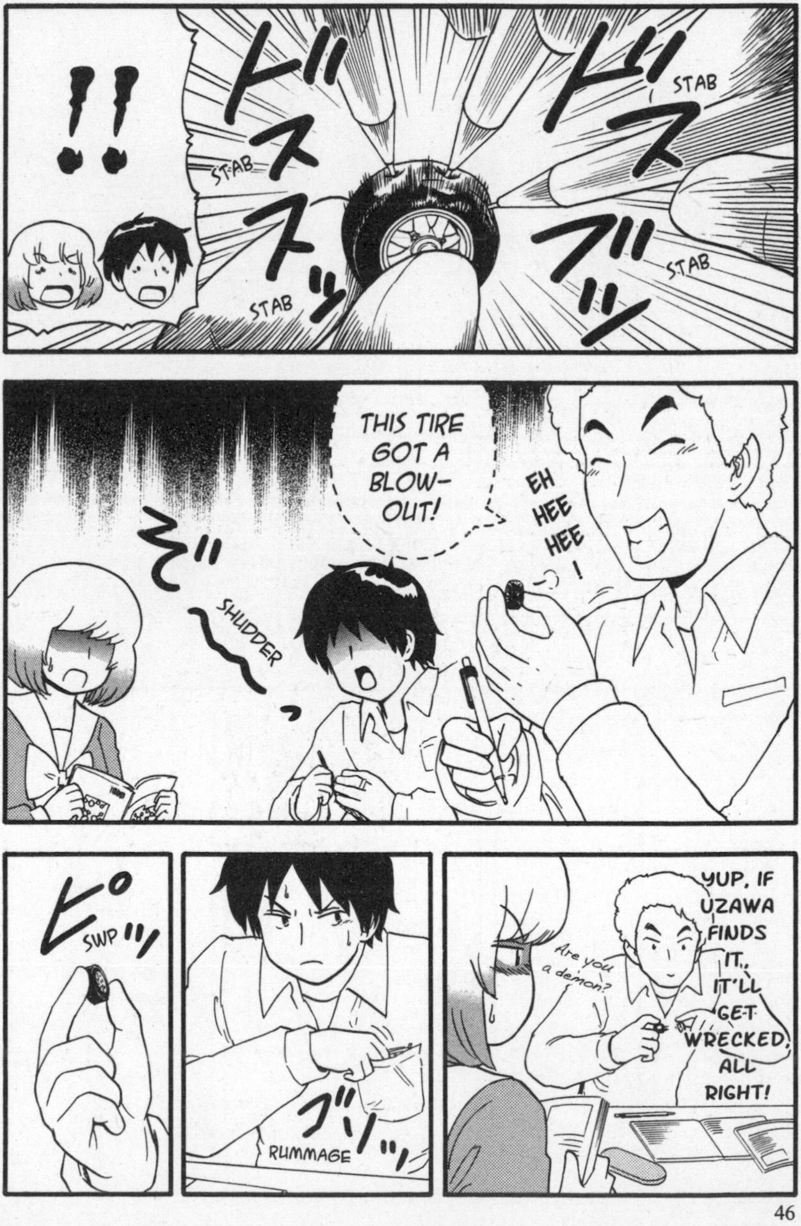
STAB
STAB
STAB
STAB
!!
THIS TIRE GOT A BLOW-OUT!
EH HEE HEE!
SHUDDER
YUP, IF UZAWA FINDS IT, IT'LL GET WRECKED, ALL RIGHT!
Are you a demon?
RUMMAGE
SWP

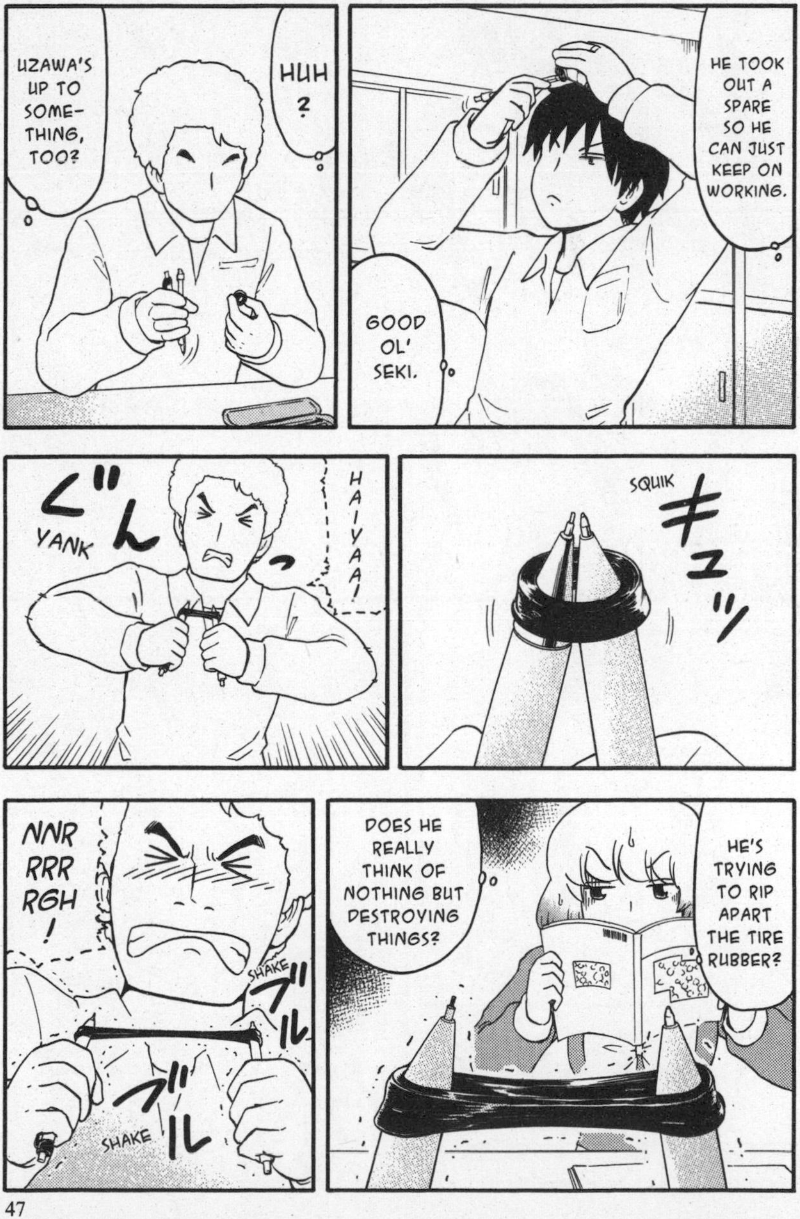

HE TOOK OUT A SPARE SO HE CAN JUST KEEP ON WORKING.
GOOD OL' SEKI.
HUH?
UZAWA'S UP TO SOMETHING, TOO?
SQUIK
キュッ
HAIYAAA!
ぐん
YANK
HE'S TRYING TO RIP APART THE TIRE RUBBER?
DOES HE REALLY THINK OF NOTHING BUT DESTROYING THINGS?
NNRRRRRGH!
SHAKE
ブル
ブル
SHAKE

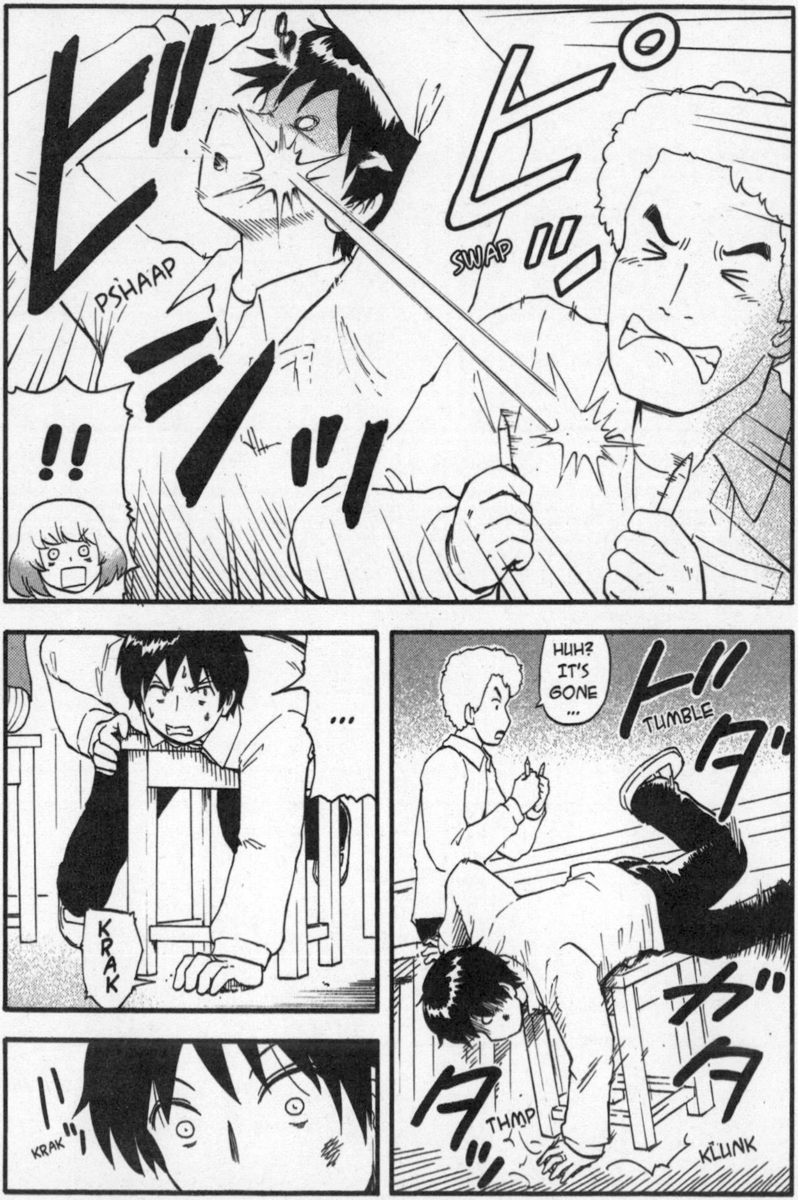
SWAP
PSHAAP
!!
HUH? IT'S GONE ...
TUMBLE
KLUNK
THMP
...
KRAK
KRAK

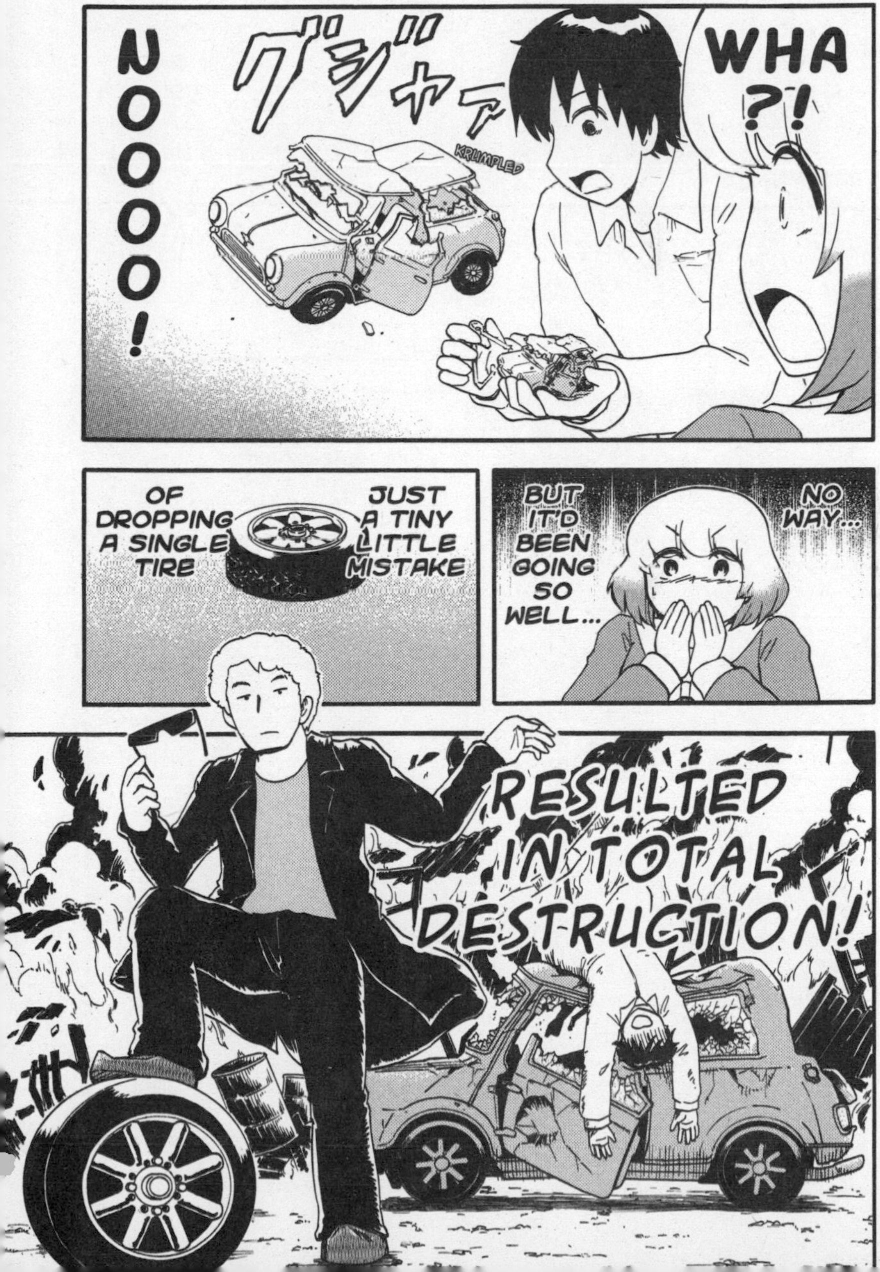
WHA ?!
グジャァ
KRUMPLED
NOOOOO!
NO WAY...
BUT IT'D BEEN GOING SO WELL...
JUST A TINY LITTLE MISTAKE
OF DROPPING A SINGLE TIRE
RESULTED IN TOTAL DESTRUCTION!

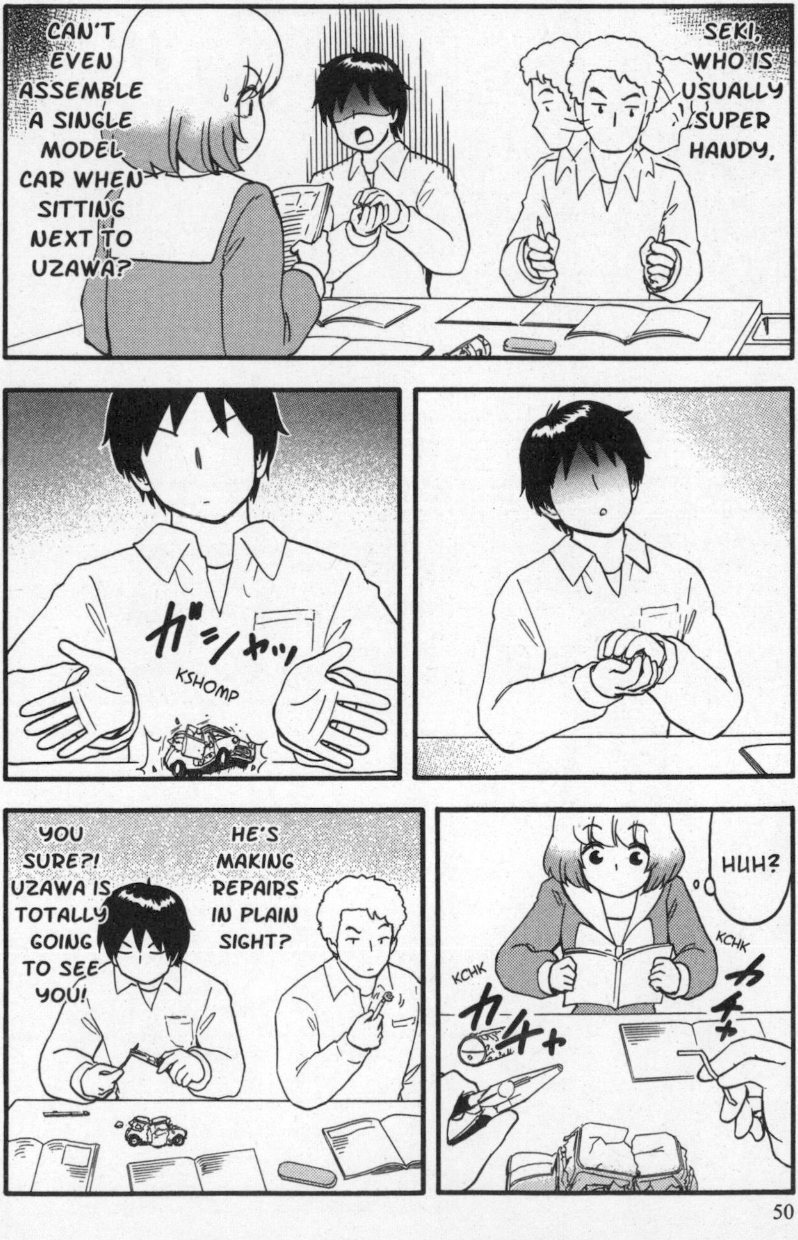
SEKI, WHO IS USUALLY SUPER HANDY,
CAN'T EVEN ASSEMBLE A SINGLE MODEL CAR WHEN SITTING NEXT TO UZAWA?
ガシャッ
KSHOMP
HUH?
カチャ
KCHK
カチャ
KCHK
HE'S MAKING REPAIRS IN PLAIN SIGHT?
YOU SURE?! UZAWA IS TOTALLY GOING TO SEE YOU!

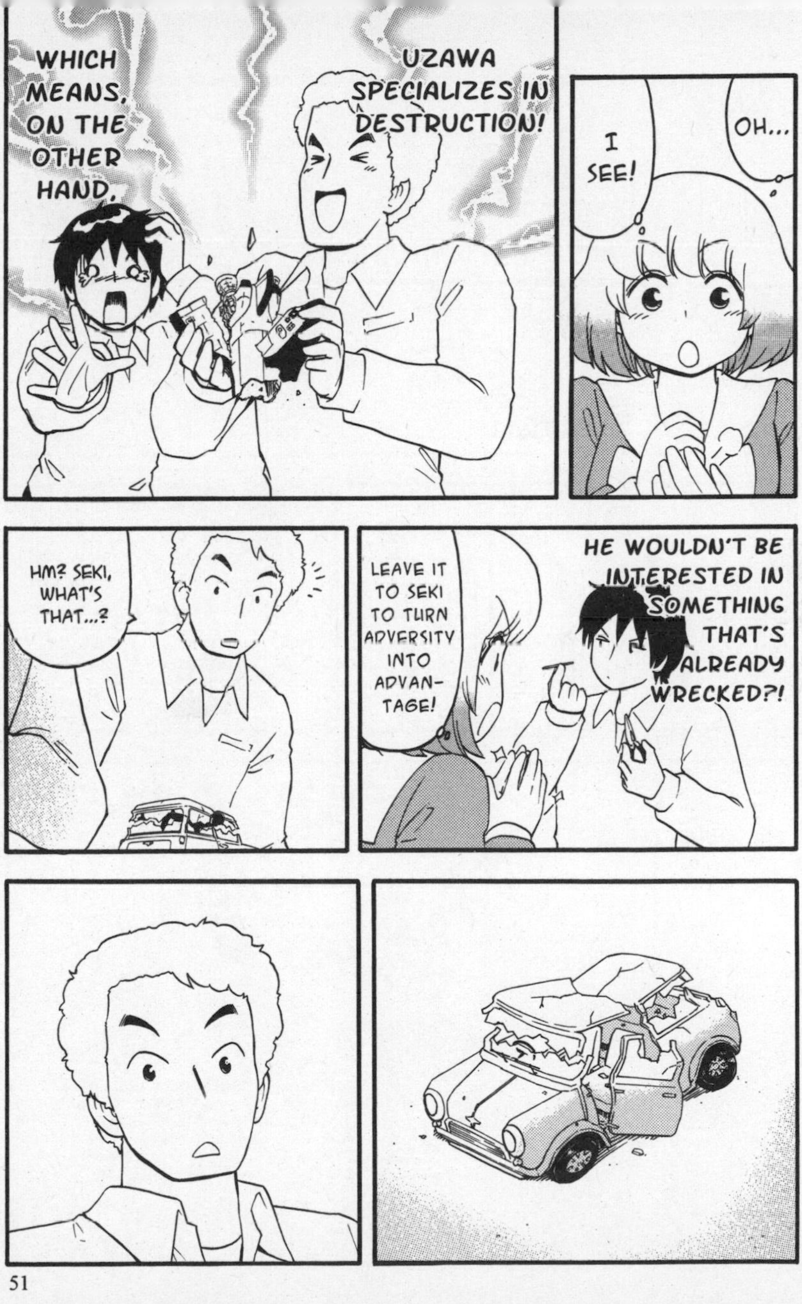
OH...
I SEE!
UZAWA SPECIALIZES IN DESTRUCTION!
WHICH MEANS, ON THE OTHER HAND,
HE WOULDN'T BE INTERESTED IN SOMETHING THAT'S ALREADY WRECKED?!
LEAVE IT TO SEKI TO TURN ADVERSITY INTO ADVAN-TAGE!
HM? SEKI, WHAT'S THAT...?

THAT'S WICKED COOL, MAN!!
SUPER AMERICAN!
GIMME.
GRAB
KCHAK
I'LL MAKE IT EVEN COOLER!
FORGET IT.
DETH
NEW YOKE
BAD
PREDICTING UZAWA'S ACTIONS IS BEYOND OUR ABILITIES...

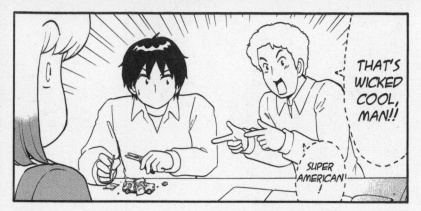

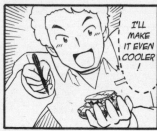

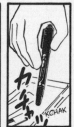

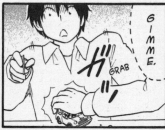

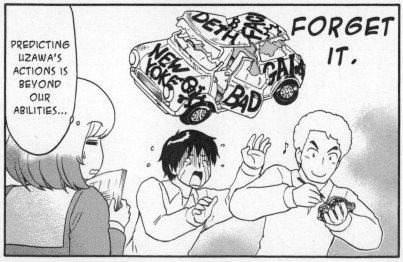

My Neighbor Seki

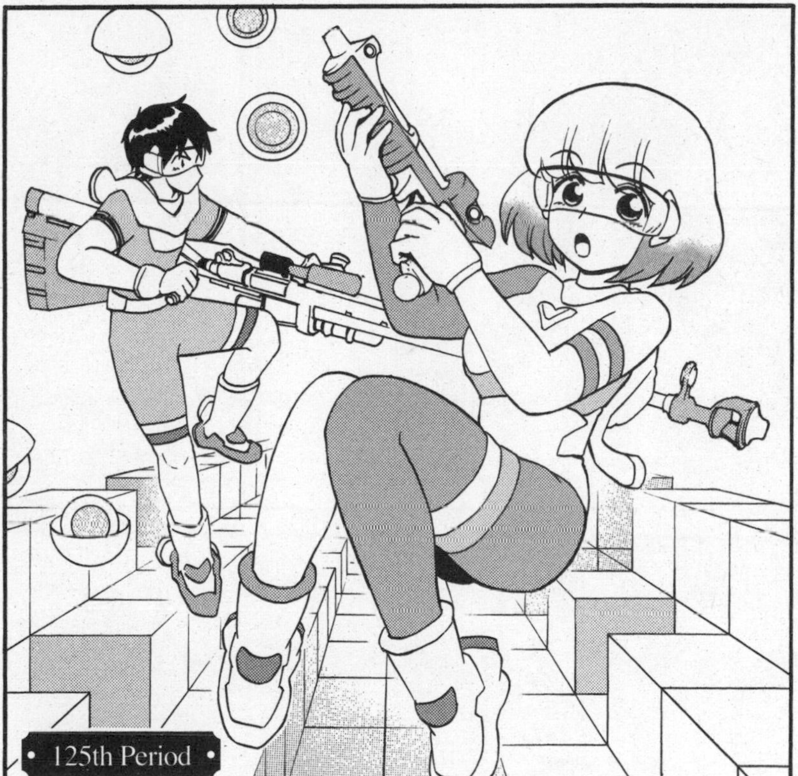
125th Period

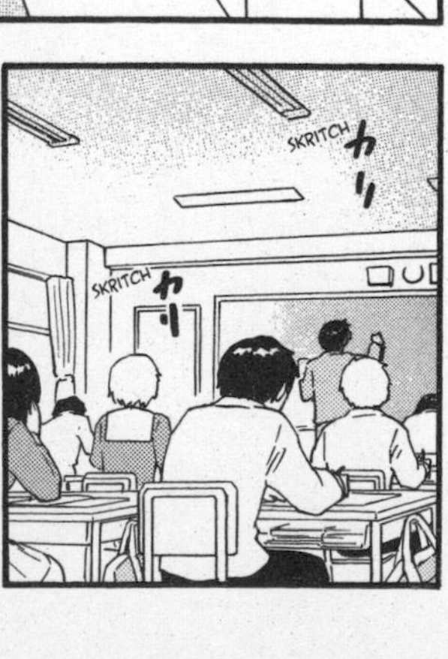
SKRITCH
カリ
SKRITCH
カリ

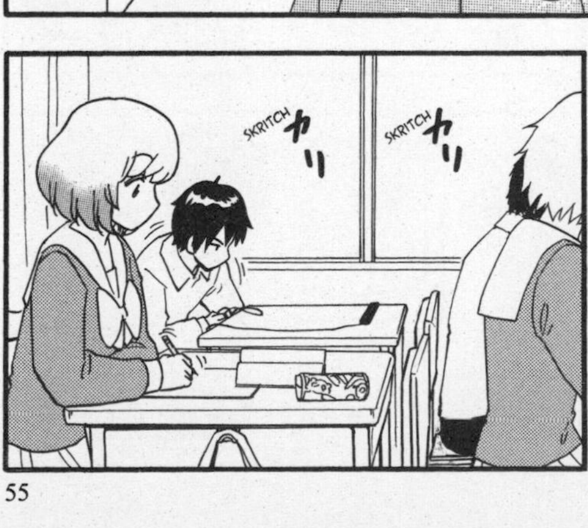
SKRITCH
カリ
SKRITCH
カリ

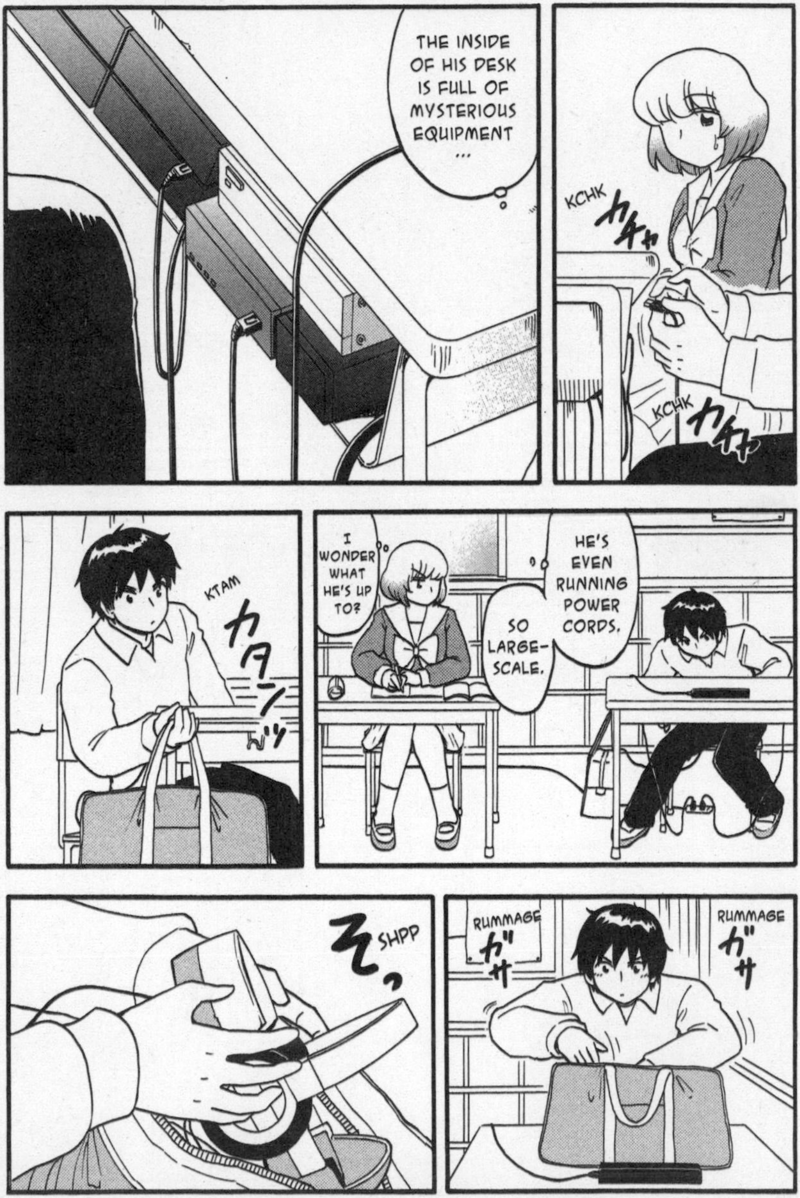
KCHK
KCHK
THE INSIDE OF HIS DESK IS FULL OF MYSTERIOUS EQUIPMENT ...
HE'S EVEN RUNNING POWER CORDS.
SO LARGE-SCALE.
I WONDER WHAT HE'S UP TO?
KTAM
RUMMAGE
RUMMAGE
SHPP

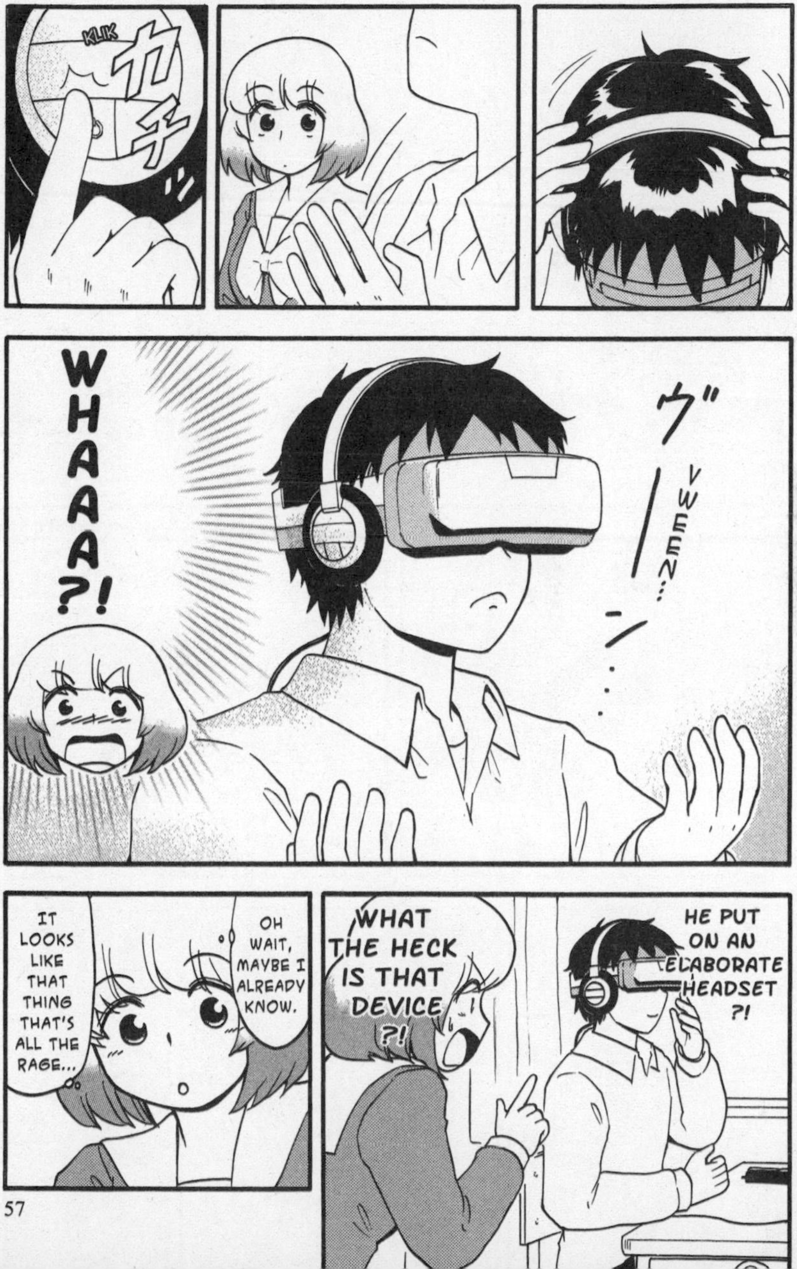
KLIK
カチッ
ヴー
VWEEN...
WHAAAA?!
HE PUT ON AN ELABORATE HEADSET ?!
WHAT THE HECK IS THAT DEVICE ?!
OH WAIT, MAYBE I ALREADY KNOW.
IT LOOKS LIKE THAT THING THAT'S ALL THE RAGE...

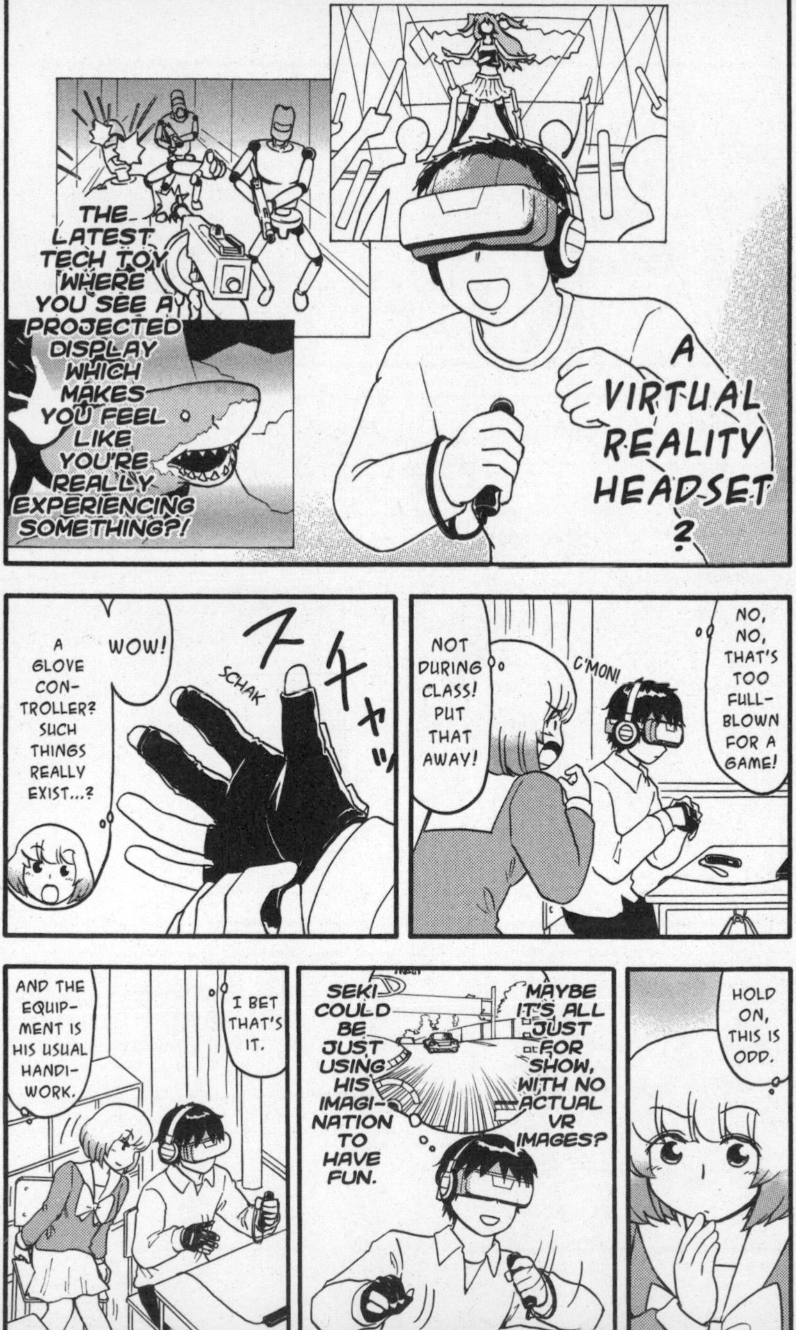
A VIRTUAL REALITY HEADSET?
THE LATEST TECH TOY WHERE YOU SEE A PROJECTED DISPLAY WHICH MAKES YOU FEEL LIKE YOU'RE REALLY EXPERIENCING SOMETHING?!
NO, NO, THAT'S TOO FULL-BLOWN FOR A GAME!
C'MON!
NOT DURING CLASS! PUT THAT AWAY!
WOW!
SCHAK
A GLOVE CONTROLLER? SUCH THINGS REALLY EXIST...?
HOLD ON, THIS IS ODD.
MAYBE IT'S ALL JUST FOR SHOW, WITH NO ACTUAL VR IMAGES?
SEKI COULD BE JUST USING HIS IMAGINATION TO HAVE FUN.
I BET THAT'S IT.
AND THE EQUIPMENT IS HIS USUAL HANDIWORK.

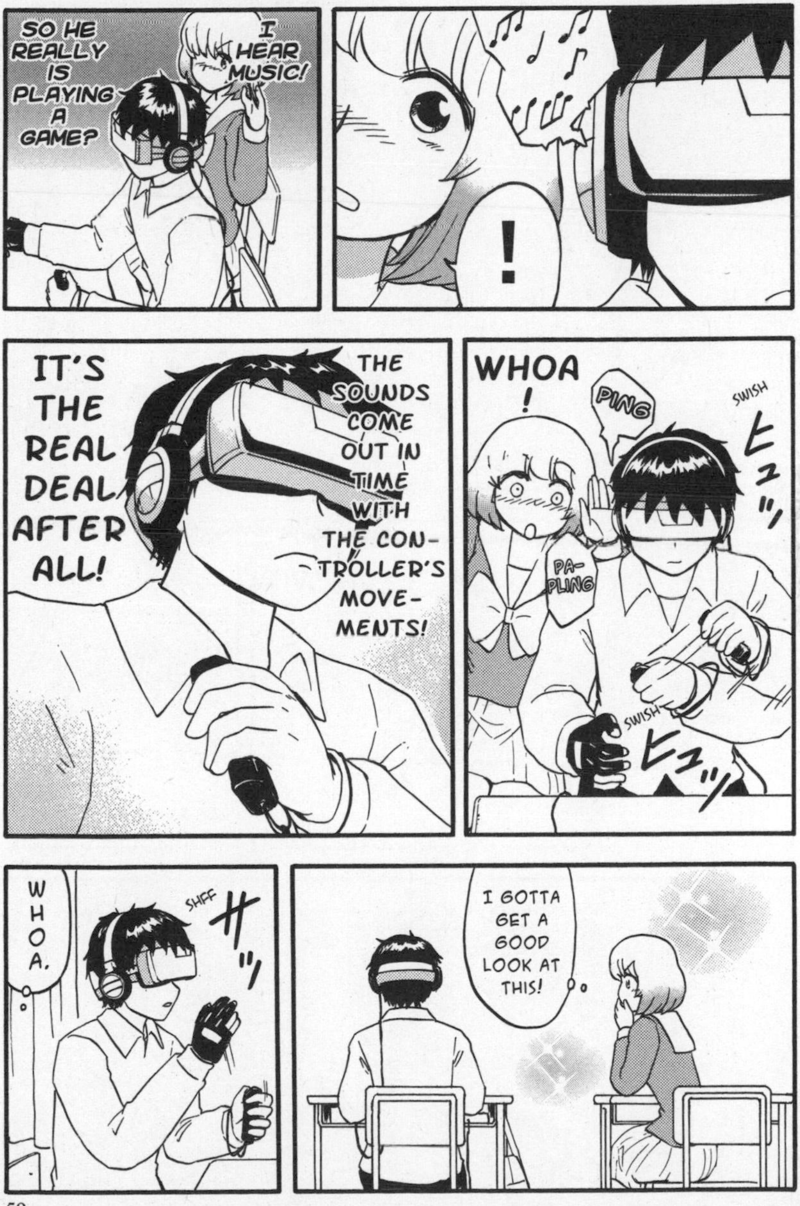
!
I HEAR MUSIC!
SO HE REALLY IS PLAYING A GAME?
WHOA !
PING
SWISH
PA-PLING
SWISH
THE SOUNDS COME OUT IN TIME WITH THE CON-TROLLER'S MOVE-MENTS!
IT'S THE REAL DEAL AFTER ALL!
I GOTTA GET A GOOD LOOK AT THIS!
SHFF
WHOA.

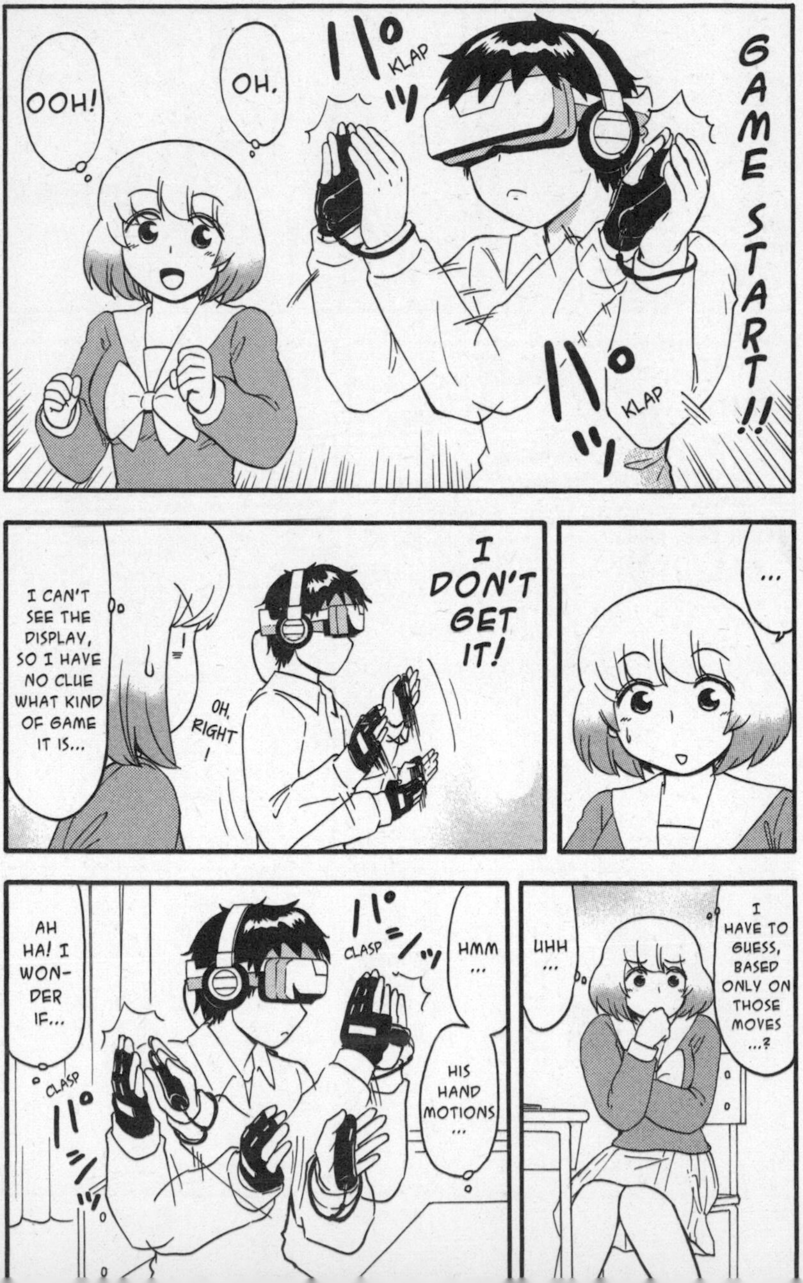
GAME START!!
KLAP
KLAP
OH.
OOH!
...
I DON'T GET IT!
OH, RIGHT!
I CAN'T SEE THE DISPLAY, SO I HAVE NO CLUE WHAT KIND OF GAME IT IS...
I HAVE TO GUESS, BASED ONLY ON THOSE MOVES ...?
UHH ...
HMM ...
HIS HAND MOTIONS ...
CLASP
AH HA! I WONDER IF...
CLASP

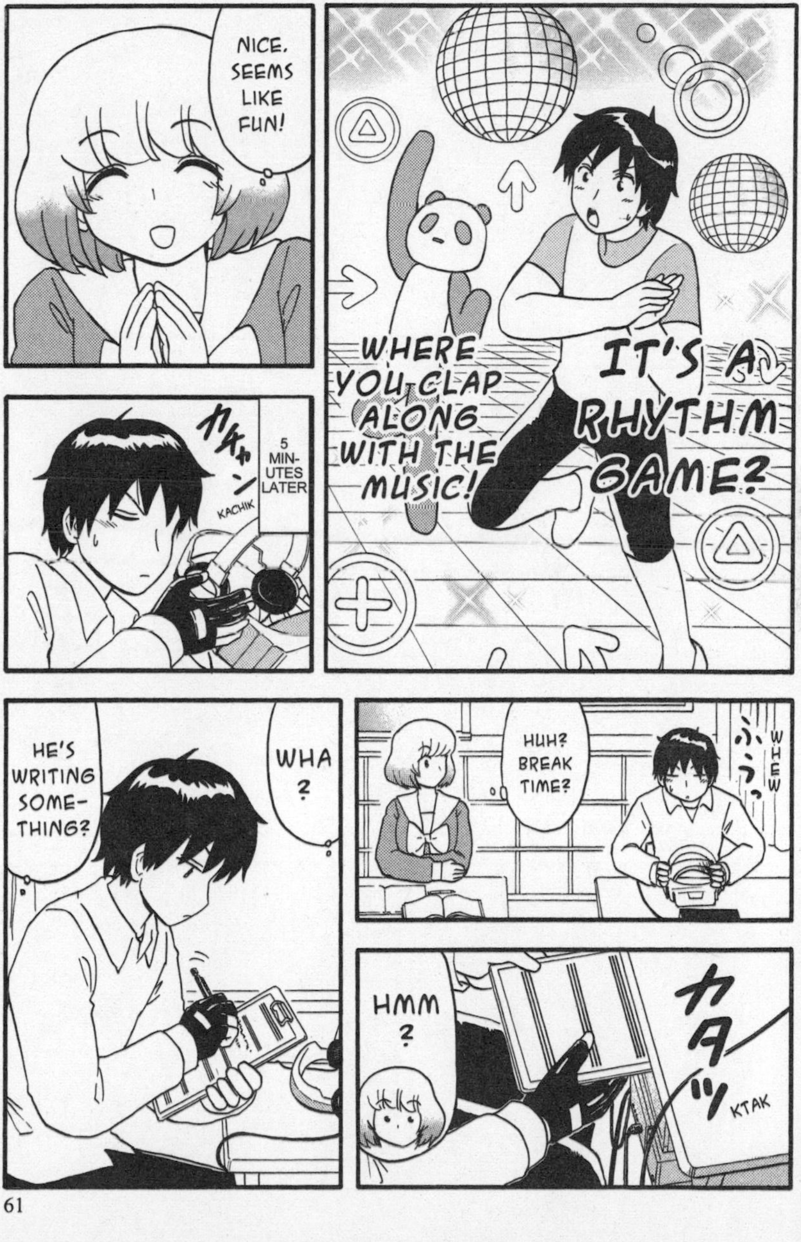
IT'S A RHYTHM GAME?
WHERE YOU CLAP ALONG WITH THE MUSIC!
NICE. SEEMS LIKE FUN!
5 MINUTES LATER
カチャン
KACHIK
ふうっ
WHEW
HUH? BREAK TIME?
カタッ
KTAK
HMM?
WHA?
HE'S WRITING SOMETHING?

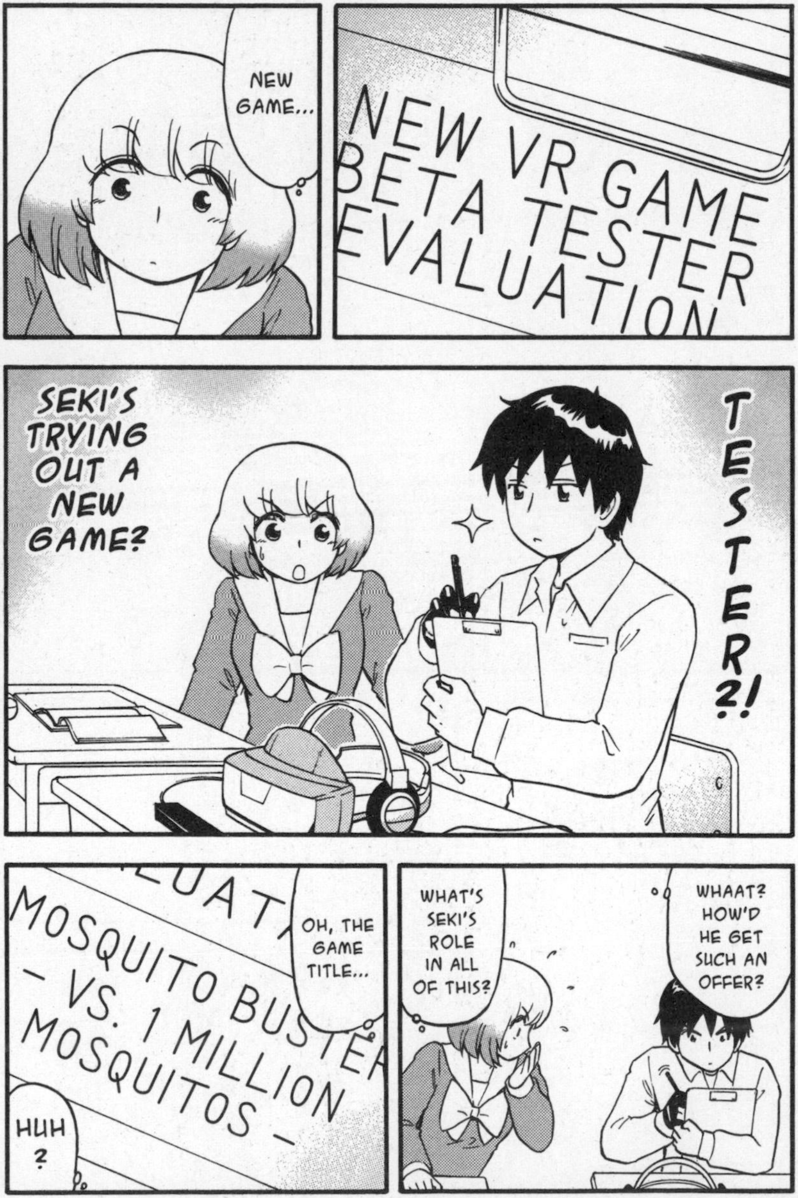
NEW VR GAME BETA TESTER EVALUATION
NEW GAME...
TESTER?!
SEKI'S TRYING OUT A NEW GAME?
WHAAT? HOW'D HE GET SUCH AN OFFER?
WHAT'S SEKI'S ROLE IN ALL OF THIS?
OH, THE GAME TITLE...
MOSQUITO BUSTE
- VS. 1 MILLION MOSQUITOS -
HUH?

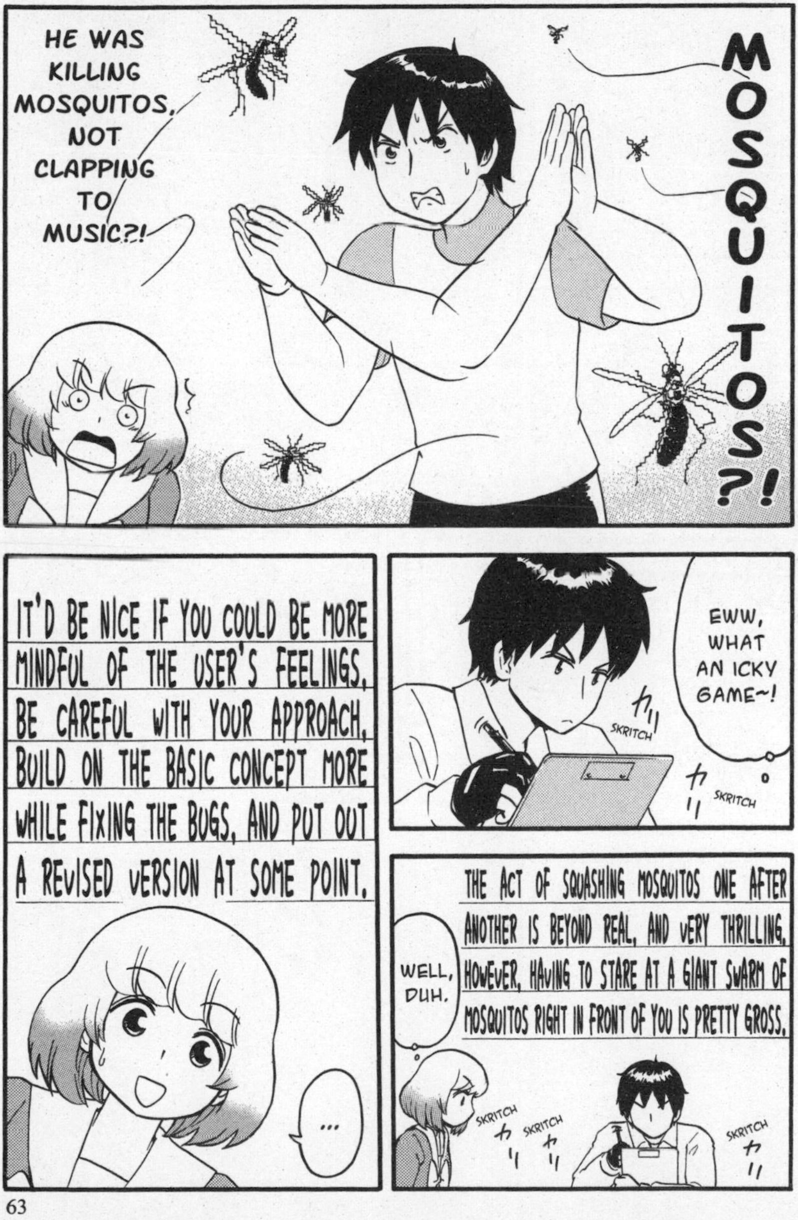
MOSQUITOS?!
HE WAS KILLING MOSQUITOS, NOT CLAPPING TO MUSIC?!
EWW, WHAT AN ICKY GAME~!
SKRITCH
SKRITCH
THE ACT OF SQUASHING MOSQUITOS ONE AFTER ANOTHER IS BEYOND REAL, AND VERY THRILLING. HOWEVER, HAVING TO STARE AT A GIANT SWARM OF MOSQUITOS RIGHT IN FRONT OF YOU IS PRETTY GROSS.
WELL, DUH.
SKRITCH
SKRITCH
SKRITCH
IT'D BE NICE IF YOU COULD BE MORE MINDFUL OF THE USER'S FEELINGS. BE CAREFUL WITH YOUR APPROACH. BUILD ON THE BASIC CONCEPT MORE WHILE FIXING THE BUGS, AND PUT OUT A REVISED VERSION AT SOME POINT.
...

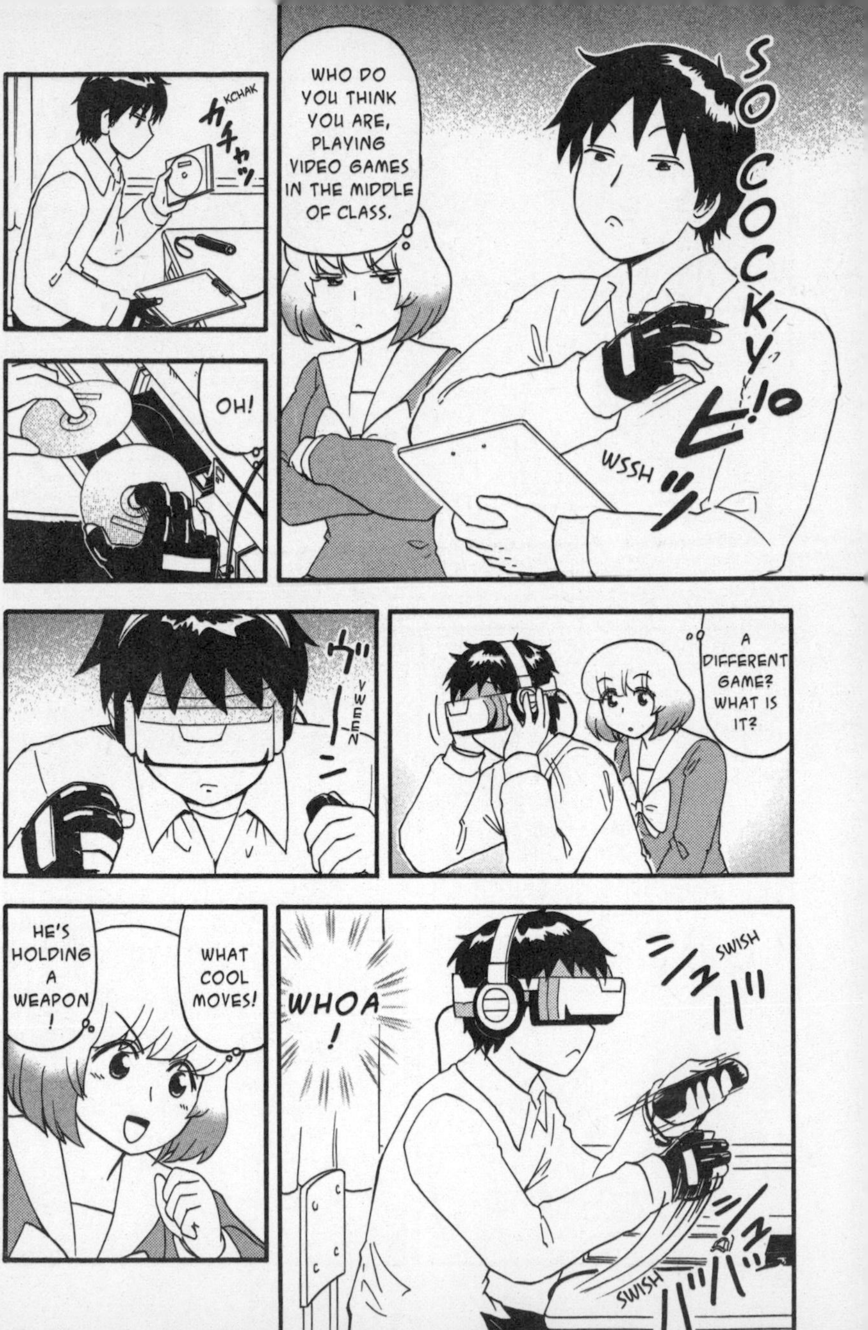
SO COCKY!
WHO DO YOU THINK YOU ARE, PLAYING VIDEO GAMES IN THE MIDDLE OF CLASS.
WSSH
KCHAK
OH!
A DIFFERENT GAME? WHAT IS IT?
VWEEN
SWISH
WHOA!
SWISH
WHAT COOL MOVES!
HE'S HOLDING A WEAPON!

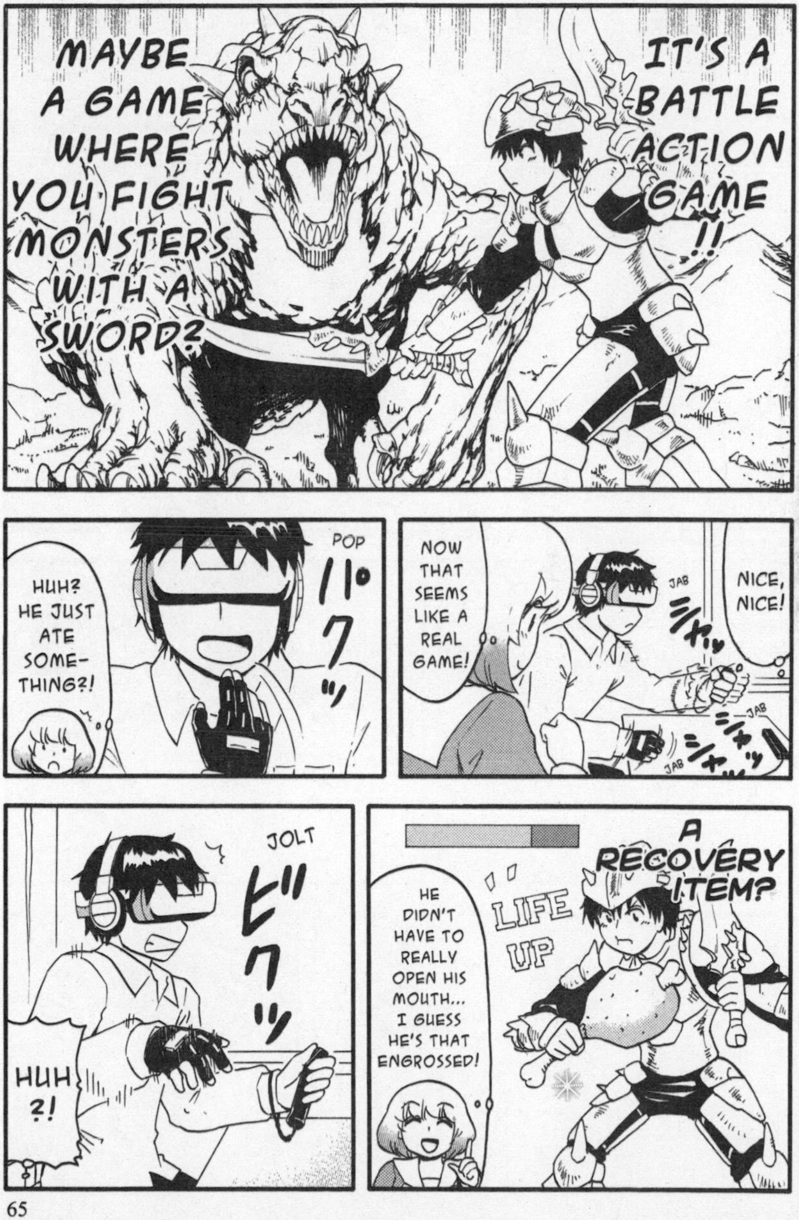
IT'S A BATTLE ACTION GAME!!
MAYBE A GAME WHERE YOU FIGHT MONSTERS WITH A SWORD?
NICE, NICE!
JAB
シャッ
JAB
シャッ
JAB
シャッ
NOW THAT SEEMS LIKE A REAL GAME!
POP
パクッ
HUH? HE JUST ATE SOME-THING?!
A RECOVERY ITEM?
LIFE UP
HE DIDN'T HAVE TO REALLY OPEN HIS MOUTH... I GUESS HE'S THAT ENGROSSED!
JOLT
ビクッ
HUH?!

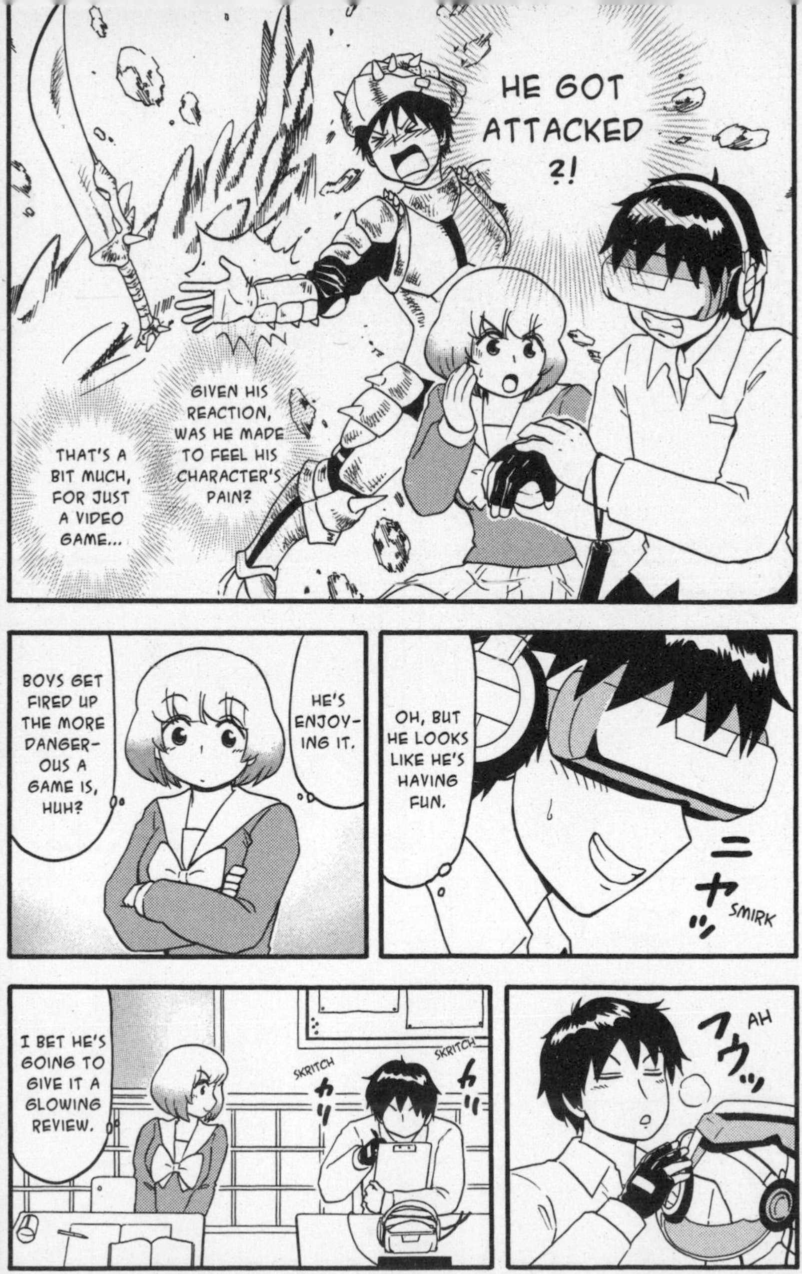
HE GOT ATTACKED?!
GIVEN HIS REACTION, WAS HE MADE TO FEEL HIS CHARACTER'S PAIN?
THAT'S A BIT MUCH, FOR JUST A VIDEO GAME...
OH, BUT HE LOOKS LIKE HE'S HAVING FUN.
ニヤッ
SMIRK
HE'S ENJOYING IT.
BOYS GET FIRED UP THE MORE DANGEROUS A GAME IS, HUH?
フウッ
AH
SKRITCH
カリ
SKRITCH
カリ
I BET HE'S GOING TO GIVE IT A GLOWING REVIEW.

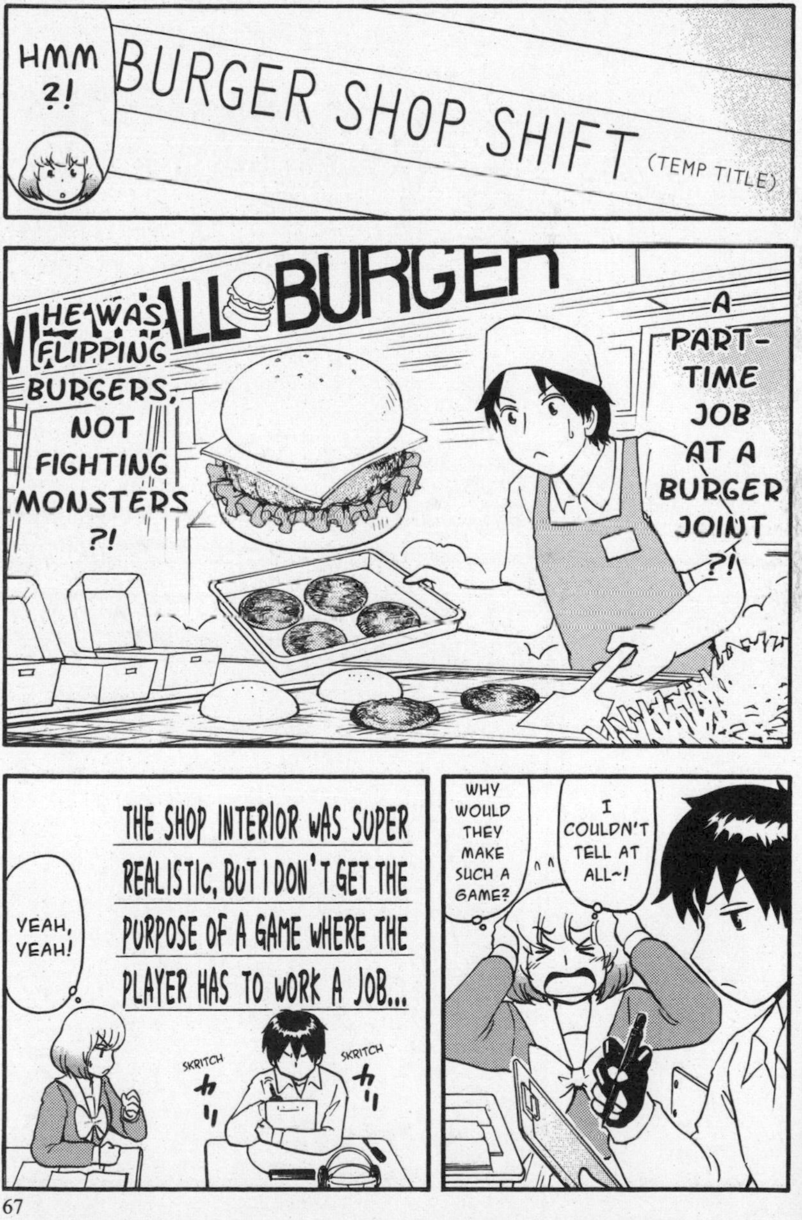
BURGER SHOP SHIFT
(TEMP TITLE)
HMM ?!
BURGER
A PART-TIME JOB AT A BURGER JOINT ?!
HE WAS FLIPPING BURGERS, NOT FIGHTING MONSTERS ?!
I COULDN'T TELL AT ALL~!
WHY WOULD THEY MAKE SUCH A GAME?
THE SHOP INTERIOR WAS SUPER REALISTIC, BUT I DON'T GET THE PURPOSE OF A GAME WHERE THE PLAYER HAS TO WORK A JOB...
YEAH, YEAH!
SKRITCH
SKRITCH

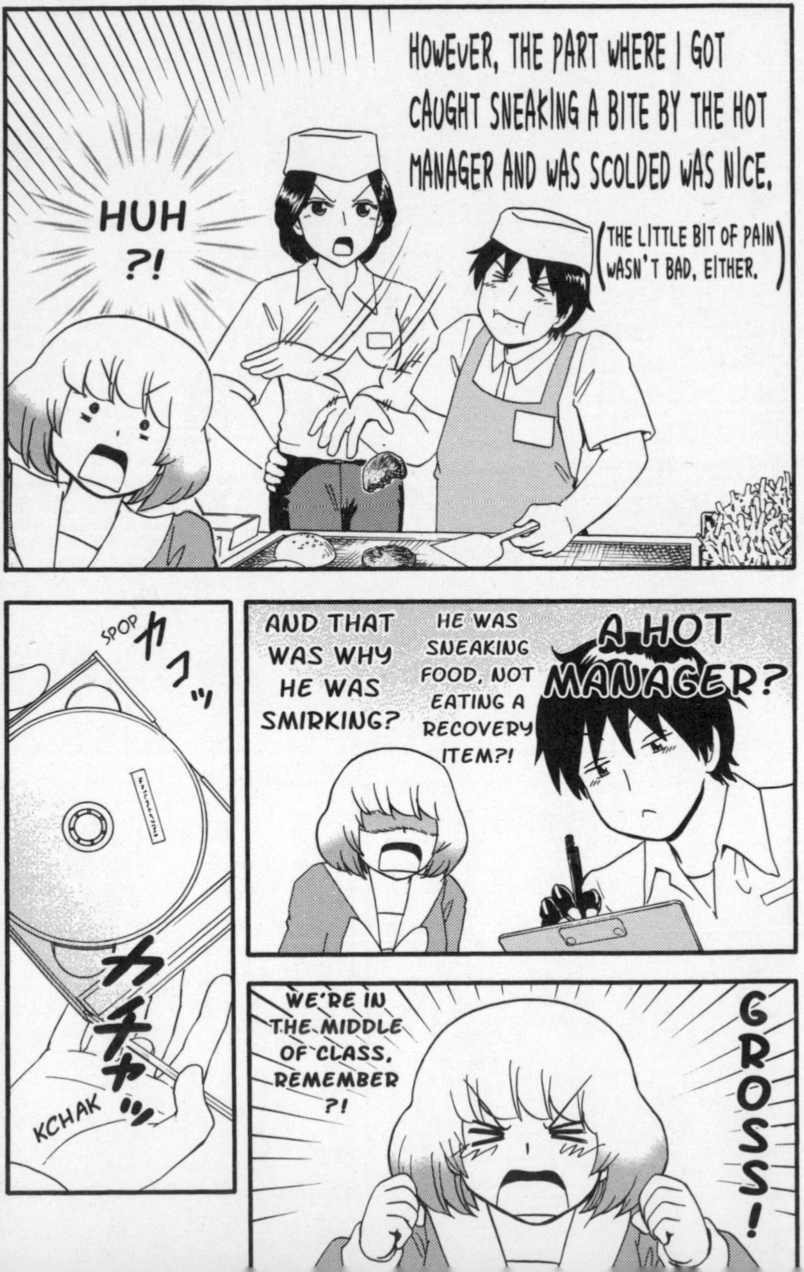
HOWEVER, THE PART WHERE I GOT CAUGHT SNEAKING A BITE BY THE HOT MANAGER AND WAS SCOLDED WAS NICE.
(THE LITTLE BIT OF PAIN WASN'T BAD, EITHER.)
HUH ?!
A HOT MANAGER?
HE WAS SNEAKING FOOD, NOT EATING A RECOVERY ITEM?!
AND THAT WAS WHY HE WAS SMIRKING?
GROSS!
WE'RE IN THE MIDDLE OF CLASS, REMEMBER ?!
カコッ
SPOP
カチャッ
KCHAK

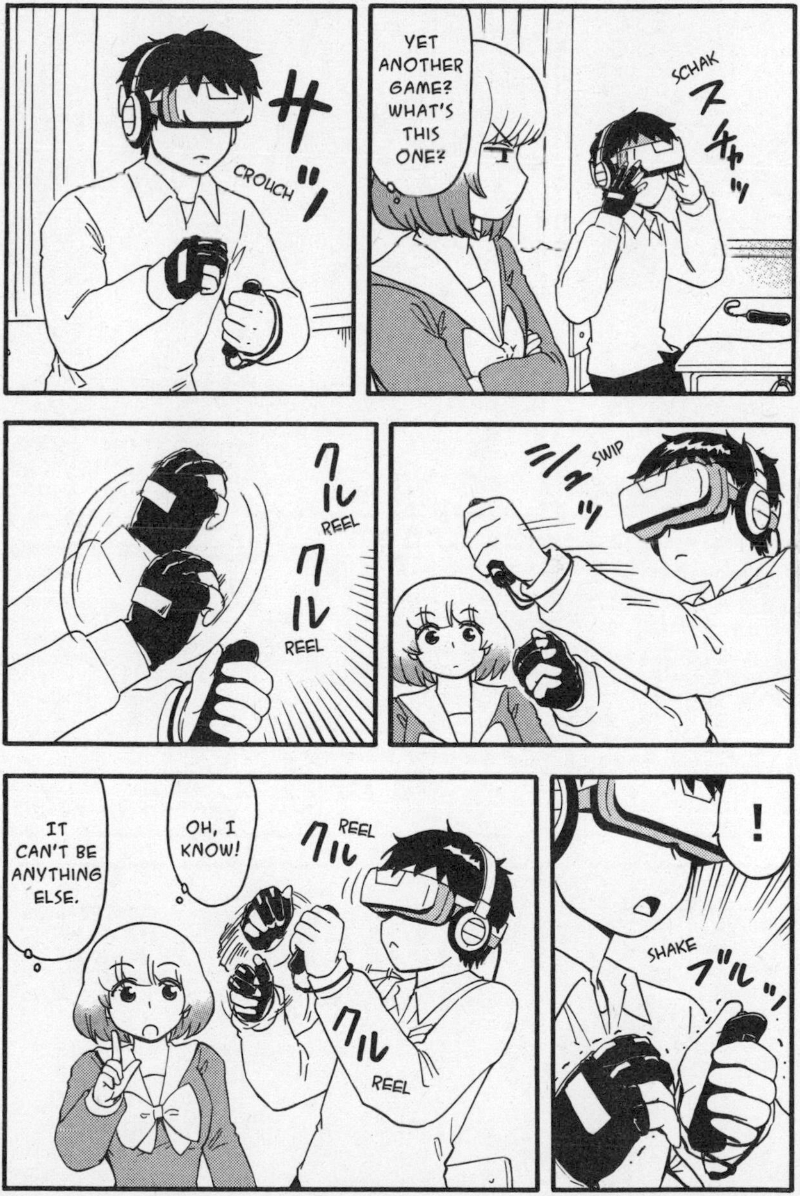
YET ANOTHER GAME? WHAT'S THIS ONE?
SCHAK
スチャッ
サッ
CROUCH
シュッ
SWIP
クル
REEL
クル
REEL
!
SHAKE
ブルッ
クル
REEL
OH, I KNOW!
IT CAN'T BE ANYTHING ELSE.
クル
REEL

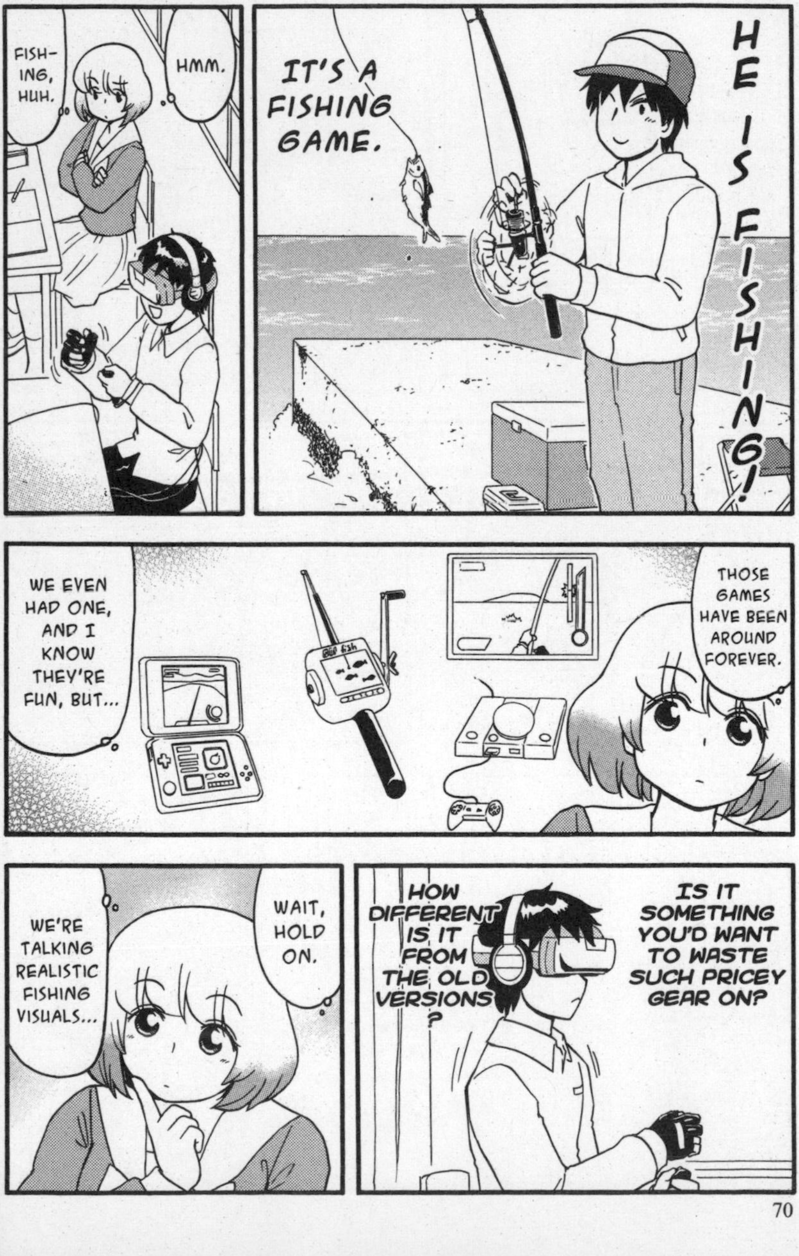
HE IS FISHING!
IT'S A FISHING GAME.
HMM.
FISHING, HUH.
THOSE GAMES HAVE BEEN AROUND FOREVER.
WE EVEN HAD ONE, AND I KNOW THEY'RE FUN, BUT...
IS IT SOMETHING YOU'D WANT TO WASTE SUCH PRICEY GEAR ON?
HOW DIFFERENT IS IT FROM THE OLD VERSIONS?
WAIT, HOLD ON.
WE'RE TALKING REALISTIC FISHING VISUALS...

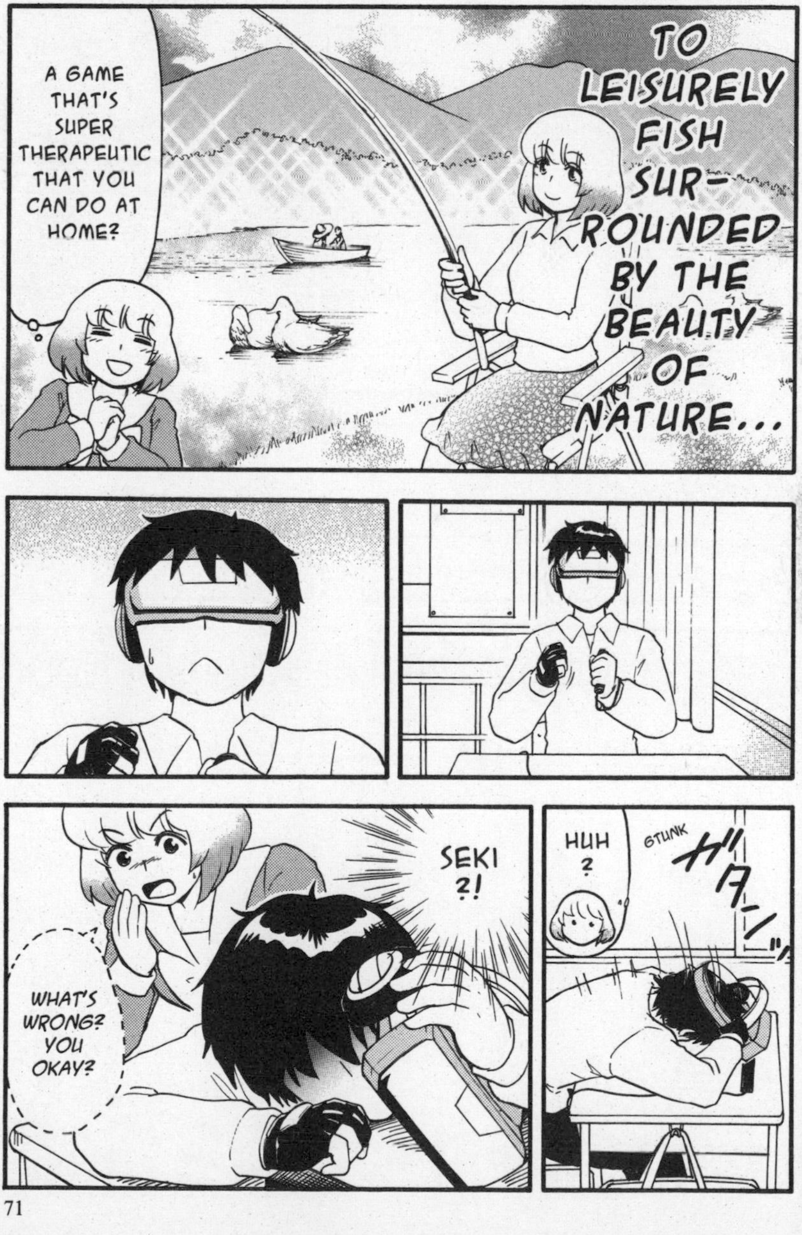
TO LEISURELY FISH SUR-ROUNDED BY THE BEAUTY OF NATURE...
A GAME THAT'S SUPER THERAPEUTIC THAT YOU CAN DO AT HOME?
GTUNK
HUH?
SEKI?!
WHAT'S WRONG? YOU OKAY?

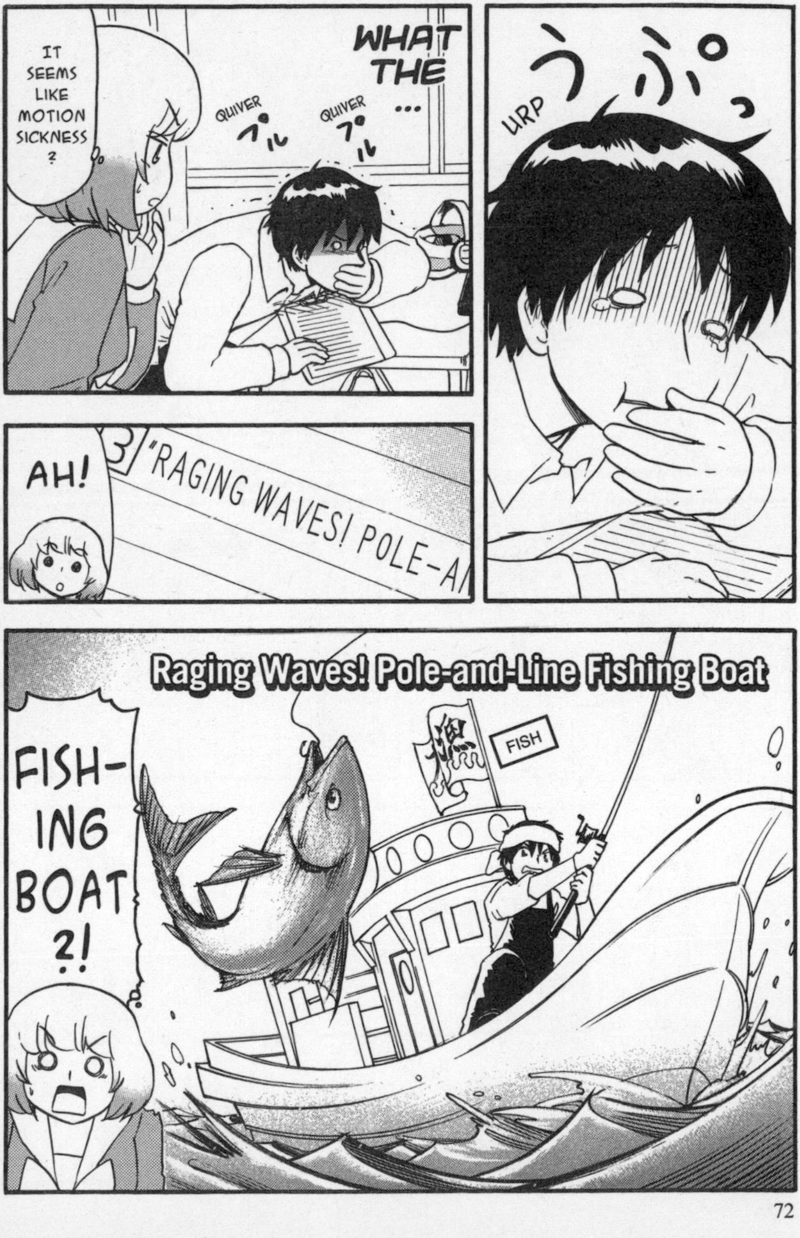

URP
うぷっ
WHAT THE ...
QUIVER プル
QUIVER プル
IT SEEMS LIKE MOTION SICKNESS?
AH!
3 "RAGING WAVES! POLE-A
Raging Waves! Pole-and-Line Fishing Boat
FISH
FISHING BOAT?!

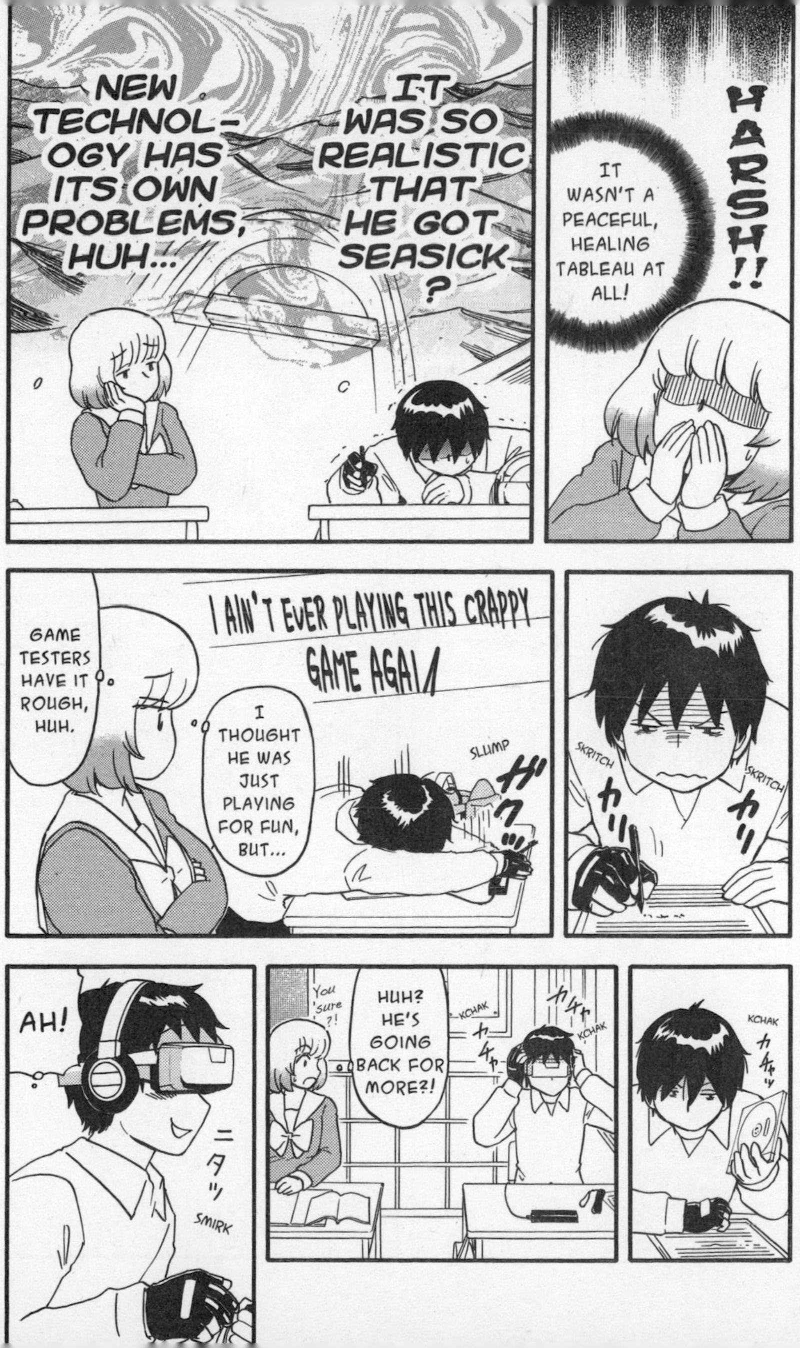
HARSH!!
IT WASN'T A PEACEFUL, HEALING TABLEAU AT ALL!
IT WAS SO REALISTIC THAT HE GOT SEASICK?
NEW TECHNOLOGY HAS ITS OWN PROBLEMS, HUH...
SKRITCH
SKRITCH
I AIN'T EVER PLAYING THIS CRAPPY GAME AGAIN
SLUMP
I THOUGHT HE WAS JUST PLAYING FOR FUN, BUT...
GAME TESTERS HAVE IT ROUGH, HUH.
KCHAK
KCHAK
KCHAK
HUH? HE'S GOING BACK FOR MORE?!
You sure?!
AH!
SMIRK

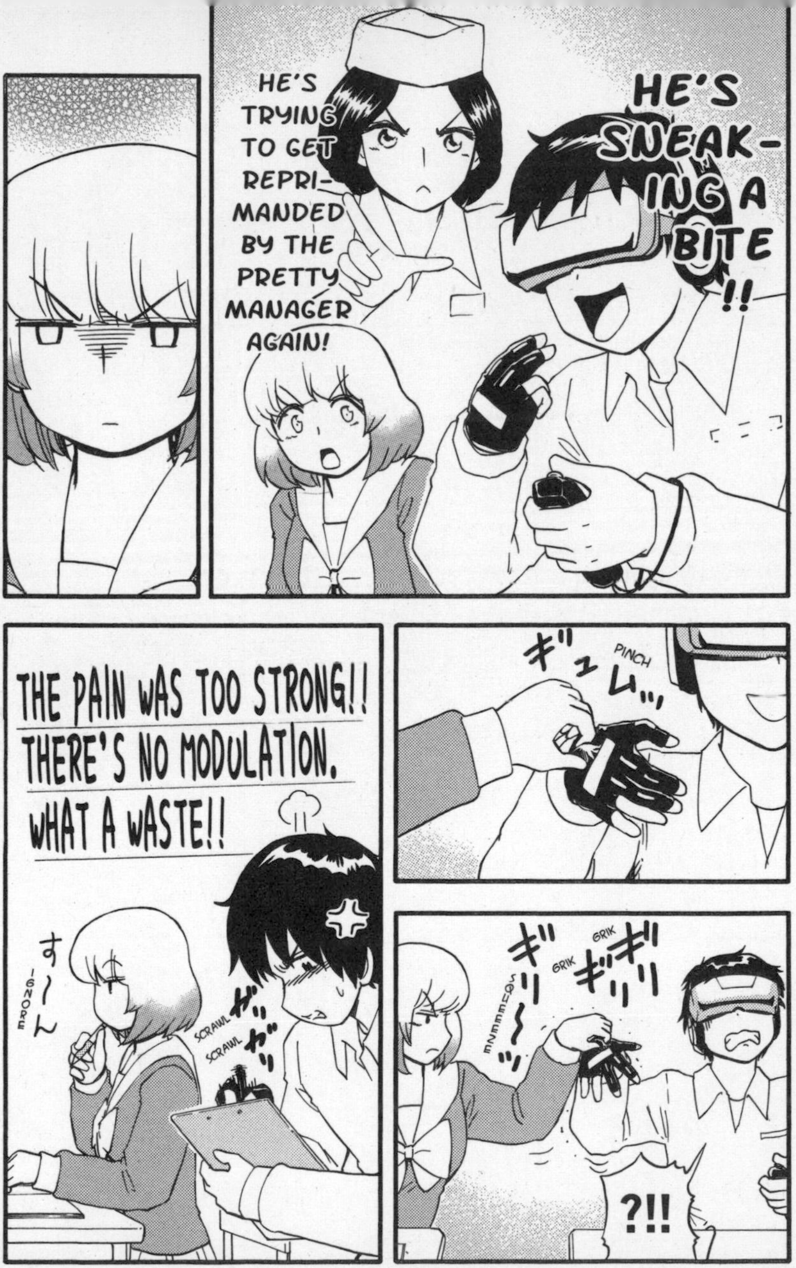
HE'S SNEAK-ING A BITE!!
HE'S TRYING TO GET REPRI-MANDED BY THE PRETTY MANAGER AGAIN!
ギュム…
PINCH
ギリギリ
GRIK GRIK
ギリ〜ッ
SQUEEEEEZE
?!!
THE PAIN WAS TOO STRONG!! THERE'S NO MODULATION. WHAT A WASTE!!
ガッガッ
SCRAWL SCRAWL
す〜ん
IGNORE

• 126th Period •

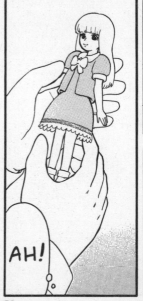

AH!

SKRITCH

SKRITCH

SO NOISY. WHAT IS IT TODAY ?

KCHK

RUSTLE

RUSTLE

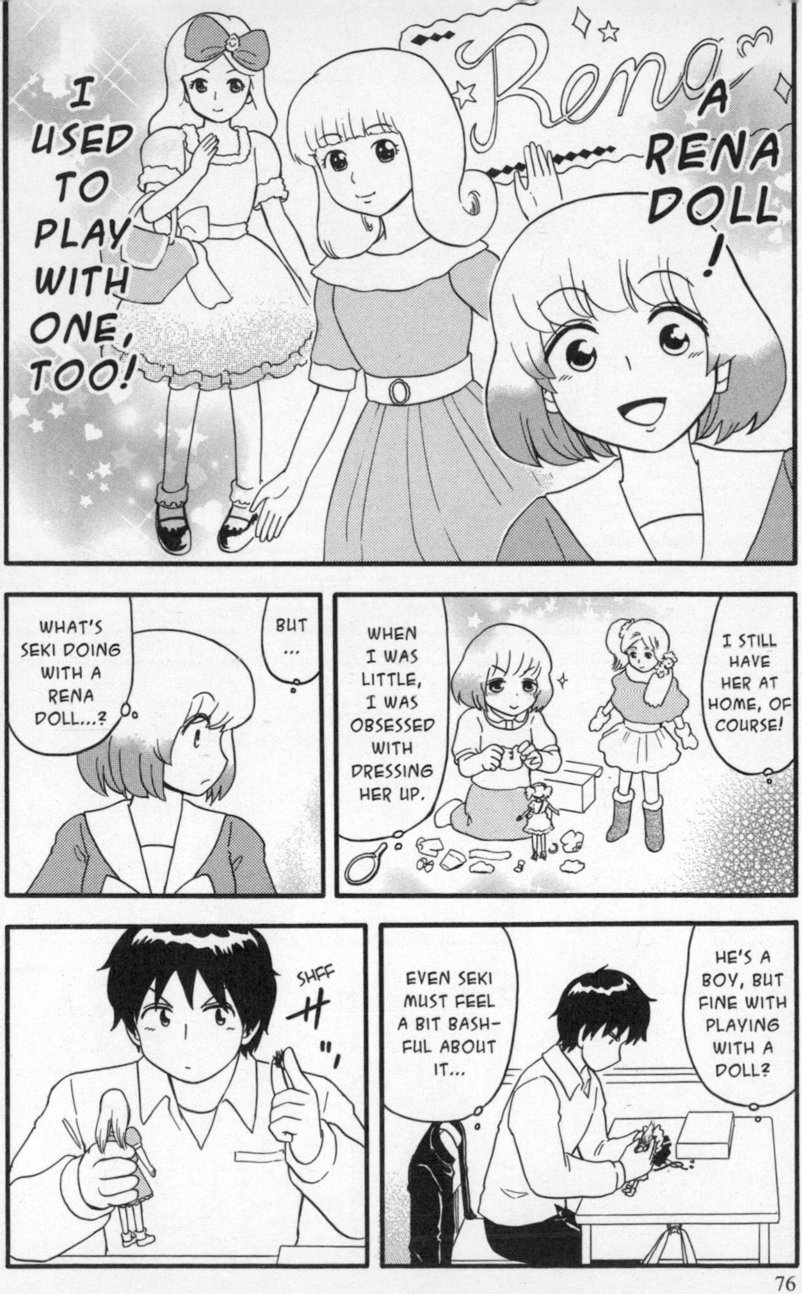
Rena
A RENA DOLL!
I USED TO PLAY WITH ONE, TOO!
I STILL HAVE HER AT HOME, OF COURSE!
WHEN I WAS LITTLE, I WAS OBSESSED WITH DRESSING HER UP.
BUT ...
WHAT'S SEKI DOING WITH A RENA DOLL...?
HE'S A BOY, BUT FINE WITH PLAYING WITH A DOLL?
EVEN SEKI MUST FEEL A BIT BASHFUL ABOUT IT...
SHFF

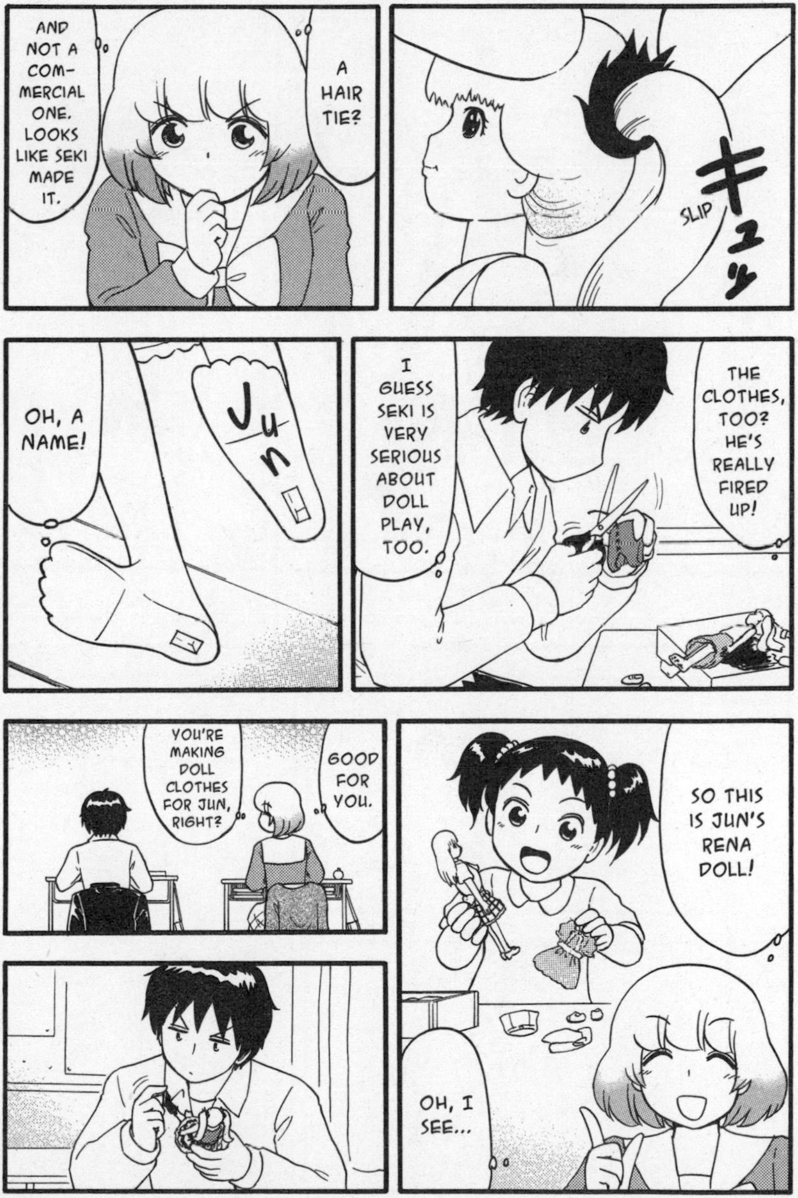

SLIP
キュッ
A HAIR TIE?
AND NOT A COM-MERCIAL ONE. LOOKS LIKE SEKI MADE IT.
THE CLOTHES, TOO? HE'S REALLY FIRED UP!
I GUESS SEKI IS VERY SERIOUS ABOUT DOLL PLAY, TOO.
Jun
OH, A NAME!
SO THIS IS JUN'S RENA DOLL!
OH, I SEE...
GOOD FOR YOU.
YOU'RE MAKING DOLL CLOTHES FOR JUN, RIGHT?

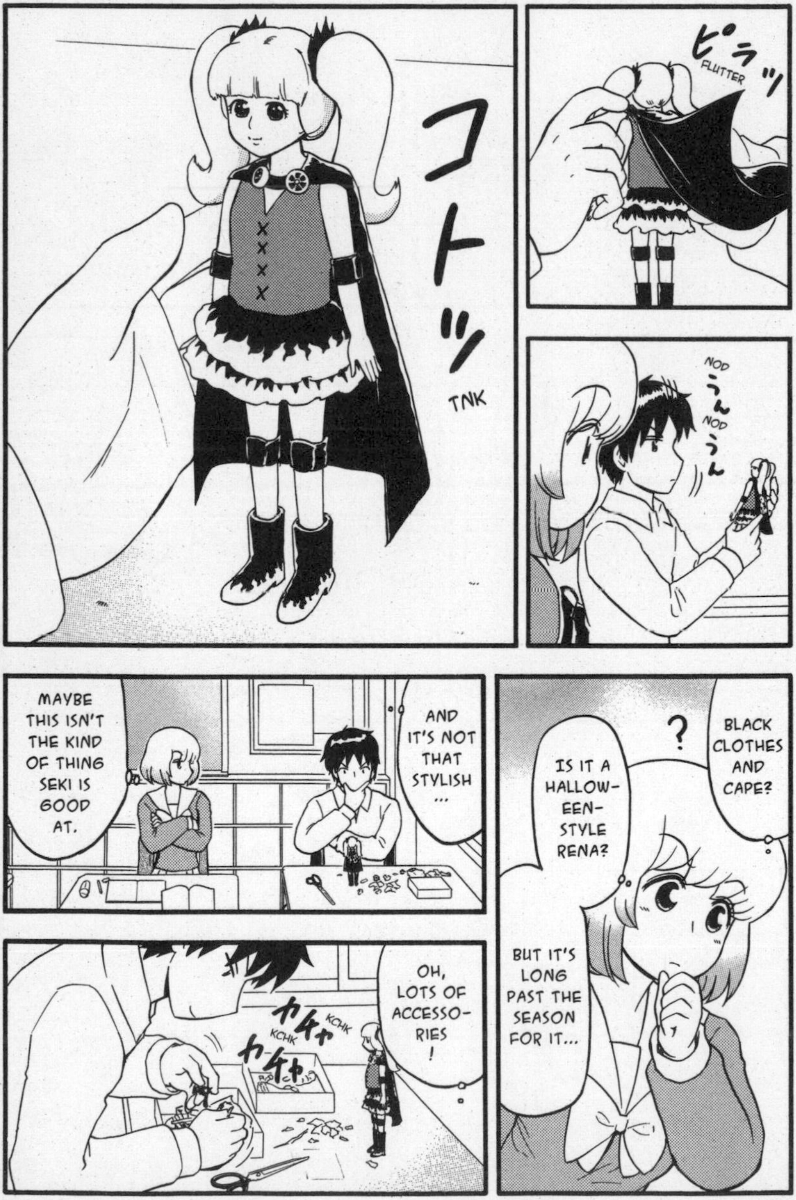
ピラッ
FLUTTER
うん NOD
うん NOD
コトッ
TNK
?
BLACK CLOTHES AND CAPE?
IS IT A HALLOWEEN-STYLE RENA?
BUT IT'S LONG PAST THE SEASON FOR IT...
AND IT'S NOT THAT STYLISH...
MAYBE THIS ISN'T THE KIND OF THING SEKI IS GOOD AT.
OH, LOTS OF ACCESSORIES!
カチャ KCHK
カチャ KCHK

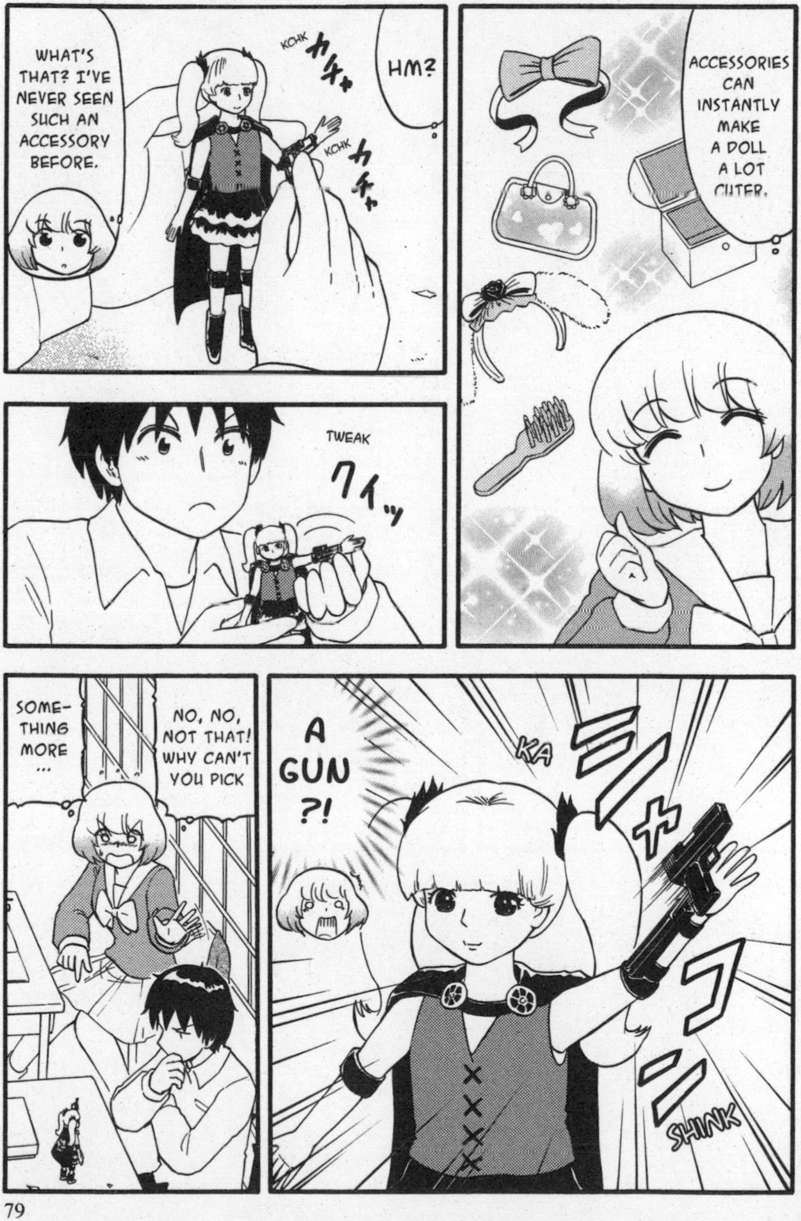
ACCESSORIES CAN INSTANTLY MAKE A DOLL A LOT CUTER.
HM?
KCHK カチャ
KCHK カチャ
WHAT'S THAT? I'VE NEVER SEEN SUCH AN ACCESSORY BEFORE.
TWEAK クイッ
KA
SHINK
A GUN ?!
NO, NO, NOT THAT! WHY CAN'T YOU PICK
SOME-THING MORE ...

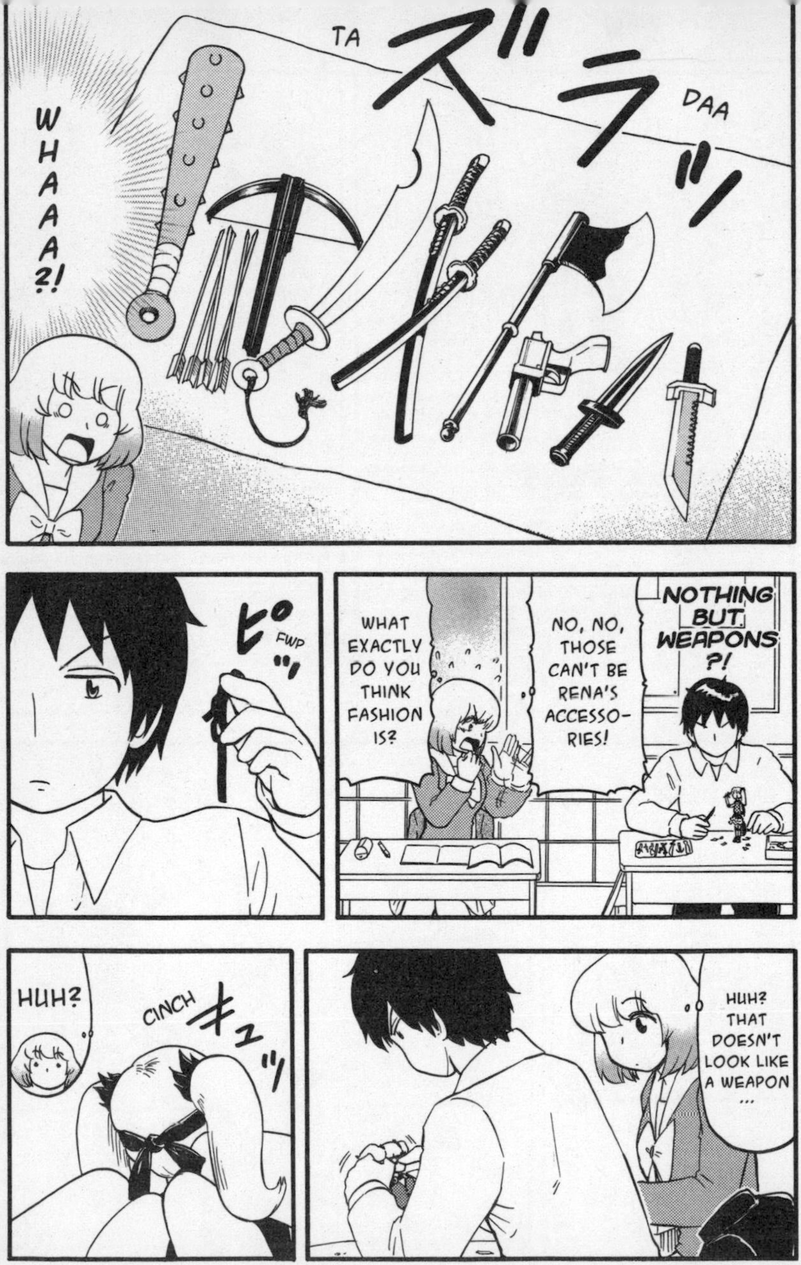
TA
DAA
WHAAAAA?!
NOTHING BUT WEAPONS?!
NO, NO, THOSE CAN'T BE RENA'S ACCESSORIES!
WHAT EXACTLY DO YOU THINK FASHION IS?
FWP
HUH? THAT DOESN'T LOOK LIKE A WEAPON ...
CINCH
HUH?

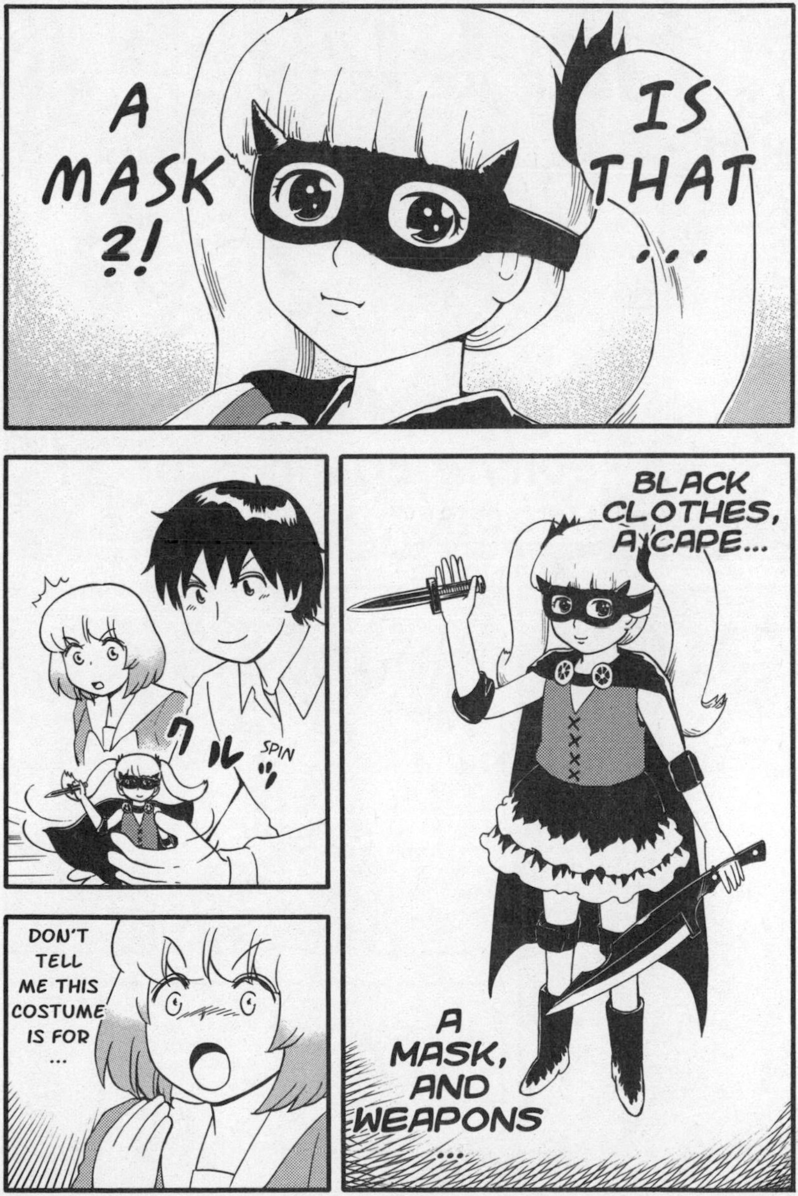
IS THAT ...
A MASK ?!
BLACK CLOTHES, A CAPE...
A MASK, AND WEAPONS ...
クルッ
SPIN
DON'T TELL ME THIS COSTUME IS FOR ...

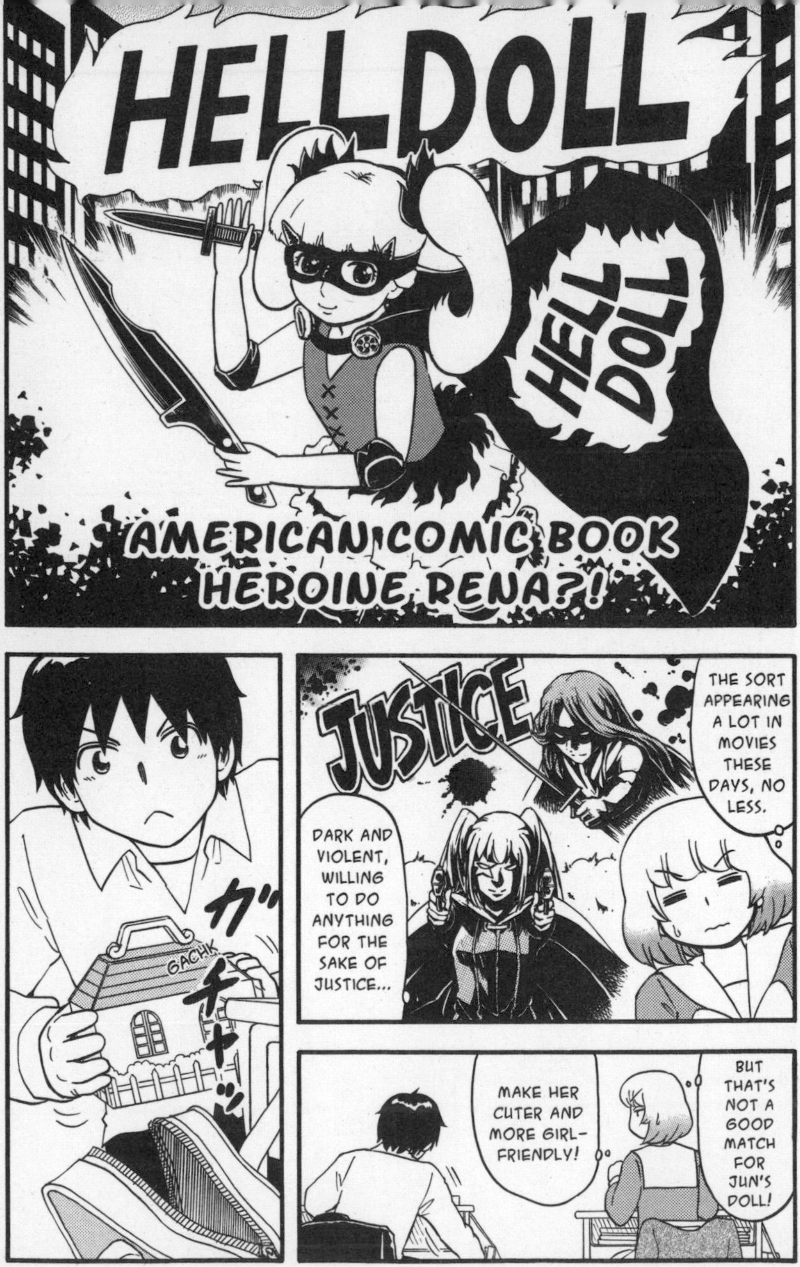
HELLDOLL
HELL DOLL
AMERICAN COMIC BOOK HEROINE RENA?!
THE SORT APPEARING A LOT IN MOVIES THESE DAYS, NO LESS.
JUSTICE
DARK AND VIOLENT, WILLING TO DO ANYTHING FOR THE SAKE OF JUSTICE...
BUT THAT'S NOT A GOOD MATCH FOR JUN'S DOLL!
MAKE HER CUTER AND MORE GIRL-FRIENDLY!
ガ
GACHK
チャッ

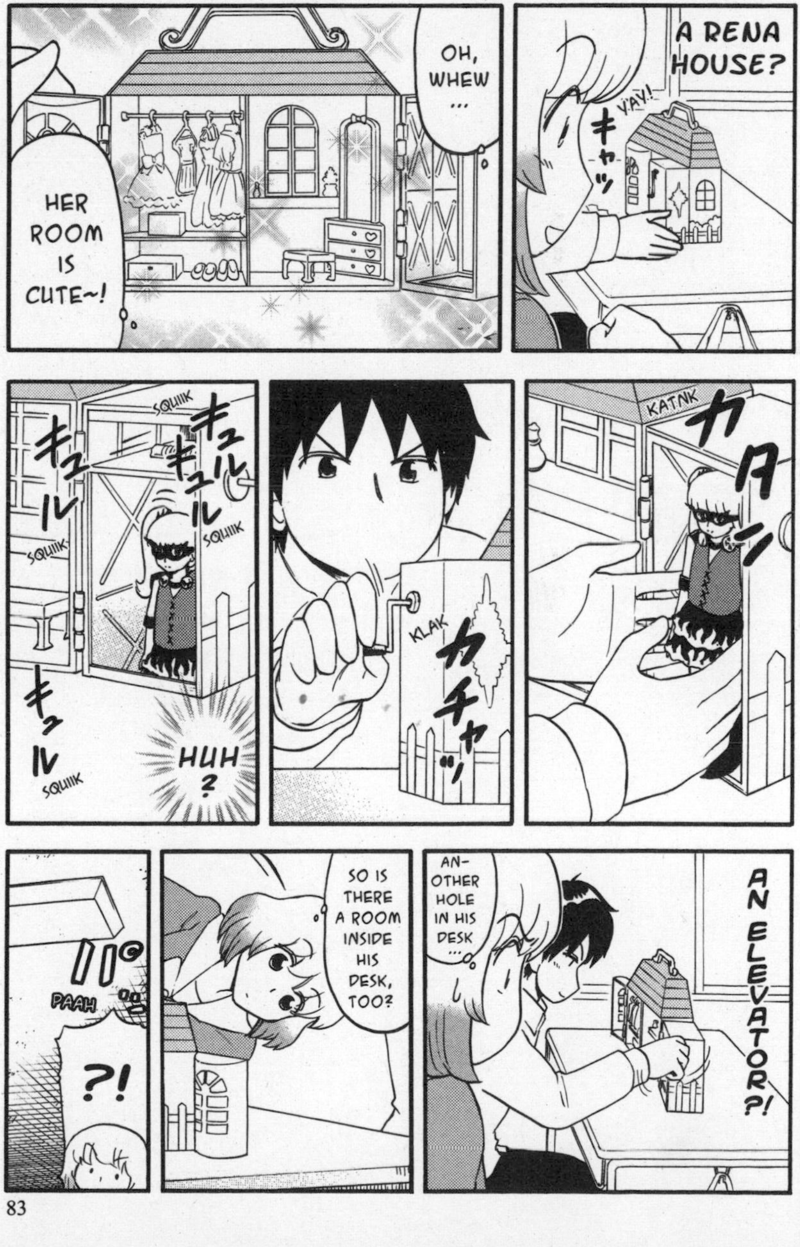
A RENA HOUSE?
YAY!
キャッ
OH, WHEW ...
HER ROOM IS CUTE~!
KATNK
カタン
KLAK
カチャッ
SQUIIK
キュルキュル
SQUIIK
SQUIIK
SQUIIK
HUH?
AN ELEVATOR?!
ANOTHER HOLE IN HIS DESK ....
SO IS THERE A ROOM INSIDE HIS DESK, TOO?
PAAH
?!

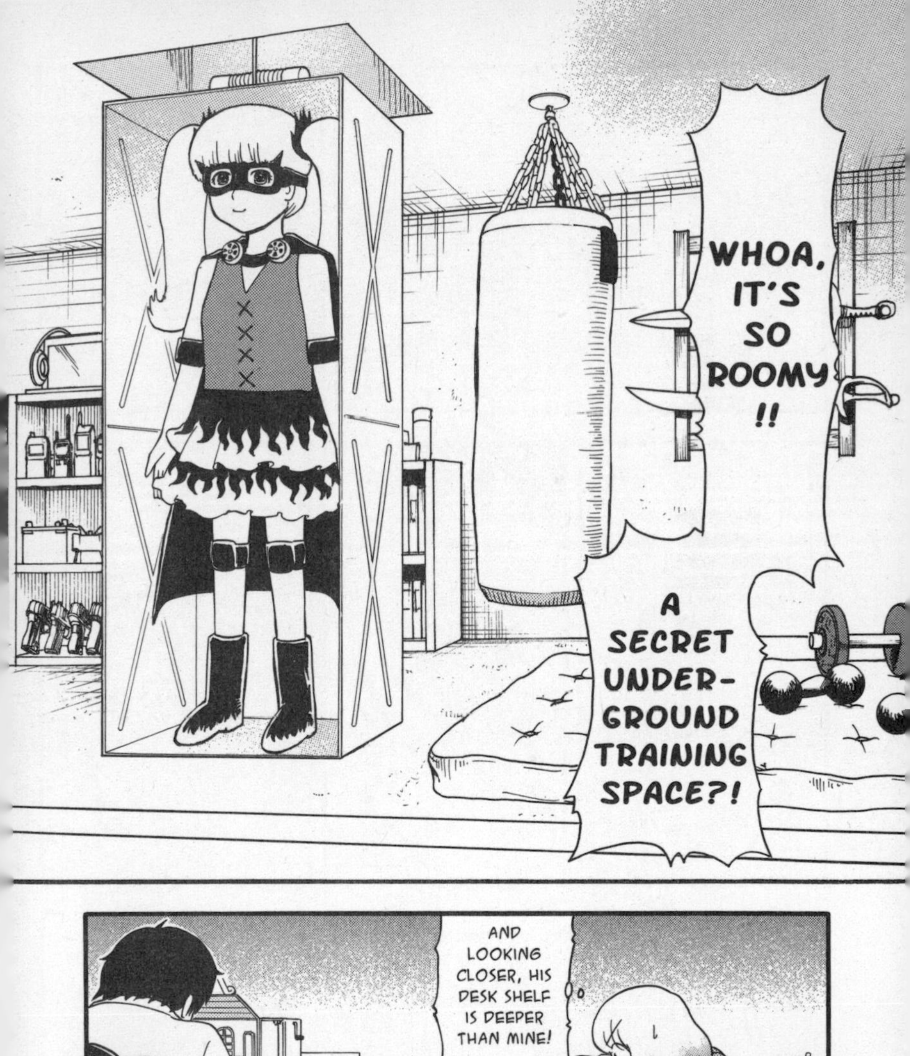
WHOA, IT'S SO ROOMY!!
A SECRET UNDER-GROUND TRAINING SPACE?!
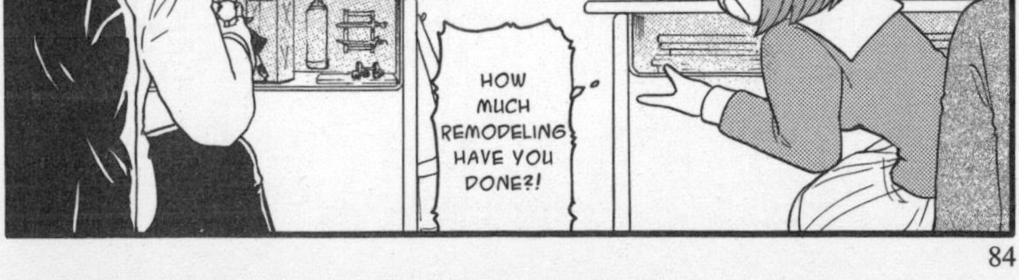
AND LOOKING CLOSER, HIS DESK SHELF IS DEEPER THAN MINE!
HOW MUCH REMODELING HAVE YOU DONE?!

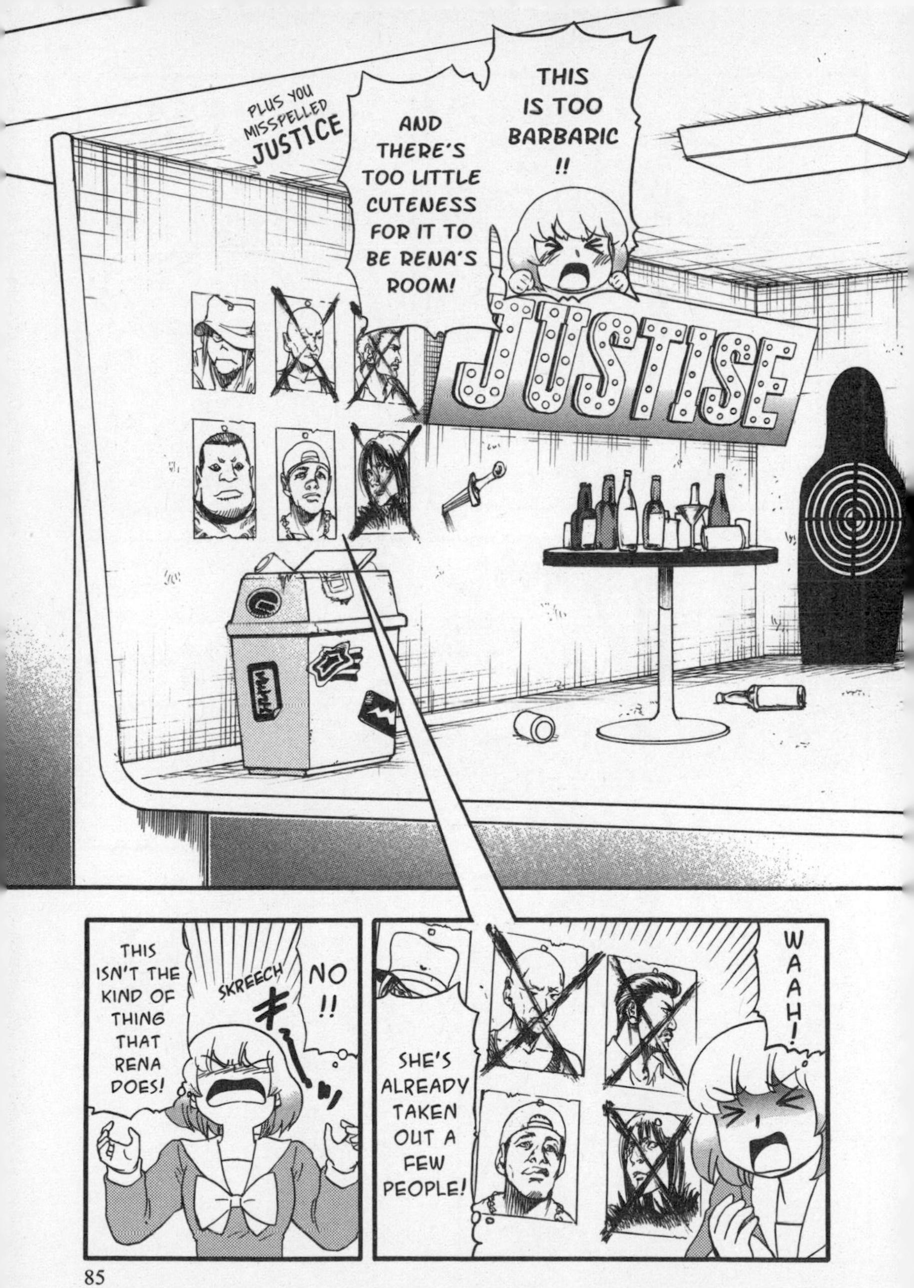
THIS IS TOO BARBARIC !!
AND THERE'S TOO LITTLE CUTENESS FOR IT TO BE RENA'S ROOM!
PLUS YOU MISSPELLED JUSTICE
JUSTISE
WAAH!
SHE'S ALREADY TAKEN OUT A FEW PEOPLE!
NO !!
SKREECH
THIS ISN'T THE KIND OF THING THAT RENA DOES!

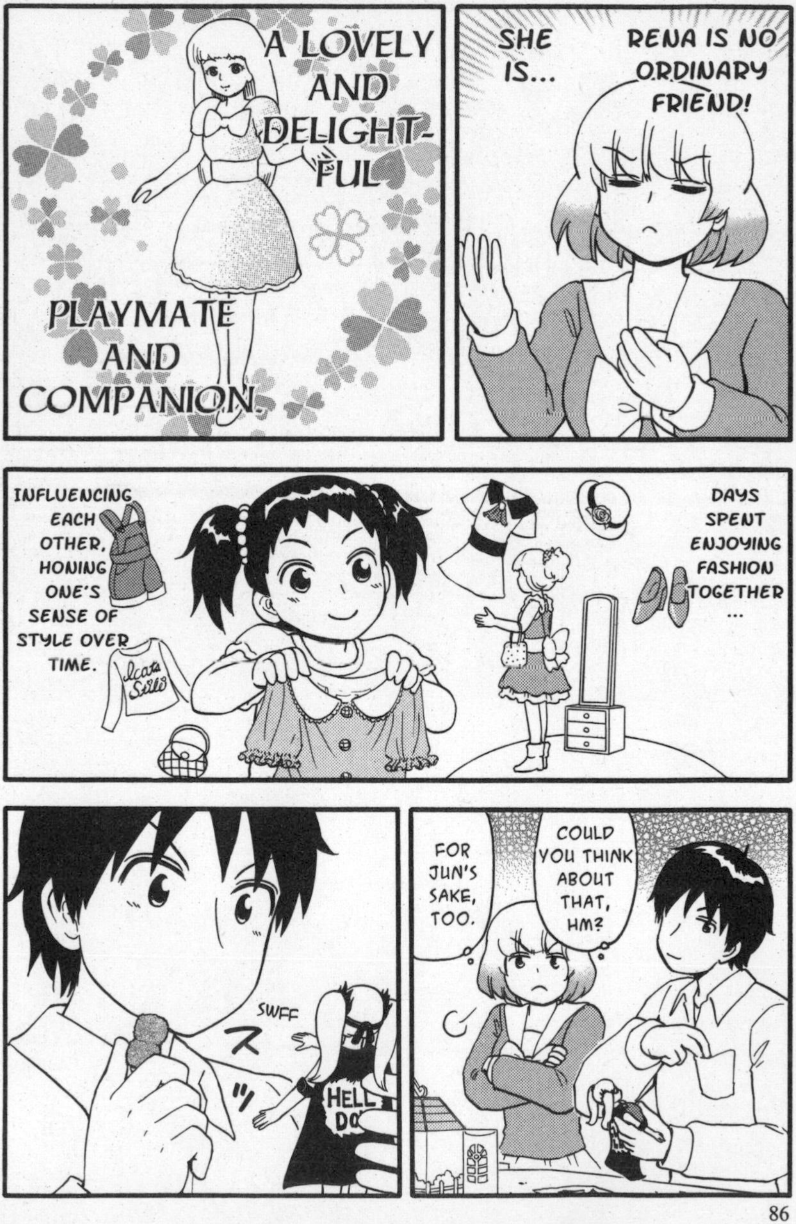
RENA IS NO ORDINARY FRIEND!
SHE IS...
A LOVELY AND DELIGHT-FUL
PLAYMATE AND COMPANION.
DAYS SPENT ENJOYING FASHION TOGETHER...
INFLUENCING EACH OTHER, HONING ONE'S SENSE OF STYLE OVER TIME.
COULD YOU THINK ABOUT THAT, HM?
FOR JUN'S SAKE, TOO.
SWFF
ス
ッ

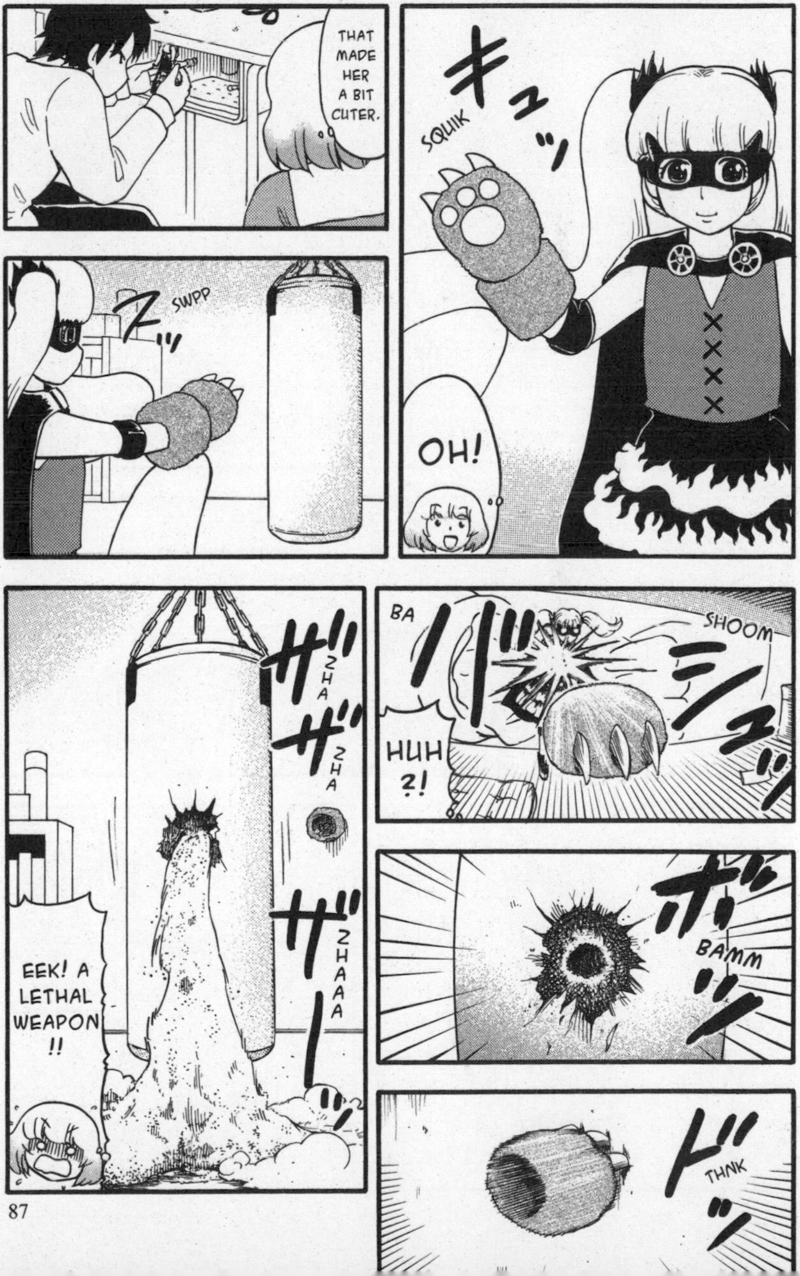
SQUIK
OH!
THAT MADE HER A BIT CUTER.
SWPP
BA
SHOOM
HUH ?!
BAMM
THNK
ZHA
ZHA
ZHAAAA
EEK! A LETHAL WEAPON !!

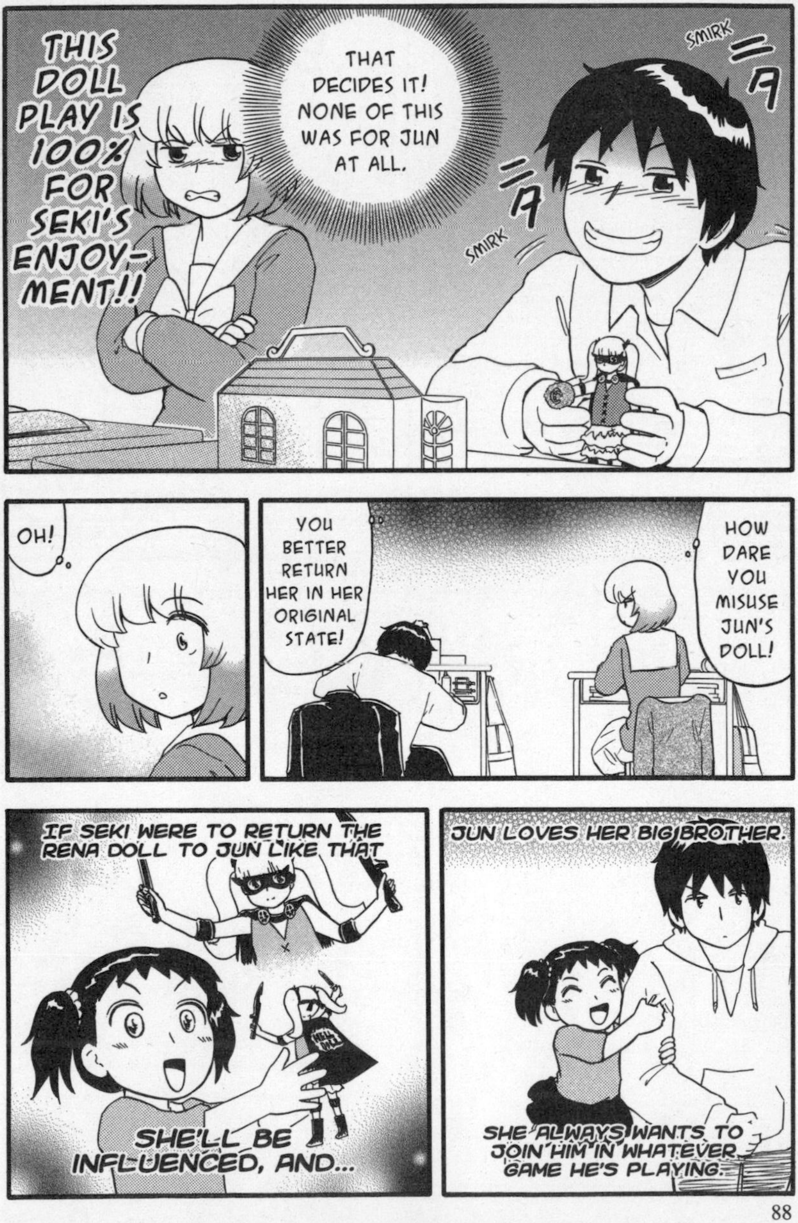
SMIRK
THAT DECIDES IT! NONE OF THIS WAS FOR JUN AT ALL.
SMIRK
THIS DOLL PLAY IS 100% FOR SEKI'S ENJOY-MENT!!
HOW DARE YOU MISUSE JUN'S DOLL!
YOU BETTER RETURN HER IN HER ORIGINAL STATE!
OH!
JUN LOVES HER BIG BROTHER.
SHE ALWAYS WANTS TO JOIN HIM IN WHATEVER GAME HE'S PLAYING.
IF SEKI WERE TO RETURN THE RENA DOLL TO JUN LIKE THAT
SHE'LL BE INFLUENCED, AND...

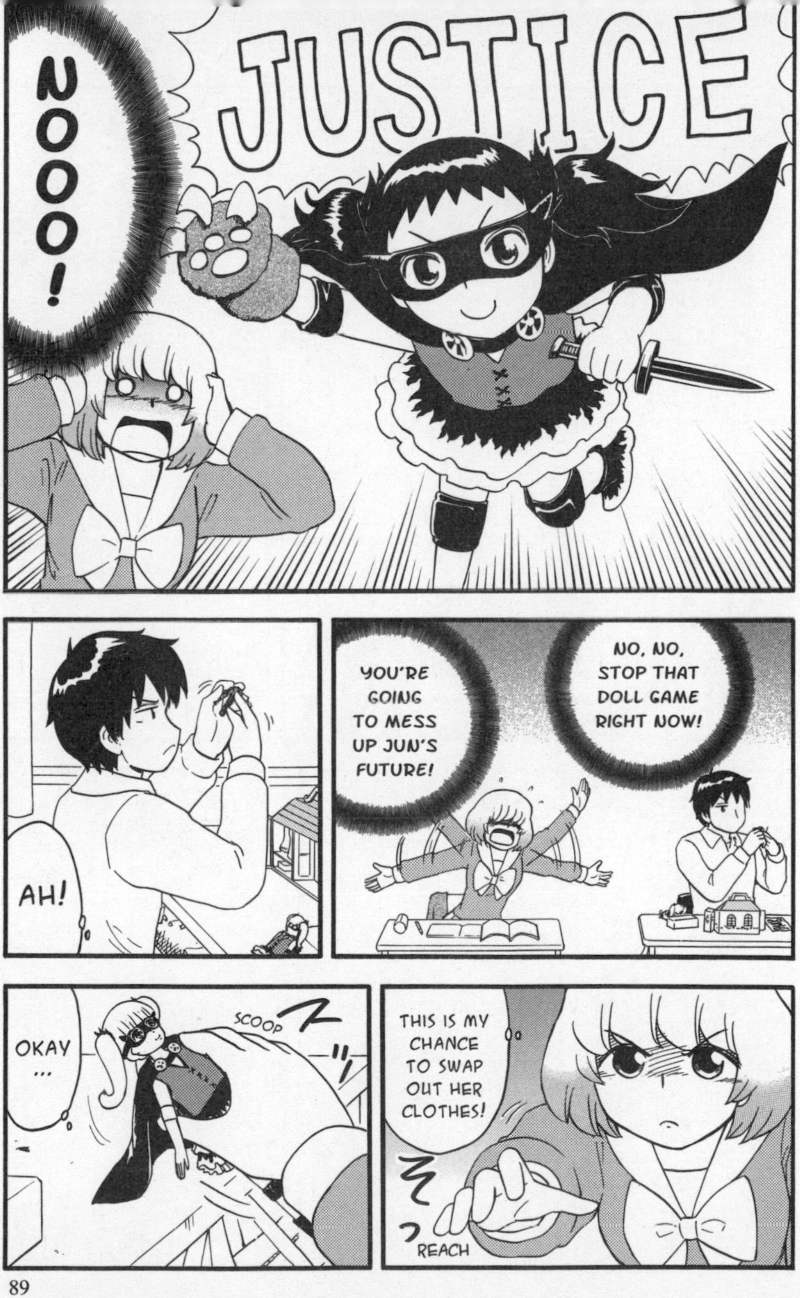
JUSTICE
NOOOO!
NO, NO, STOP THAT DOLL GAME RIGHT NOW!
YOU'RE GOING TO MESS UP JUN'S FUTURE!
AH!
THIS IS MY CHANCE TO SWAP OUT HER CLOTHES!
REACH
SCOOP
OKAY ...

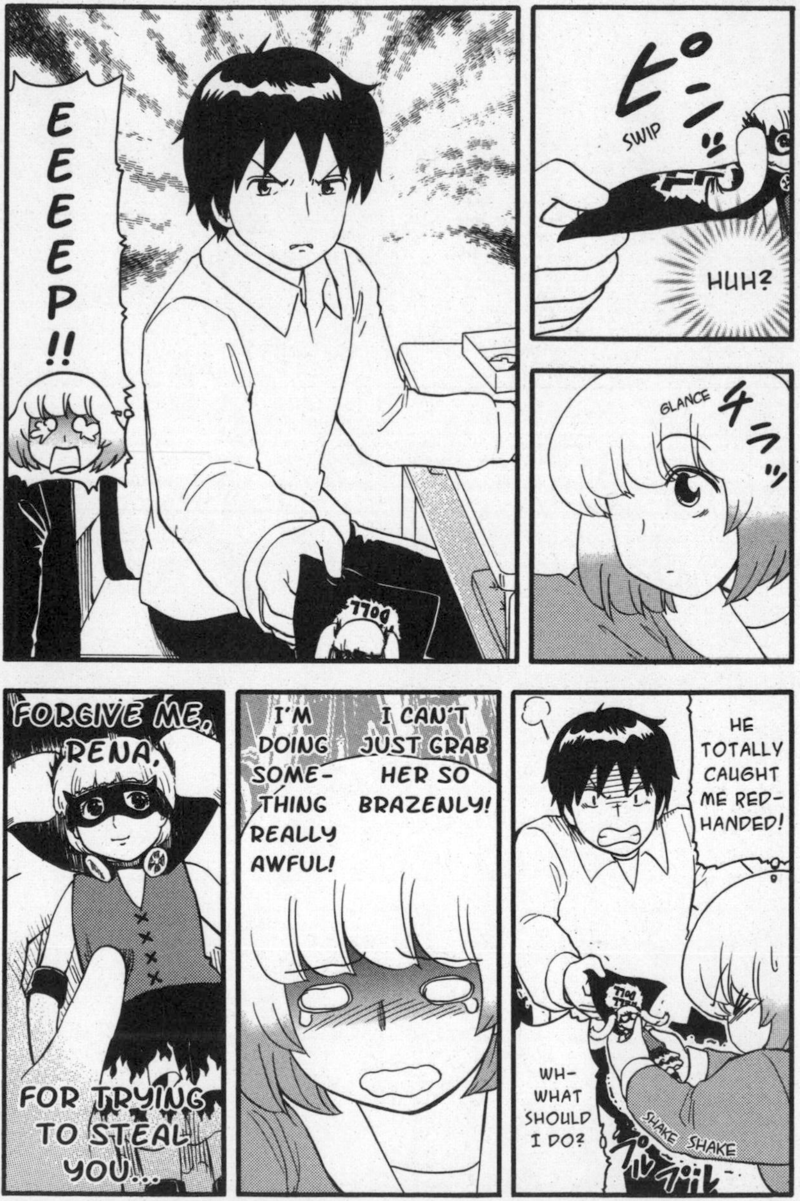

SWIP
HUH?
GLANCE
EEEEEP!!
HE TOTALLY CAUGHT ME RED-HANDED!
WH- WHAT SHOULD I DO?
SHAKE SHAKE
I CAN'T JUST GRAB HER SO BRAZENLY!
I'M DOING SOMETHING REALLY AWFUL!
FORGIVE ME, RENA,
FOR TRYING TO STEAL YOU...

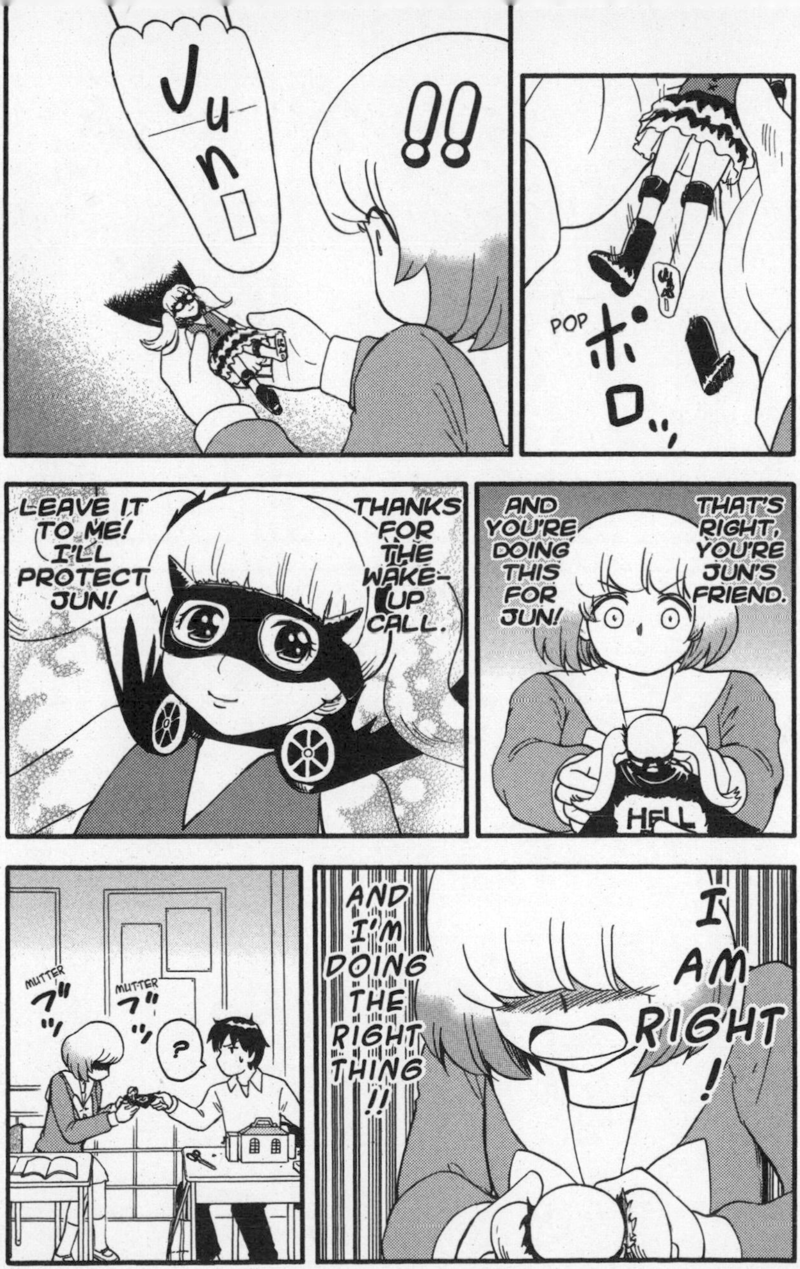
POP
ボロ
Jun!
!!
THAT'S RIGHT, YOU'RE JUN'S FRIEND.
AND YOU'RE DOING THIS FOR JUN!
HELL
THANKS FOR THE WAKE-UP CALL.
LEAVE IT TO ME! I'LL PROTECT JUN!
I AM RIGHT!
AND I'M DOING THE RIGHT THING!!
MUTTER
ブツ
MUTTER
ブツ
?

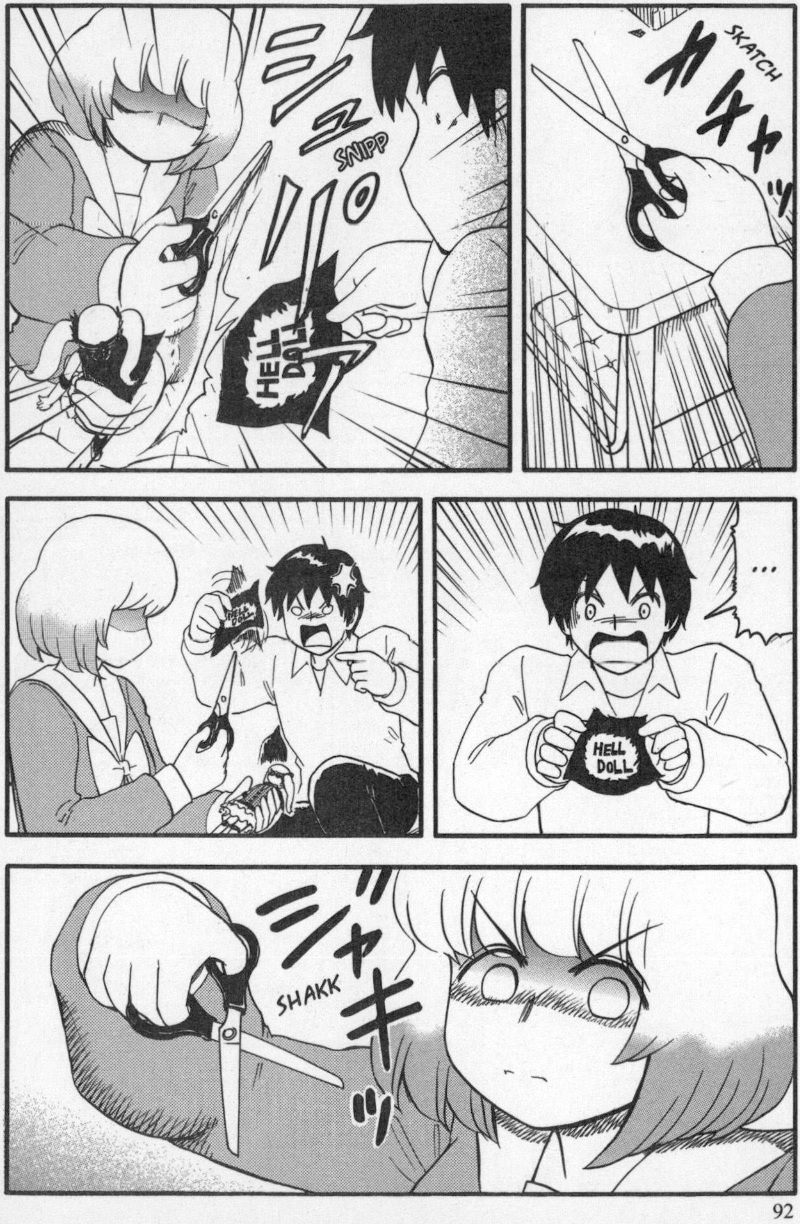

SKATCH
SNIPP
HELL DOLL
...
HELL DOLL
HELL DOLL
SHAKK

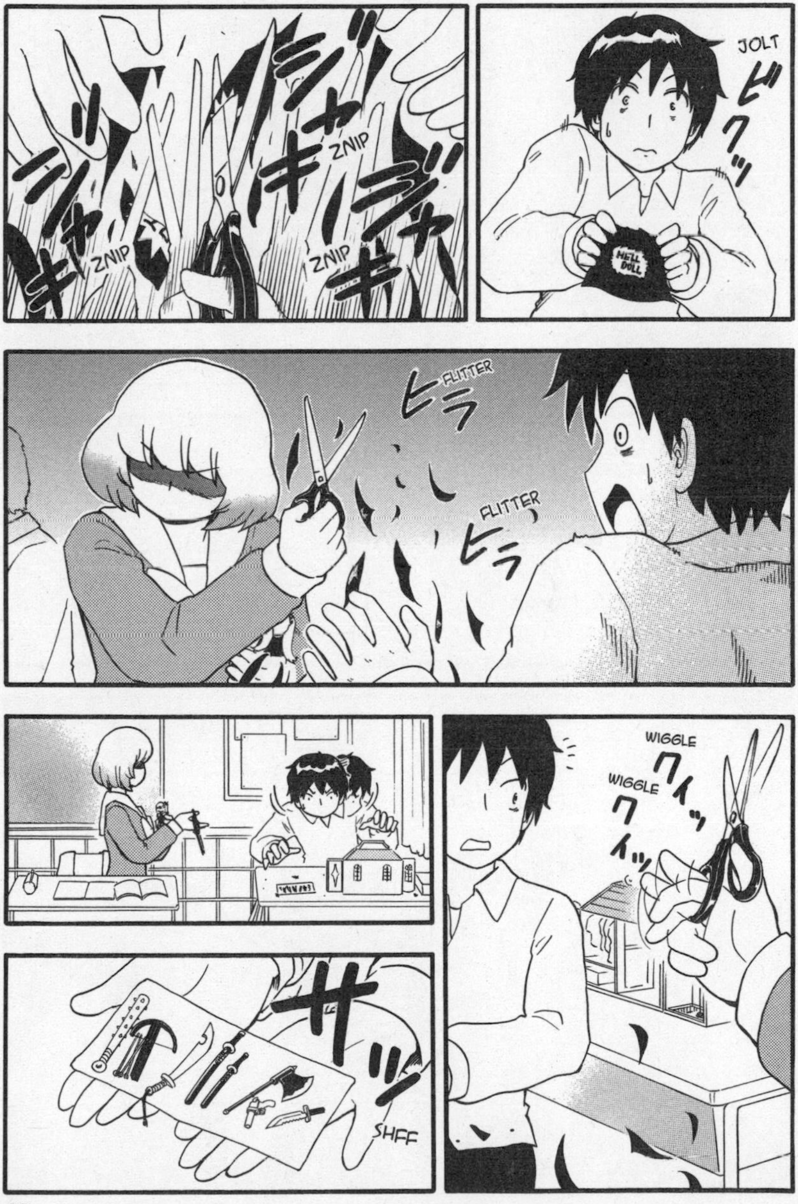

JOLT
ビクッ
HELL DOLL
ZNIP
ZNIP
ZNIP
FLITTER
ヒラ
FLITTER
ヒラ
WIGGLE
クイッ
WIGGLE
クイッ
サッ
SHFF

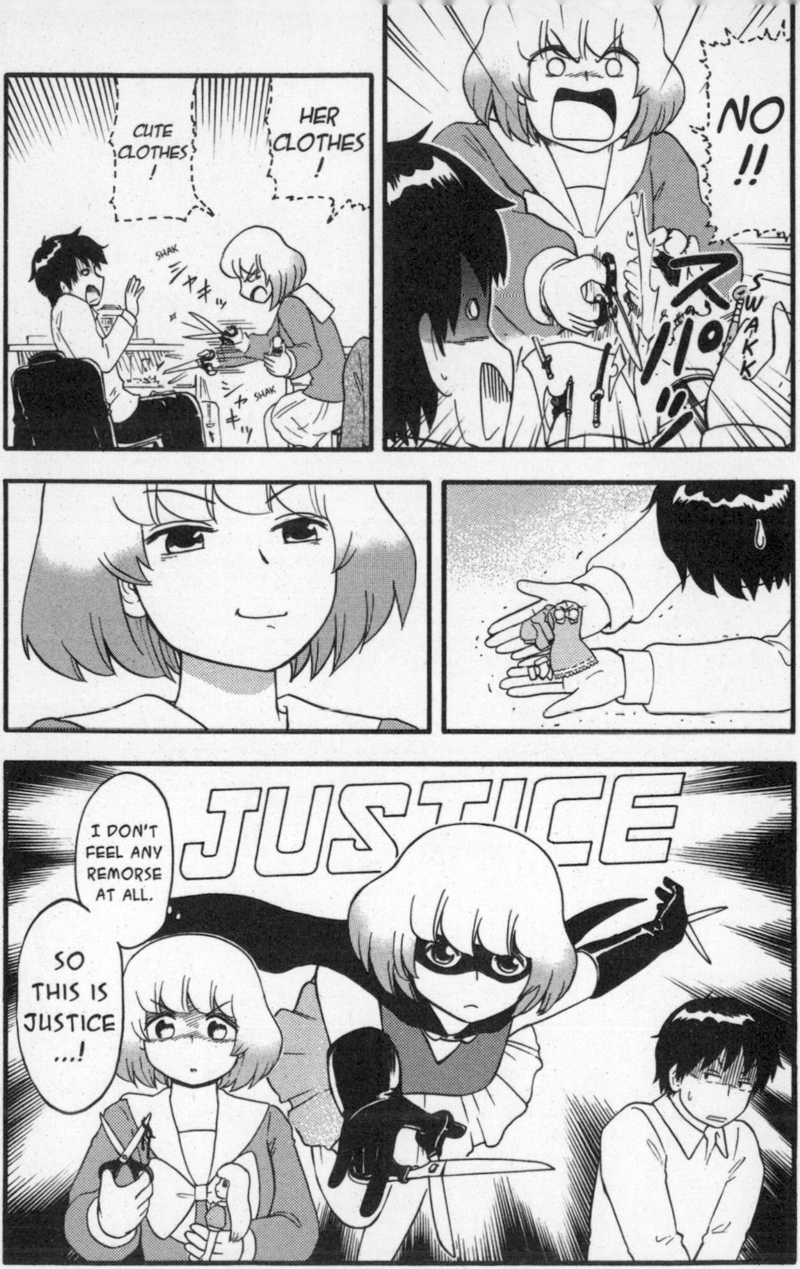
NO !!
スパッ
SWAKK
HER CLOTHES !
CUTE CLOTHES !
SHAK
シャキッ
シャキッ
SHAK
JUSTICE
I DON'T FEEL ANY REMORSE AT ALL.
SO THIS IS JUSTICE ...!

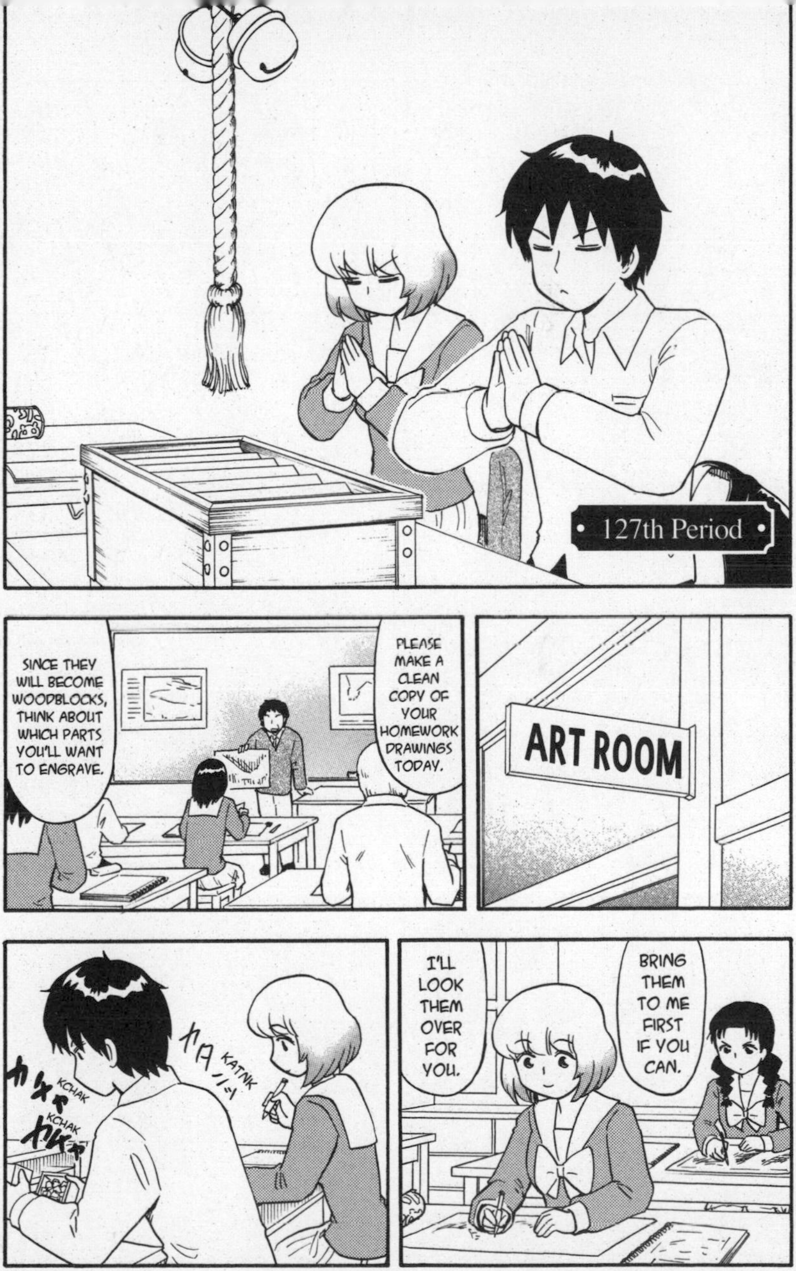
• 127th Period •
ART ROOM
PLEASE MAKE A CLEAN COPY OF YOUR HOMEWORK DRAWINGS TODAY.
SINCE THEY WILL BECOME WOODBLOCKS, THINK ABOUT WHICH PARTS YOU'LL WANT TO ENGRAVE.
BRING THEM TO ME FIRST IF YOU CAN.
I'LL LOOK THEM OVER FOR YOU.
KATNK
KCHAK
KCHAK

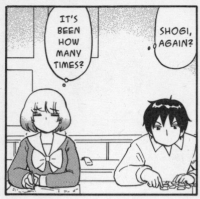

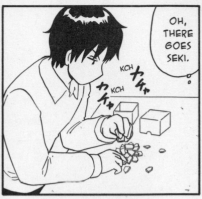

OH, THERE GOES SEKI.
KCH
KCH
SHOGI, AGAIN?
IT'S BEEN HOW MANY TIMES?
BUT HE SEEMS TO ENJOY IT.
I CAN'T BELIEVE HE HASN'T GOTTEN BORED WITH IT YET.
YOU'D THINK DRAWING WOULD BE A LOT MORE FUN...
HM?
KCHK
KCHK
THEY ALL SEEM TO BE THE SAME PIECES.
WHAT'S WRITTEN ON THEM? UHM...

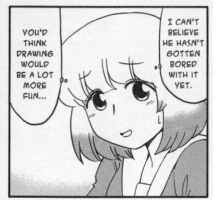

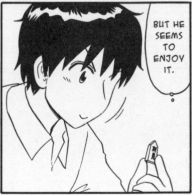

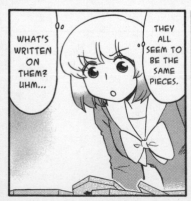

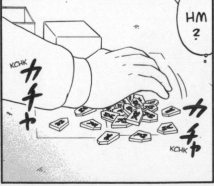

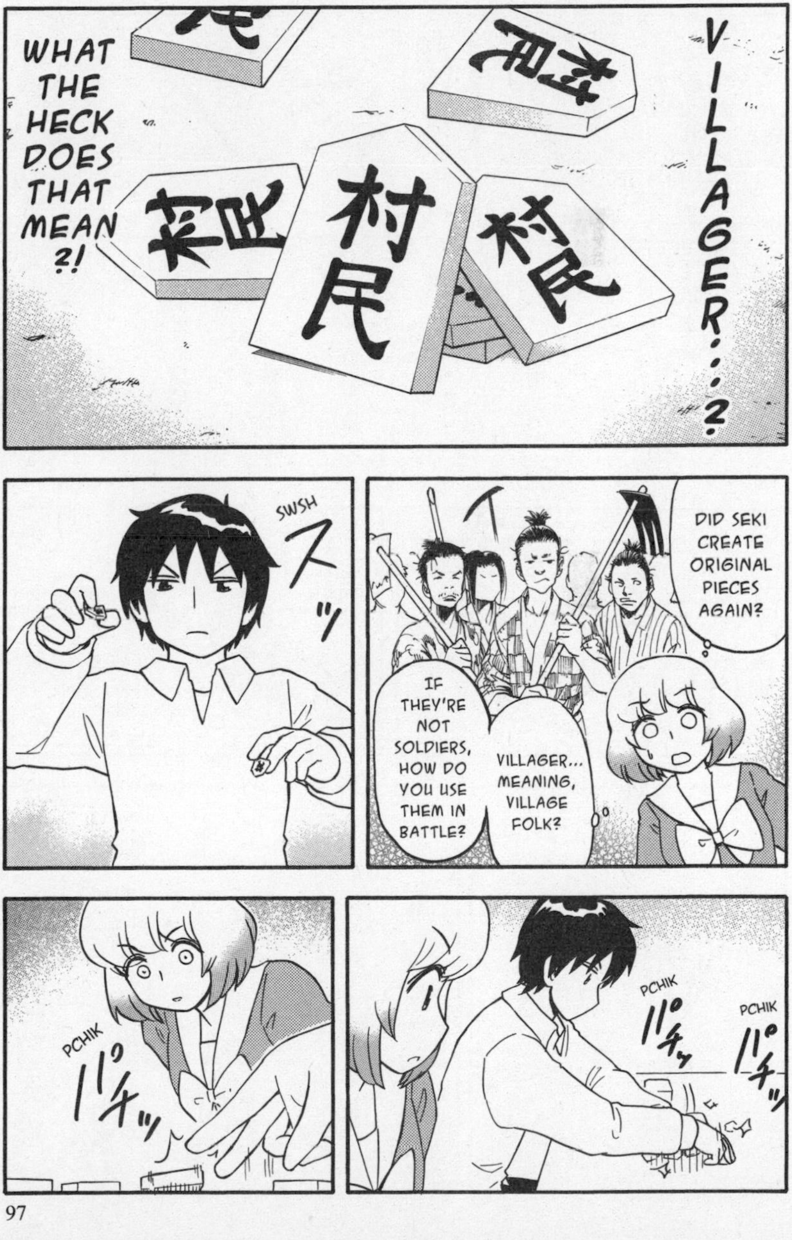
VILLAGER...?
WHAT THE HECK DOES THAT MEAN?!
DID SEKI CREATE ORIGINAL PIECES AGAIN?
VILLAGER... MEANING, VILLAGE FOLK?
IF THEY'RE NOT SOLDIERS, HOW DO YOU USE THEM IN BATTLE?
SWSH
PCHIK
PCHIK
PCHIK

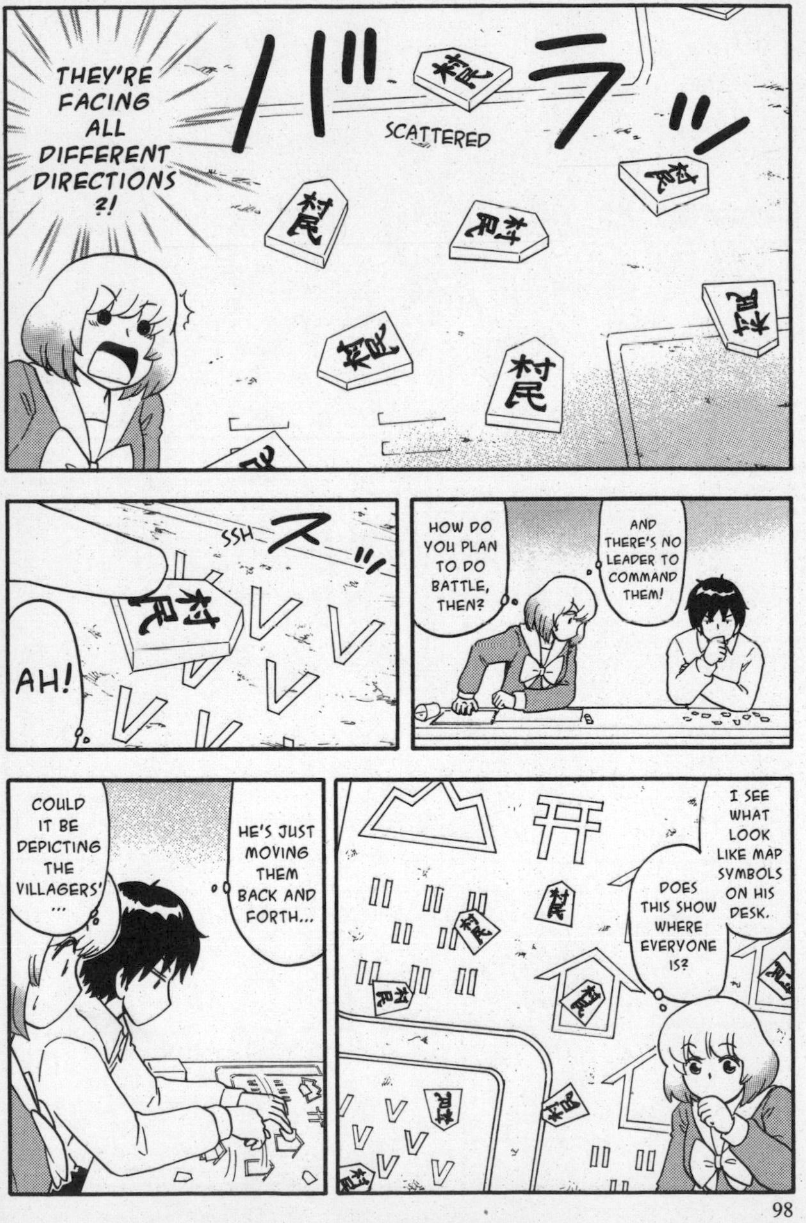
THEY'RE FACING ALL DIFFERENT DIRECTIONS?!
バラッ
SCATTERED
AND THERE'S NO LEADER TO COMMAND THEM!
HOW DO YOU PLAN TO DO BATTLE, THEN?
スッ
SSH
AH!
I SEE WHAT LOOK LIKE MAP SYMBOLS ON HIS DESK.
DOES THIS SHOW WHERE EVERYONE IS?
HE'S JUST MOVING THEM BACK AND FORTH...
COULD IT BE DEPICTING THE VILLAGERS' ...

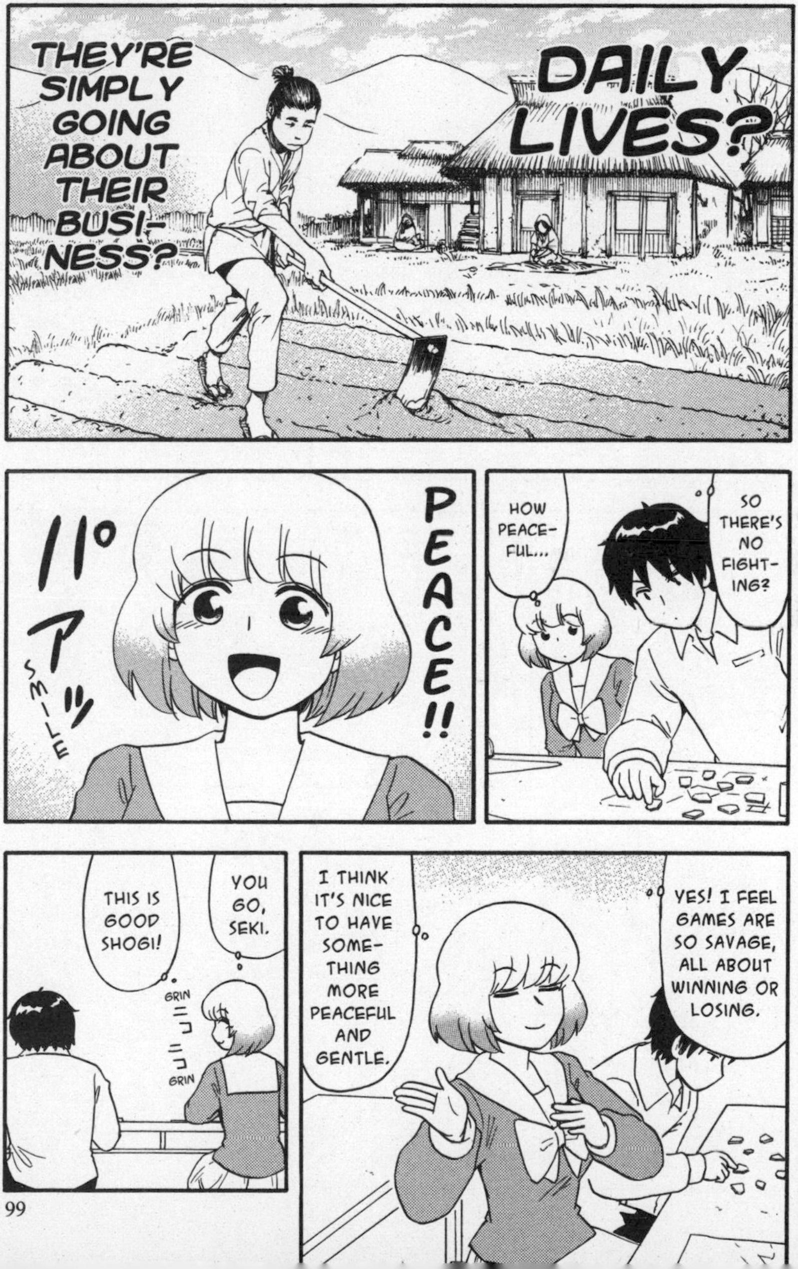
DAILY LIVES?
THEY'RE SIMPLY GOING ABOUT THEIR BUSI-NESS?
SO THERE'S NO FIGHT-ING?
HOW PEACE-FUL...
PEACE!!
パアッ
SMILE
YES! I FEEL GAMES ARE SO SAVAGE, ALL ABOUT WINNING OR LOSING.
I THINK IT'S NICE TO HAVE SOME-THING MORE PEACEFUL AND GENTLE.
YOU GO, SEKI.
THIS IS GOOD SHOGI!
GRIN
ニコ
ニコ
GRIN

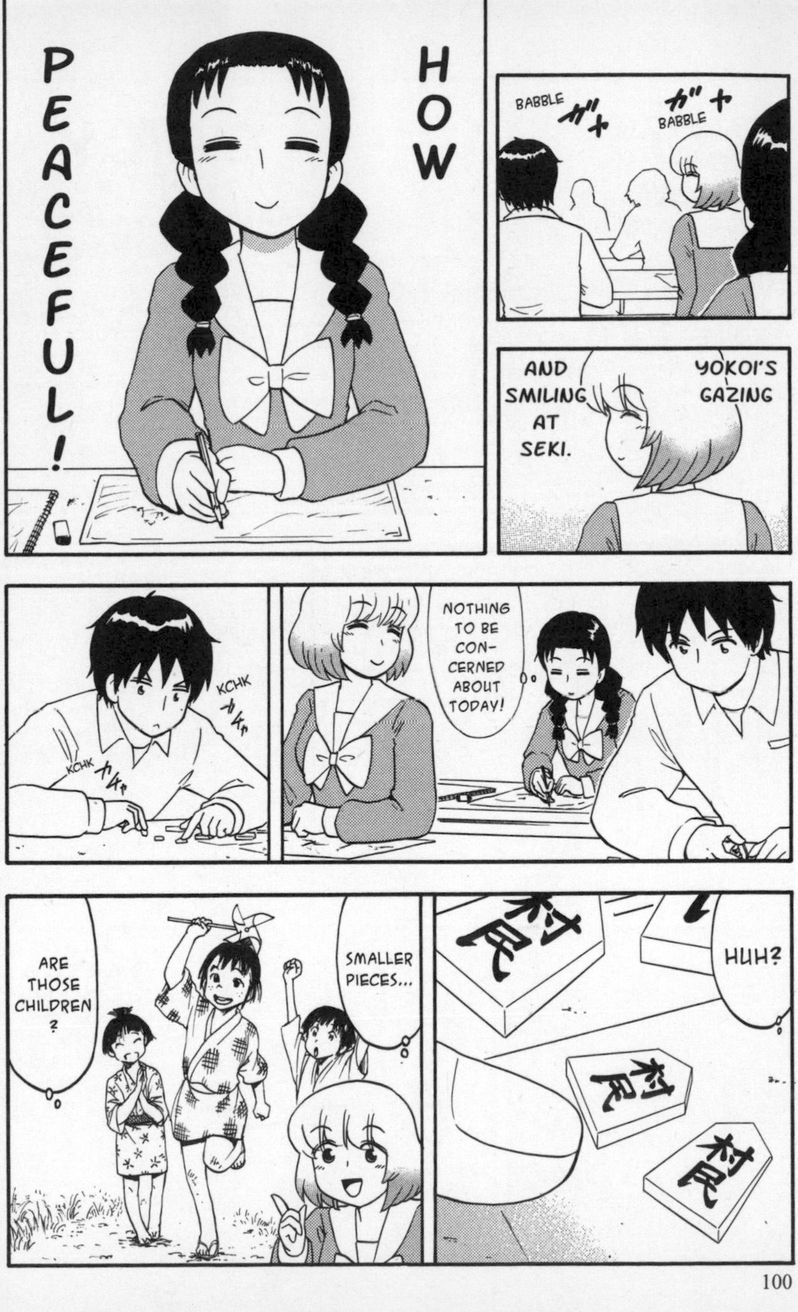
ガヤ BABBLE
BABBLE ガヤ
YOKOI'S GAZING
AND SMILING AT SEKI.
HOW
PEACEFUL!
NOTHING TO BE CON-CERNED ABOUT TODAY!
KCHK カチャ
KCHK カチャ
HUH?
村民
村民
村民
SMALLER PIECES...
ARE THOSE CHILDREN?

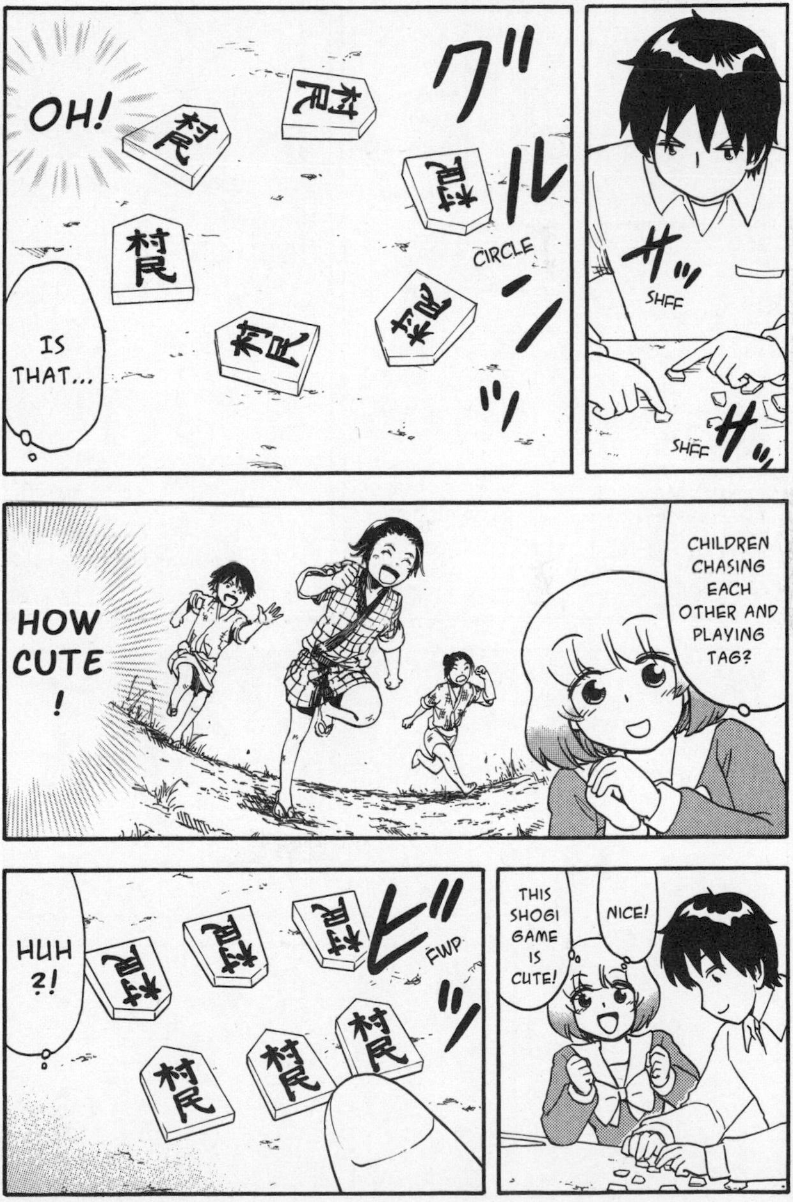
サッ
SHFF
サッ
SHFF
グルンッ
CIRCLE
OH!
IS THAT...
CHILDREN CHASING EACH OTHER AND PLAYING TAG?
HOW CUTE!
NICE!
THIS SHOGI GAME IS CUTE!
ビッ
FWP
HUH?!

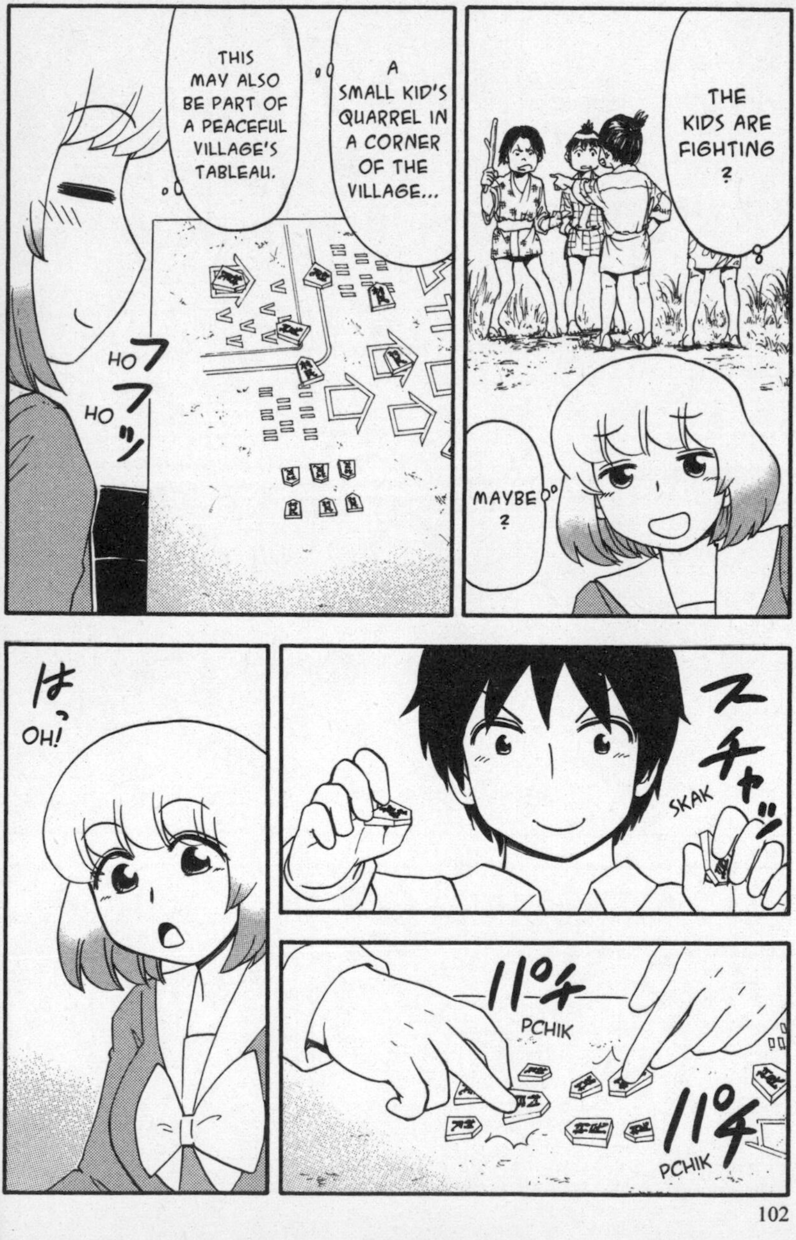

THE KIDS ARE FIGHTING?
MAYBE?
A SMALL KID'S QUARREL IN A CORNER OF THE VILLAGE...
THIS MAY ALSO BE PART OF A PEACEFUL VILLAGE'S TABLEAU.
フフッ
HO HO
スチャッ
SKAK
パチ
PCHIK
パチ
PCHIK
はっ
OH!

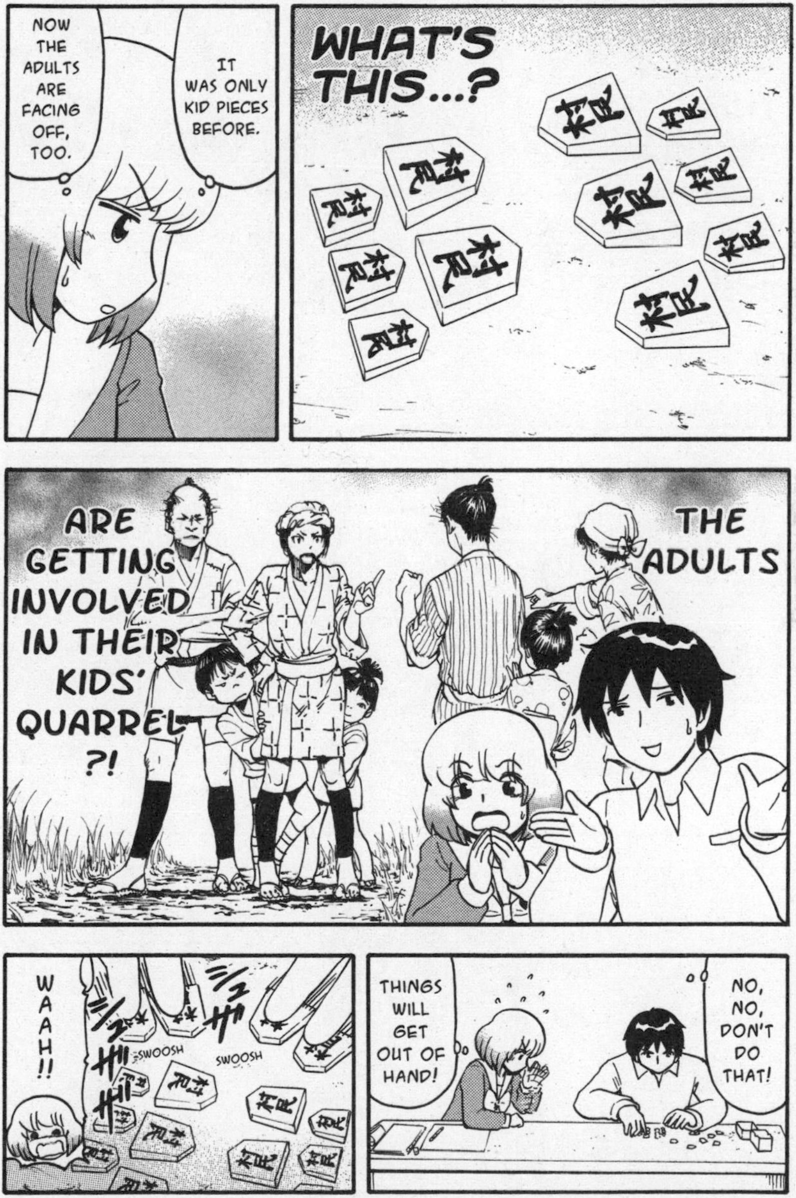
WHAT'S THIS...?
IT WAS ONLY KID PIECES BEFORE.
NOW THE ADULTS ARE FACING OFF, TOO.
THE ADULTS
ARE GETTING INVOLVED IN THEIR KIDS' QUARREL ?!
NO, NO, DON'T DO THAT!
THINGS WILL GET OUT OF HAND!
SWOOSH
SWOOSH
WAAAH!!

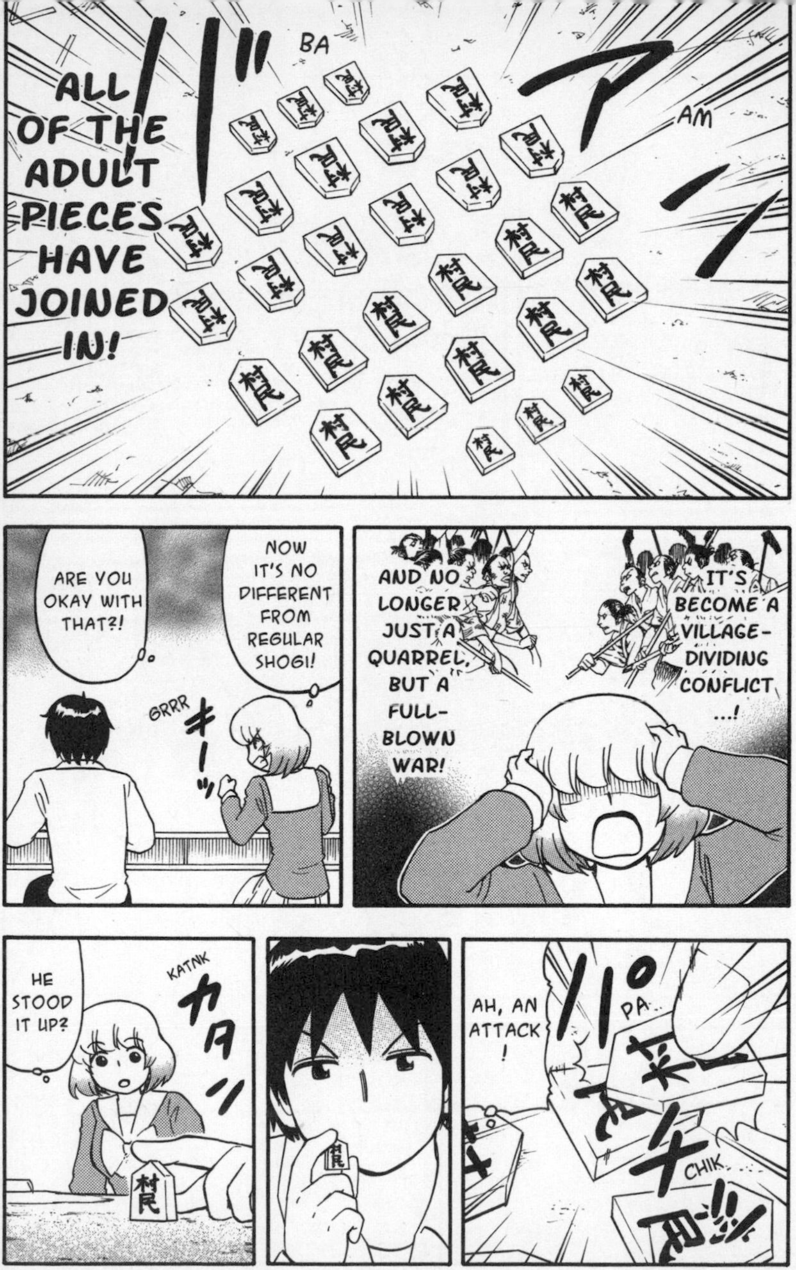
BA
AM
ALL OF THE ADULT PIECES HAVE JOINED IN!
IT'S BECOME A VILLAGE-DIVIDING CONFLICT ...!
AND NO LONGER JUST A QUARREL, BUT A FULL-BLOWN WAR!
NOW IT'S NO DIFFERENT FROM REGULAR SHOGI!
GRRR
ARE YOU OKAY WITH THAT?!
PA
AH, AN ATTACK!
CHIK
KATNK
HE STOOD IT UP?

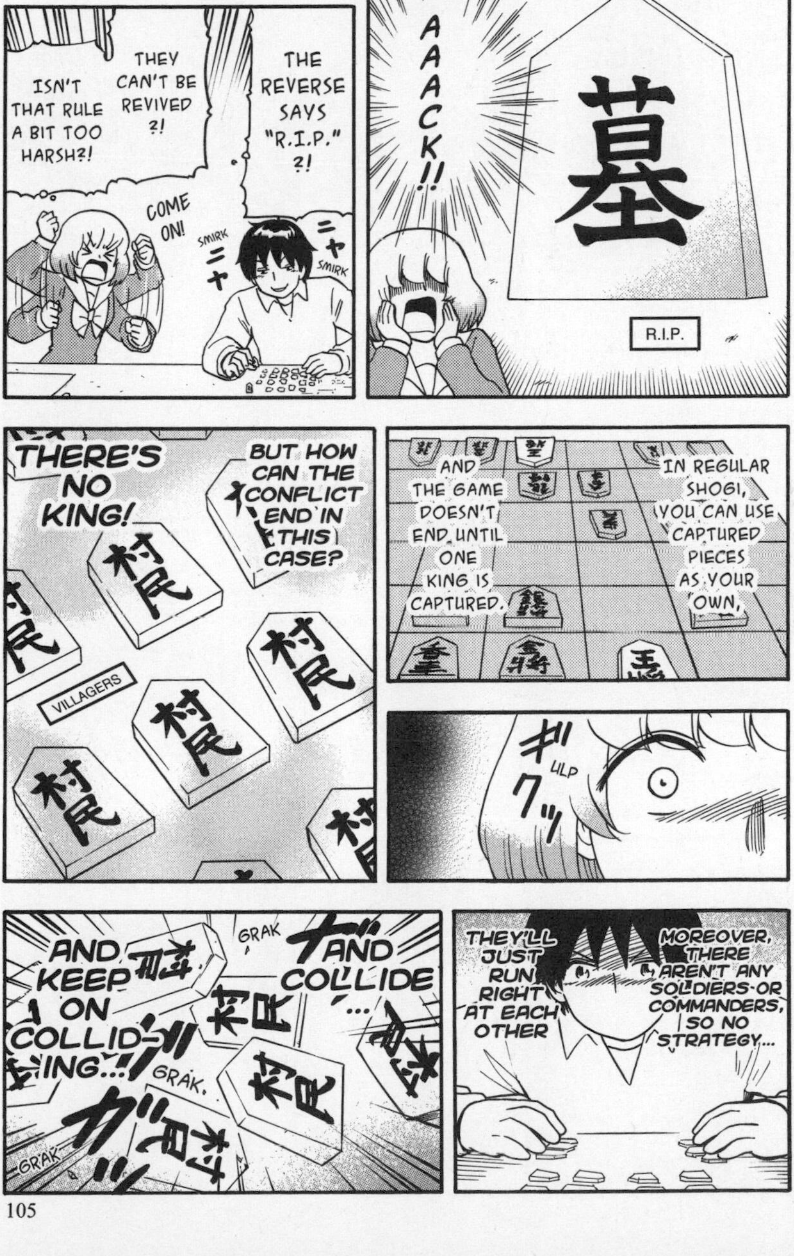
AAAACK!!
墓
R.I.P.
THE REVERSE SAYS "R.I.P."?!
THEY CAN'T BE REVIVED?!
ISN'T THAT RULE A BIT TOO HARSH?!
COME ON!
ニヤ SMIRK
ニヤ SMIRK
IN REGULAR SHOGI, YOU CAN USE CAPTURED PIECES AS YOUR OWN,
AND THE GAME DOESN'T END UNTIL ONE KING IS CAPTURED.
ギクッ ULP
BUT HOW CAN THE CONFLICT END IN THIS CASE?
THERE'S NO KING!
VILLAGERS
MOREOVER, THERE AREN'T ANY SOLDIERS OR COMMANDERS, SO NO STRATEGY...
THEY'LL JUST RUN RIGHT AT EACH OTHER
AND COLLIDE...
GRAK
AND KEEP ON COLLIDING...!
GRAK
GRAK

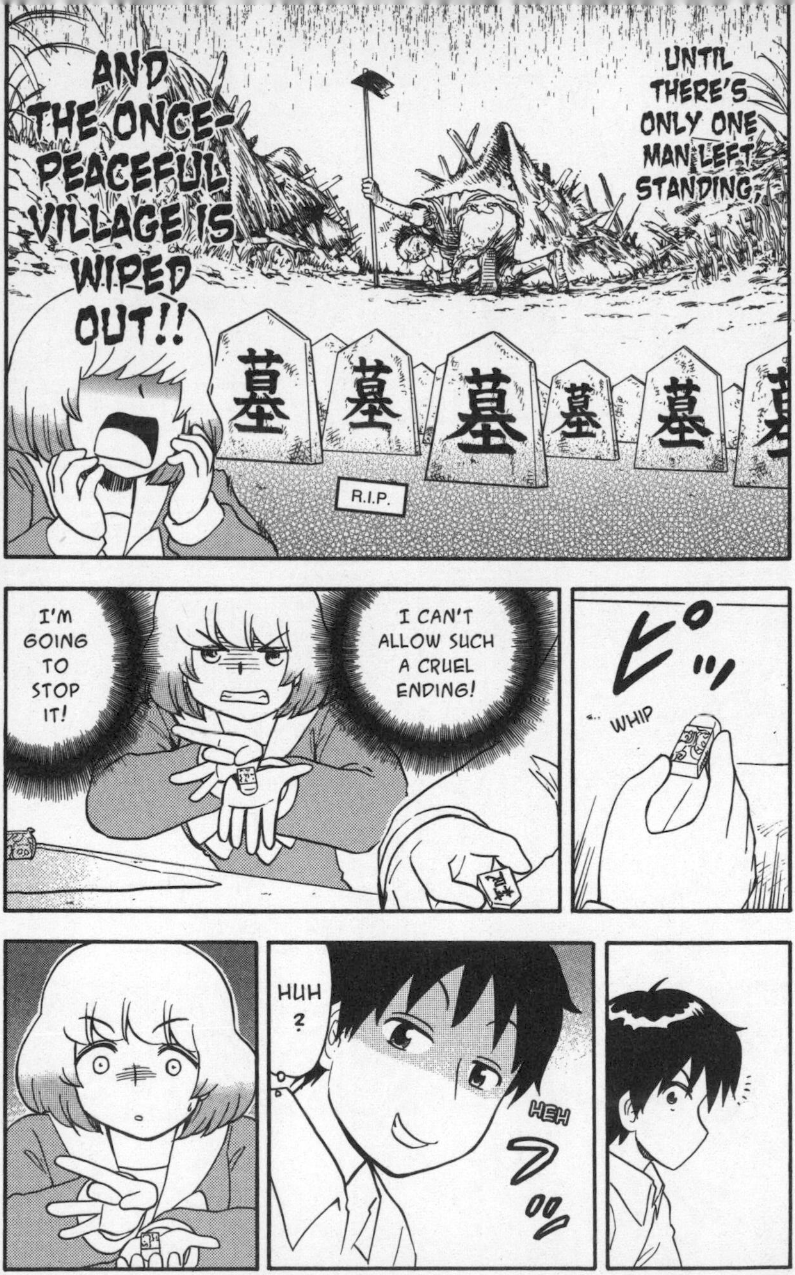
UNTIL THERE'S ONLY ONE MAN LEFT STANDING,
AND THE ONCE-PEACEFUL VILLAGE IS WIPED OUT!!
墓
墓
墓
墓
墓
R.I.P.
ピッ
WHIP
I CAN'T ALLOW SUCH A CRUEL ENDING!
I'M GOING TO STOP IT!
HUH?
HEH

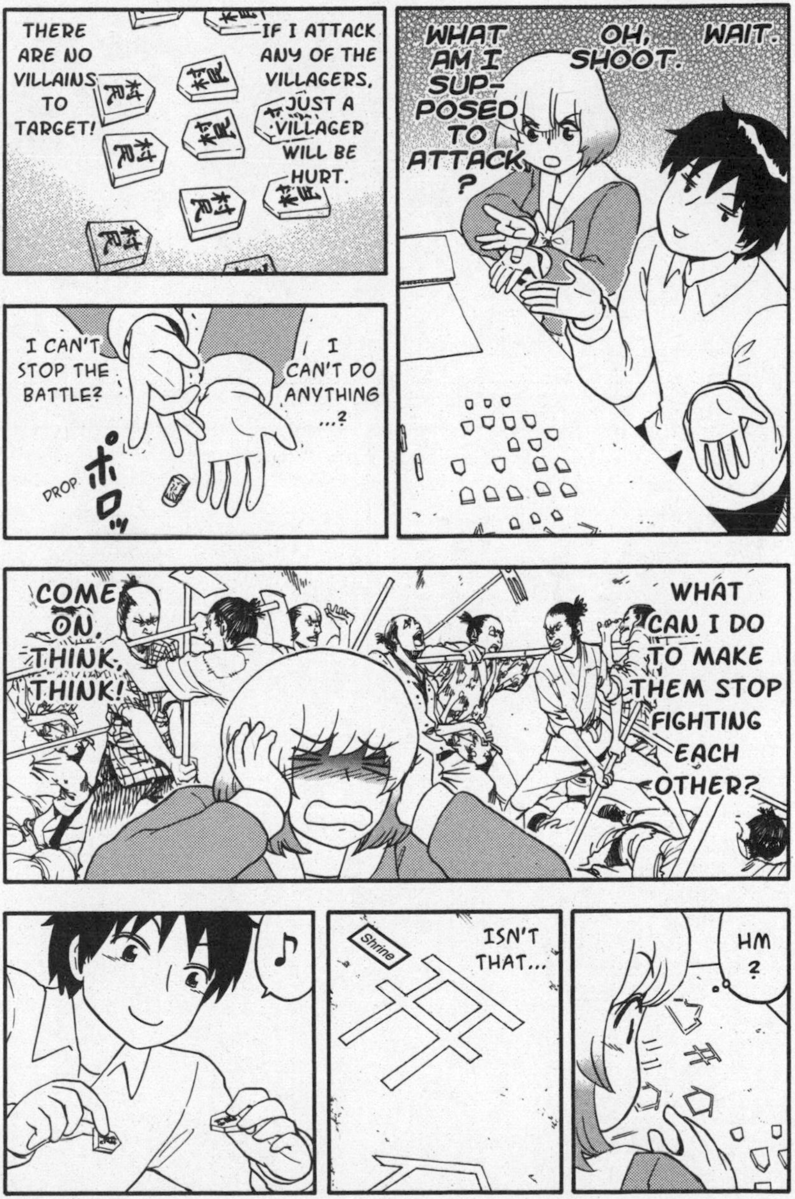
WAIT.
OH, SHOOT.
WHAT AM I SUP-POSED TO ATTACK?
IF I ATTACK ANY OF THE VILLAGERS, JUST A VILLAGER WILL BE HURT.
THERE ARE NO VILLAINS TO TARGET!
I CAN'T DO ANYTHING ...?
I CAN'T STOP THE BATTLE?
ポロッ
DROP
WHAT CAN I DO TO MAKE THEM STOP FIGHTING EACH OTHER?
COME ON, THINK, THINK!
HM?
ISN'T THAT...
Shrine
♪

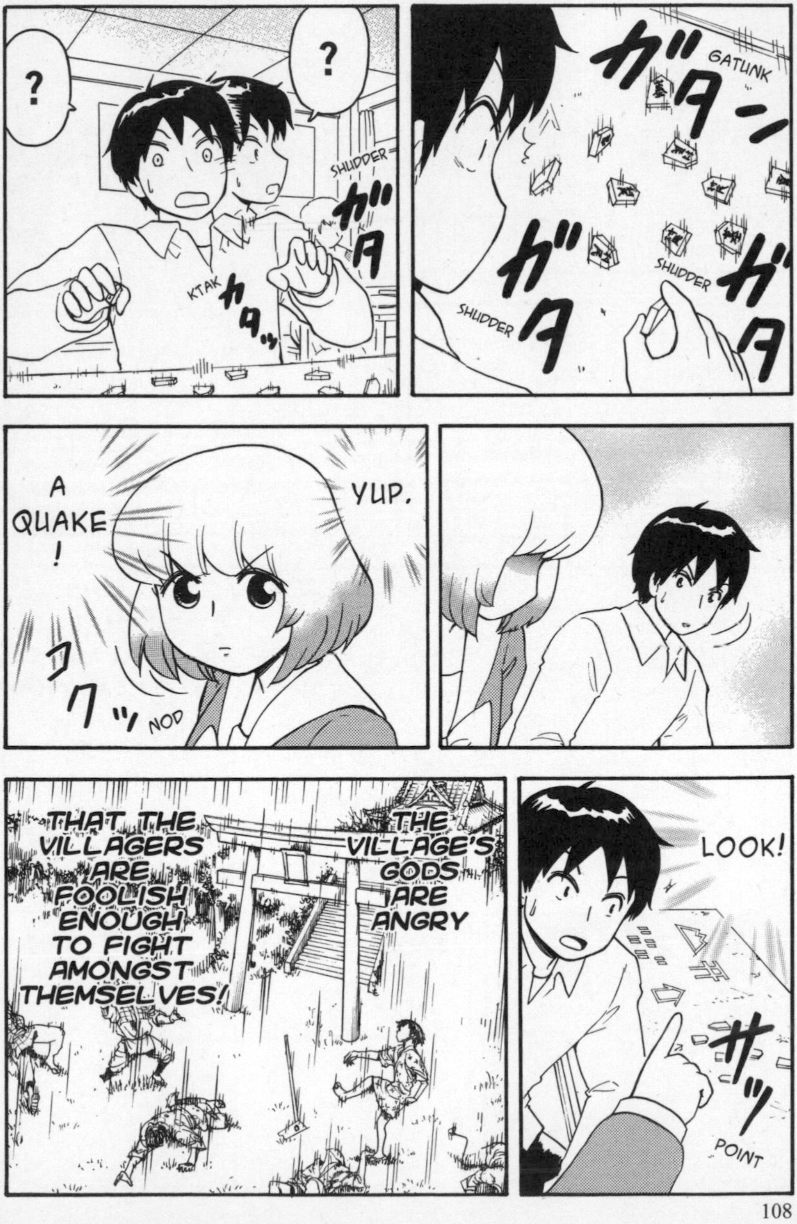
ガタン
GATUNK
ガタ
SHUDDER
ガタ
SHUDDER
?
?
SHUDDER
ガタ
KTAK
カタッ
YUP.
A QUAKE!
コクッ
NOD
LOOK!
サッ
POINT
THE VILLAGE'S GODS ARE ANGRY
THAT THE VILLAGERS ARE FOOLISH ENOUGH TO FIGHT AMONGST THEMSELVES!

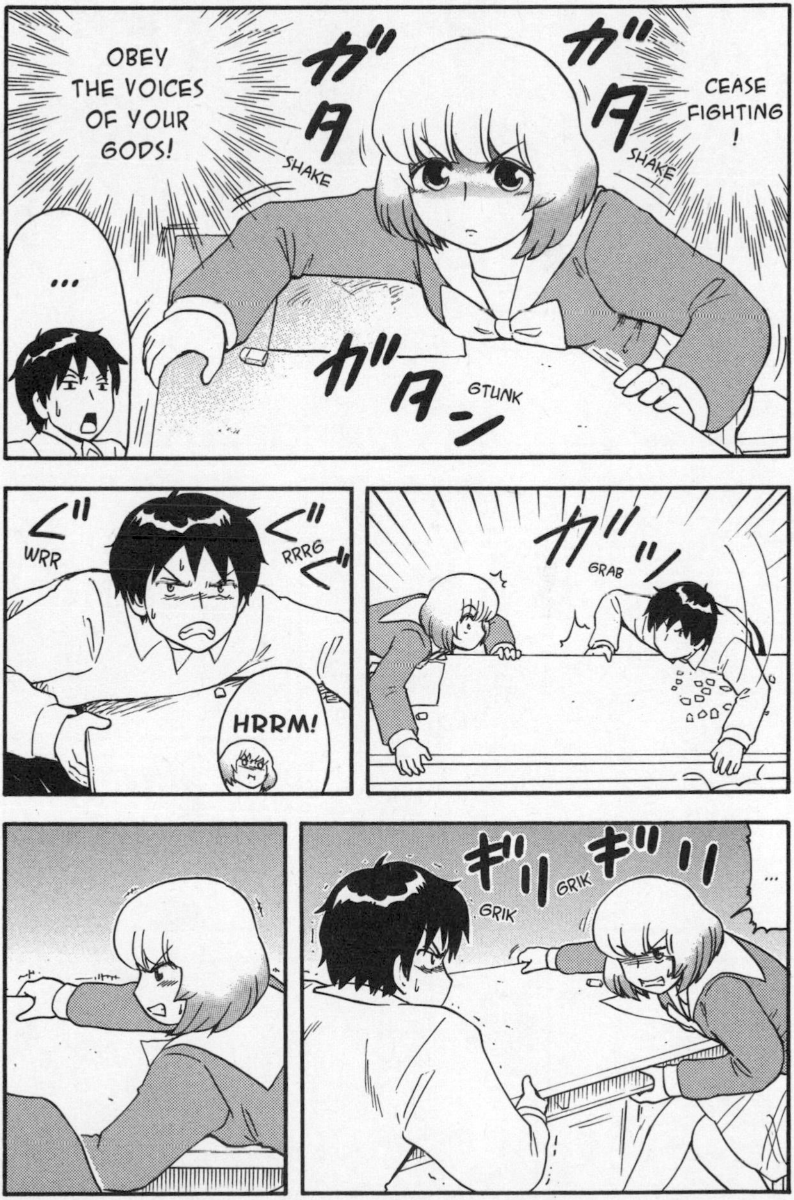

CEASE FIGHTING !
ガタ
SHAKE
ガタ
SHAKE
OBEY THE VOICES OF YOUR GODS!
ガタン
GTUNK
...
ガッ
GRAB
ぐぐ
RRRG
ぐ
WRR
HRRM!
ギリ
GRIK
ギリ
GRIK
...

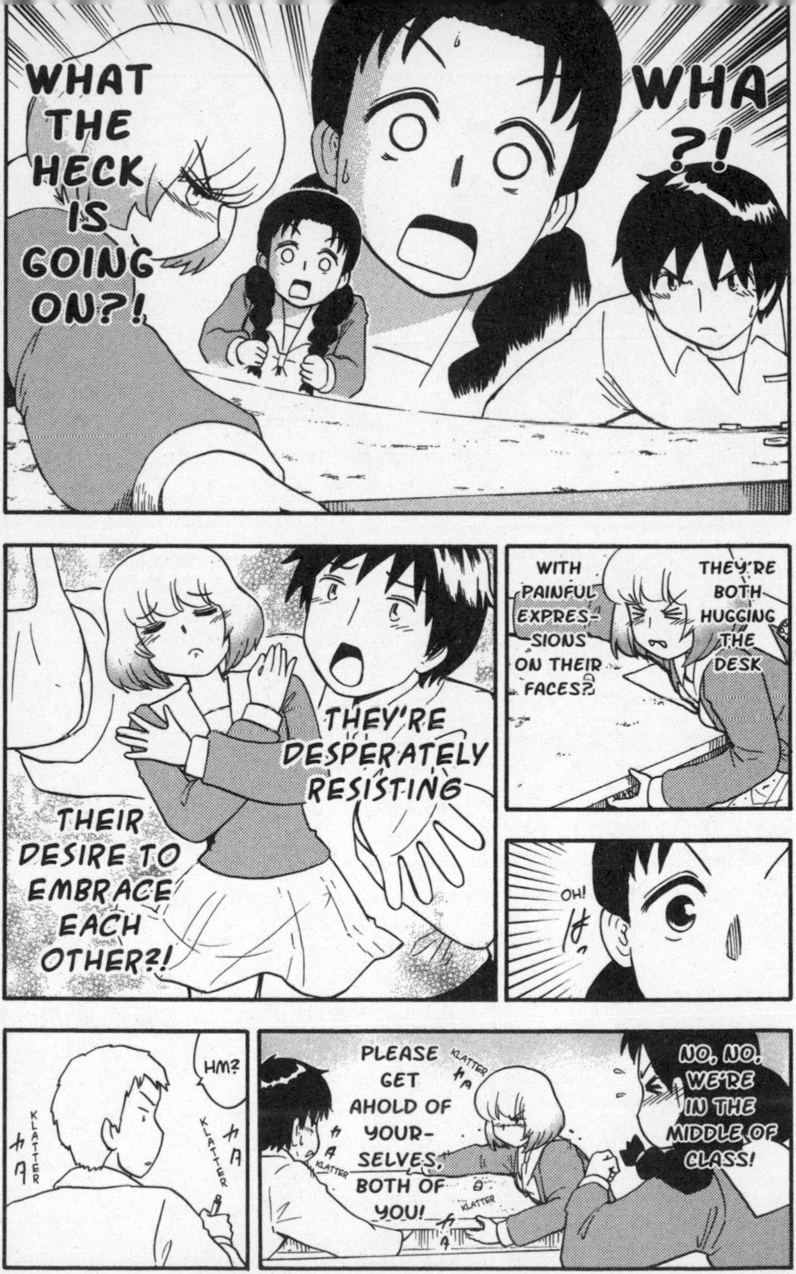
WHA ?!
WHAT THE HECK IS GOING ON?!
THEY'RE BOTH HUGGING THE DESK
WITH PAINFUL EXPRES-SIONS ON THEIR FACES?
OH!
THEY'RE DESPERATELY RESISTING
THEIR DESIRE TO EMBRACE EACH OTHER?!
NO, NO, WE'RE IN THE MIDDLE OF CLASS!
KLATTER
PLEASE GET AHOLD OF YOUR-SELVES, BOTH OF YOU!
KLATTER
KLATTER
HM?
KLATTER
KLATTER

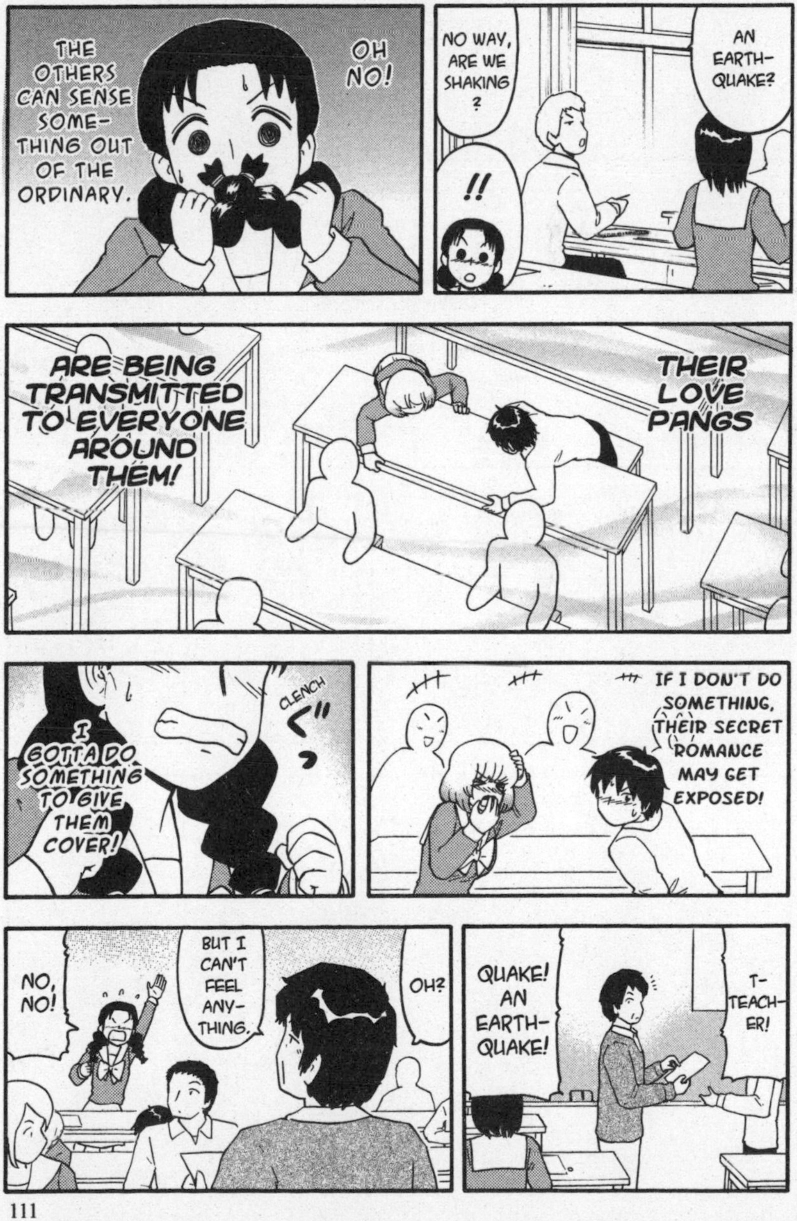
AN EARTH-QUAKE?
NO WAY, ARE WE SHAKING?
!!
OH NO!
THE OTHERS CAN SENSE SOME-THING OUT OF THE ORDINARY.
THEIR LOVE PANGS
ARE BEING TRANSMITTED TO EVERYONE AROUND THEM!
IF I DON'T DO SOMETHING, THEIR SECRET ROMANCE MAY GET EXPOSED!
CLENCH
I GOTTA DO SOMETHING TO GIVE THEM COVER!
T-TEACHER!
QUAKE! AN EARTH-QUAKE!
OH?
BUT I CAN'T FEEL ANY-THING.
NO, NO!

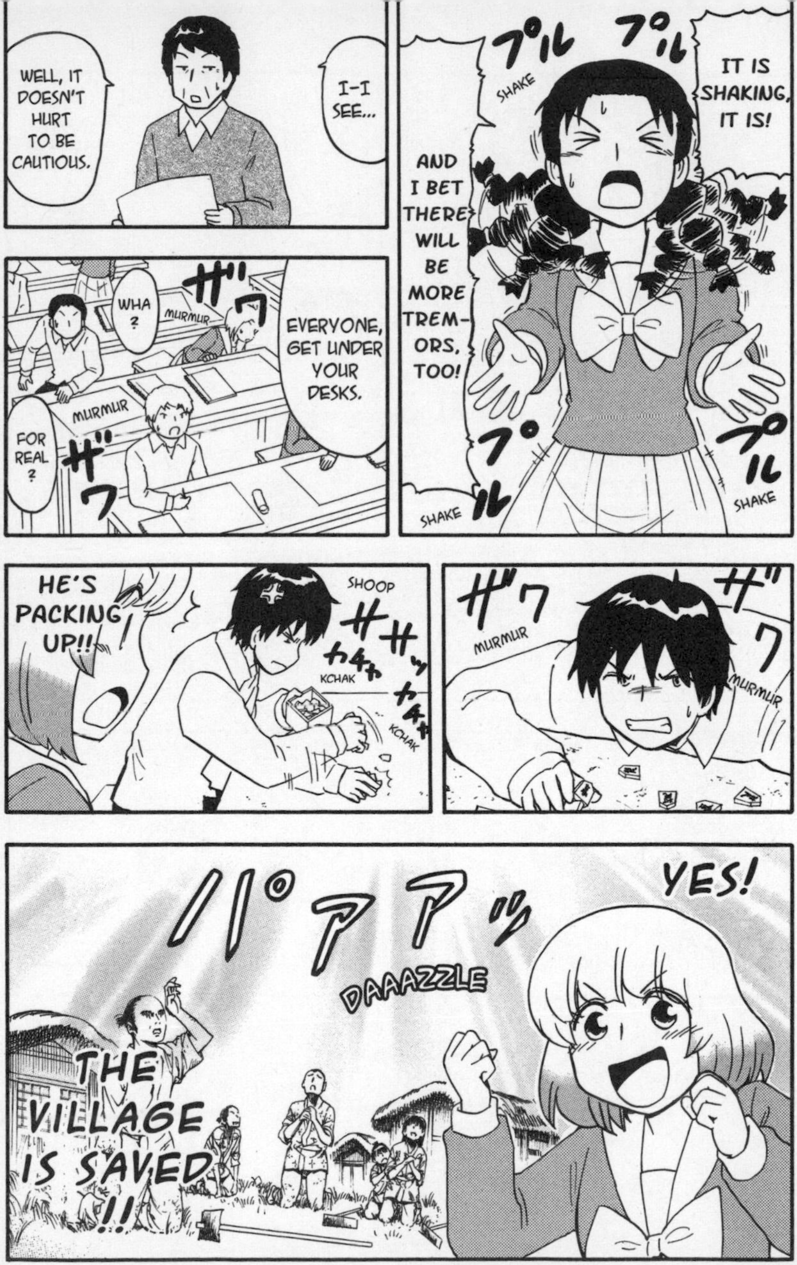
プル プル
SHAKE
IT IS SHAKING, IT IS!
AND I BET THERE WILL BE MORE TREM-ORS, TOO!
プル
SHAKE
プル
SHAKE
WELL, IT DOESN'T HURT TO BE CAUTIOUS.
I-I SEE...
EVERYONE, GET UNDER YOUR DESKS.
ザワ
MURMUR
WHA?
ザワ
MURMUR
FOR REAL?
ザワ
MURMUR
ザワ
MURMUR
SHOOP
サッ サッ
カチャ
KCHAK
カチャ
KCHAK
HE'S PACKING UP!!
YES!
パアアッ
DAAAZZLE
THE VILLAGE IS SAVED!!

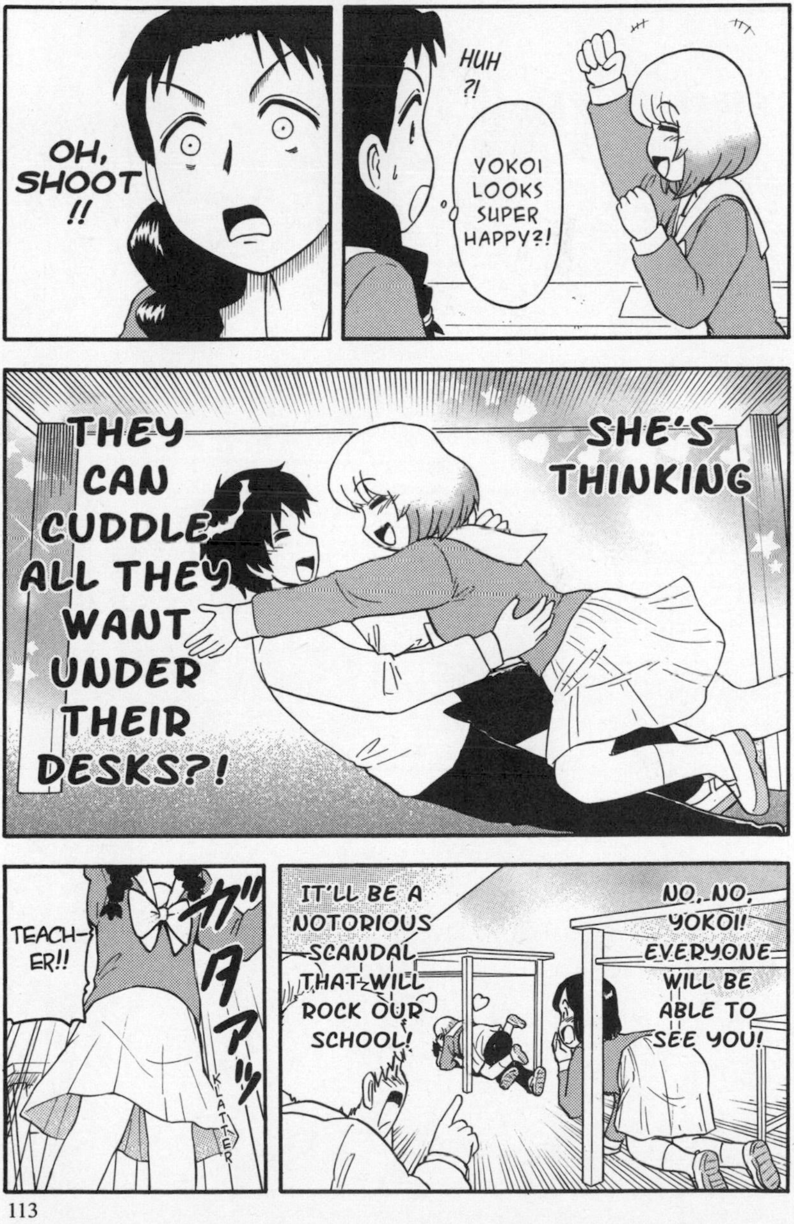
HUH ?!
YOKOI LOOKS SUPER HAPPY?!
OH, SHOOT !!
SHE'S THINKING
THEY CAN CUDDLE ALL THEY WANT UNDER THEIR DESKS?!
NO, NO, YOKOI! EVERYONE WILL BE ABLE TO SEE YOU!
IT'LL BE A NOTORIOUS SCANDAL THAT WILL ROCK OUR SCHOOL!
TEACHER!!
KLATTER

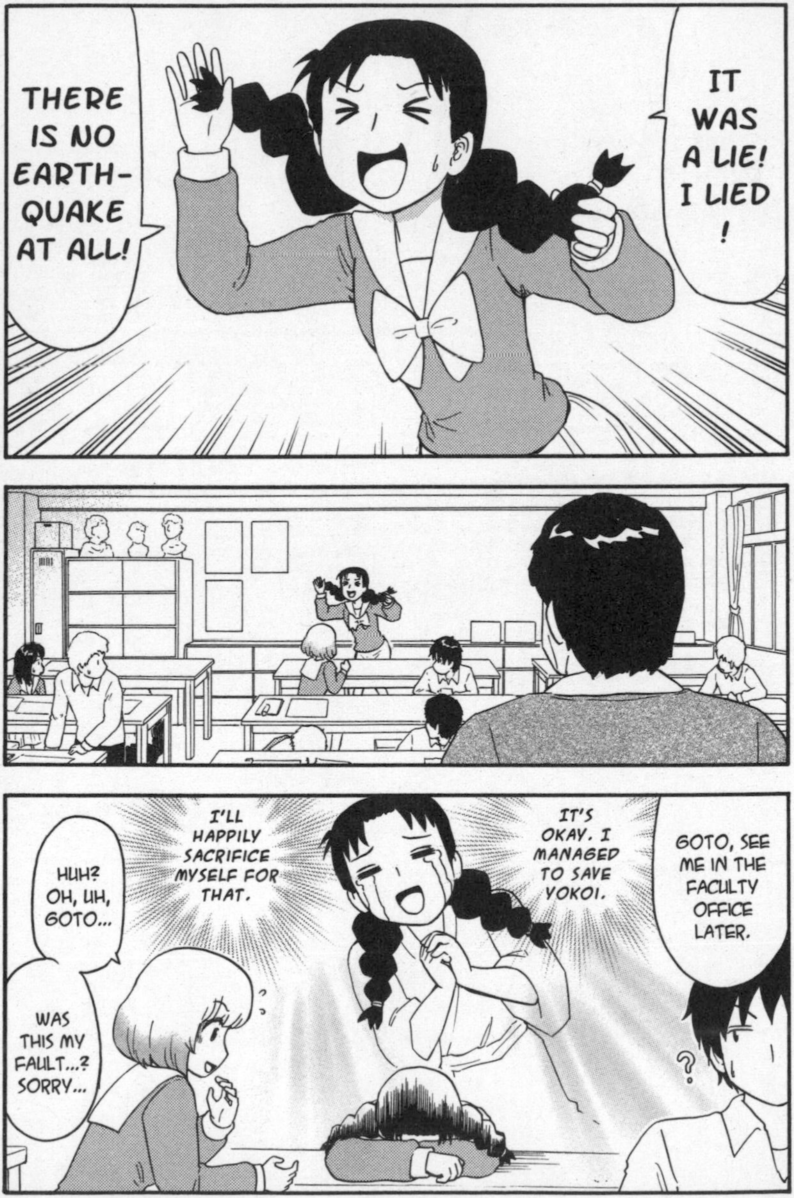
IT WAS A LIE! I LIED!
THERE IS NO EARTH-QUAKE AT ALL!
GOTO, SEE ME IN THE FACULTY OFFICE LATER.
IT'S OKAY. I MANAGED TO SAVE YOKOI.
I'LL HAPPILY SACRIFICE MYSELF FOR THAT.
HUH? OH, UH, GOTO...
WAS THIS MY FAULT...? SORRY...

My Neighbor Seki

HOW-
EVER...

TODAY IN
HOME-
ROOM,
WE'RE
DISCUSSING
THE
UPCOMING
SCHOOL
FESTIVAL.

SCHOOL
FESTIVAL

CLASS
PRESENTATION

117

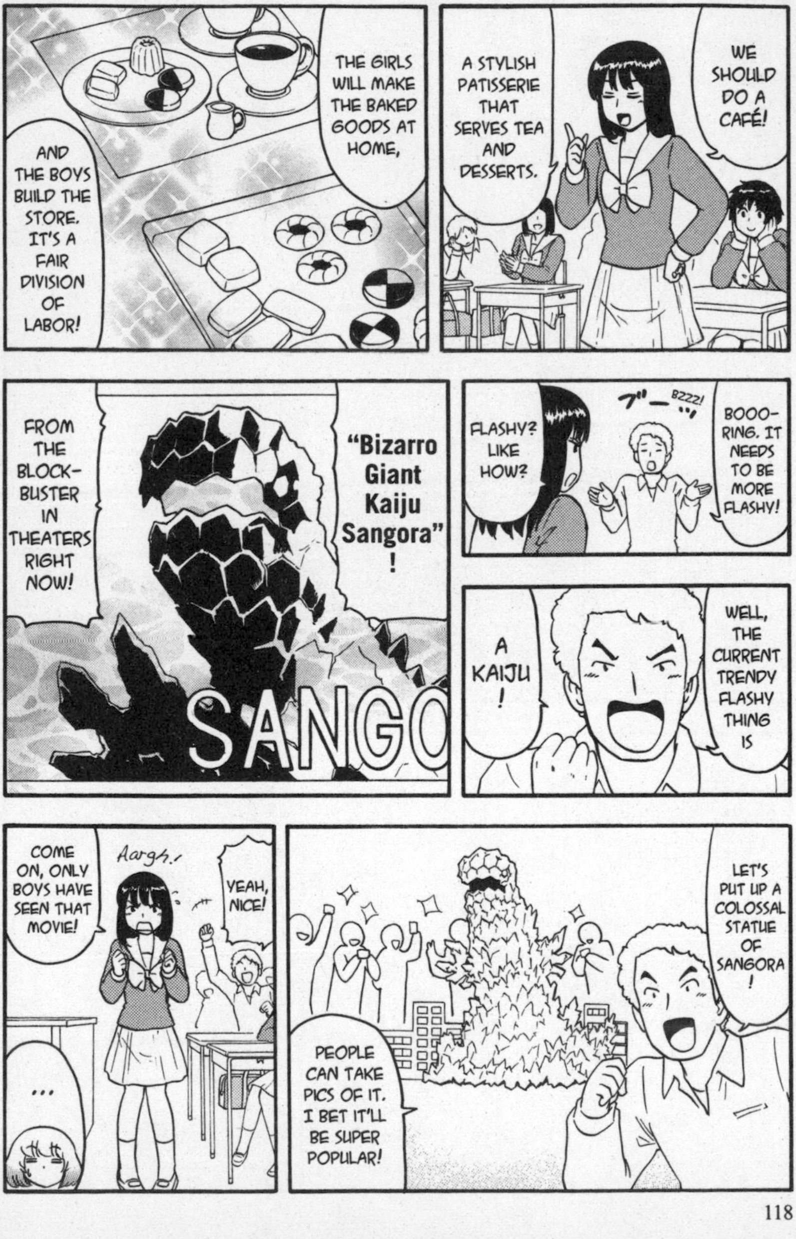
WE SHOULD DO A CAFÉ!
A STYLISH PATISSERIE THAT SERVES TEA AND DESSERTS.
THE GIRLS WILL MAKE THE BAKED GOODS AT HOME,
AND THE BOYS BUILD THE STORE. IT'S A FAIR DIVISION OF LABOR!
ブー BZZZ!
BOOO-RING. IT NEEDS TO BE MORE FLASHY!
FLASHY? LIKE HOW?
WELL, THE CURRENT TRENDY FLASHY THING IS
A KAIJU!
"Bizarro Giant Kaiju Sangora"!
FROM THE BLOCK-BUSTER IN THEATERS RIGHT NOW!
SANGO
LET'S PUT UP A COLOSSAL STATUE OF SANGORA!
PEOPLE CAN TAKE PICS OF IT. I BET IT'LL BE SUPER POPULAR!
YEAH, NICE!
Aargh!
COME ON, ONLY BOYS HAVE SEEN THAT MOVIE!
...

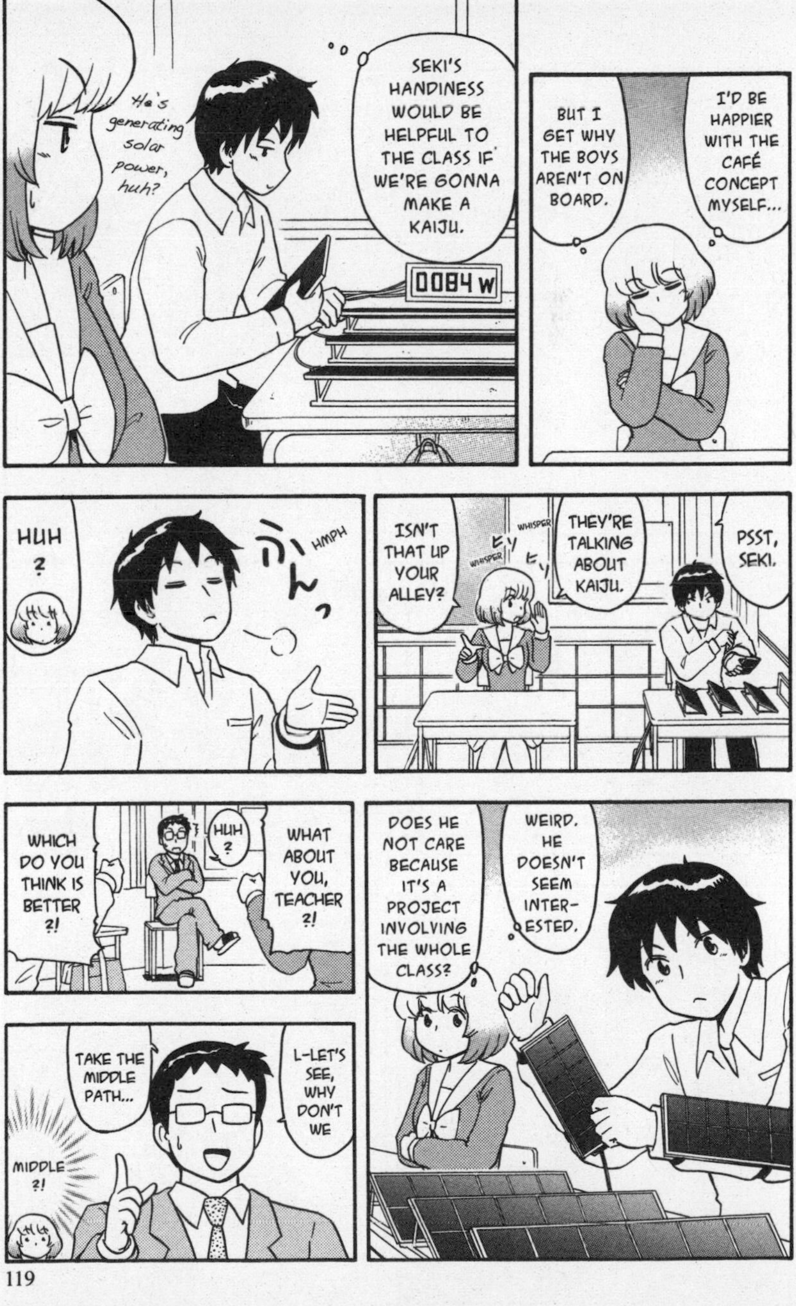
I'D BE HAPPIER WITH THE CAFÉ CONCEPT MYSELF...
BUT I GET WHY THE BOYS AREN'T ON BOARD.
SEKI'S HANDINESS WOULD BE HELPFUL TO THE CLASS IF WE'RE GONNA MAKE A KAIJU.
He's generating solar power, huh?
0084 W
PSST, SEKI.
THEY'RE TALKING ABOUT KAIJU.
ヒソ ヒソ
WHISPER WHISPER
ISN'T THAT UP YOUR ALLEY?
ふんっ
HMPH
HUH?
WEIRD. HE DOESN'T SEEM INTER-ESTED.
DOES HE NOT CARE BECAUSE IT'S A PROJECT INVOLVING THE WHOLE CLASS?
WHAT ABOUT YOU, TEACHER?!
HUH?
WHICH DO YOU THINK IS BETTER?!
L-LET'S SEE, WHY DON'T WE
TAKE THE MIDDLE PATH...
MIDDLE?!

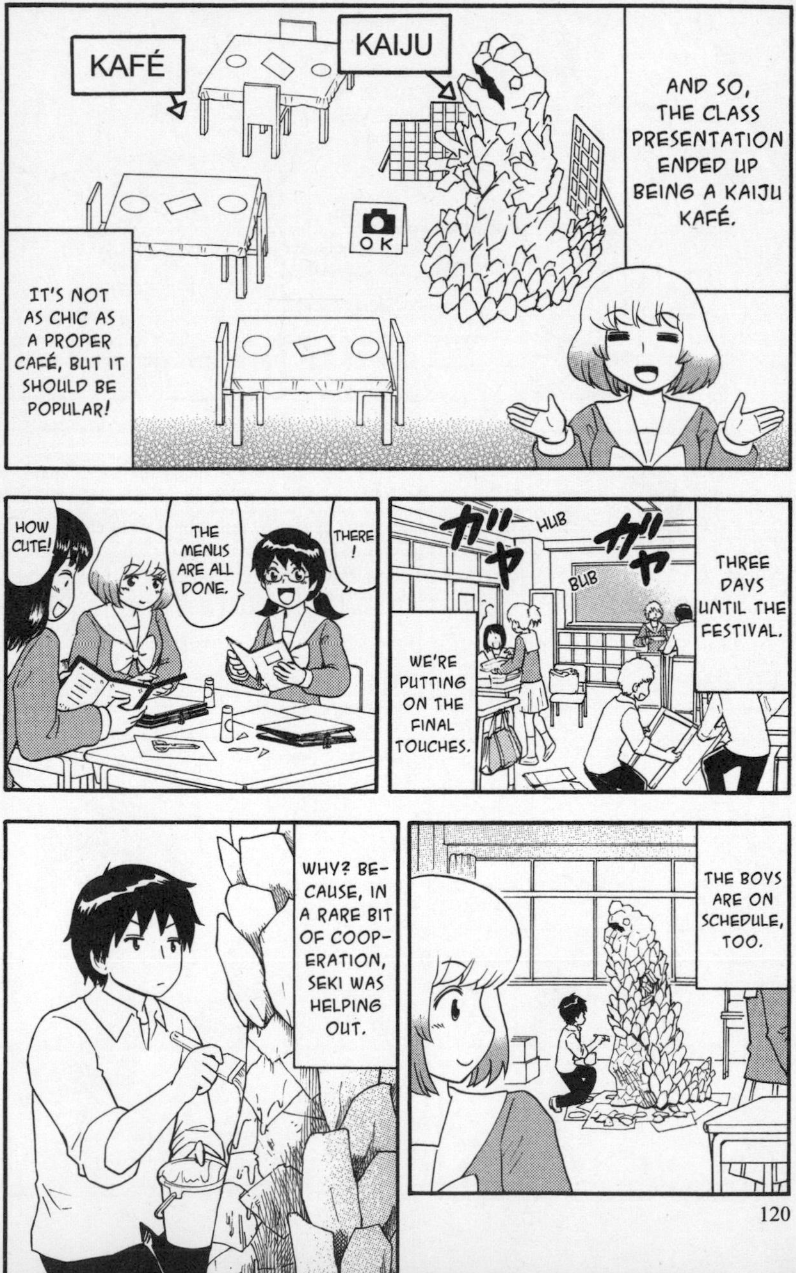
AND SO, THE CLASS PRESENTATION ENDED UP BEING A KAIJU KAFÉ.
KAIJU
KAFÉ
OK
IT'S NOT AS CHIC AS A PROPER CAFÉ, BUT IT SHOULD BE POPULAR!
THREE DAYS UNTIL THE FESTIVAL.
ガヤ
BUB
ガヤ
HUB
WE'RE PUTTING ON THE FINAL TOUCHES.
THERE!
THE MENUS ARE ALL DONE.
HOW CUTE!
THE BOYS ARE ON SCHEDULE, TOO.
WHY? BE-CAUSE, IN A RARE BIT OF COOP-ERATION, SEKI WAS HELPING OUT.

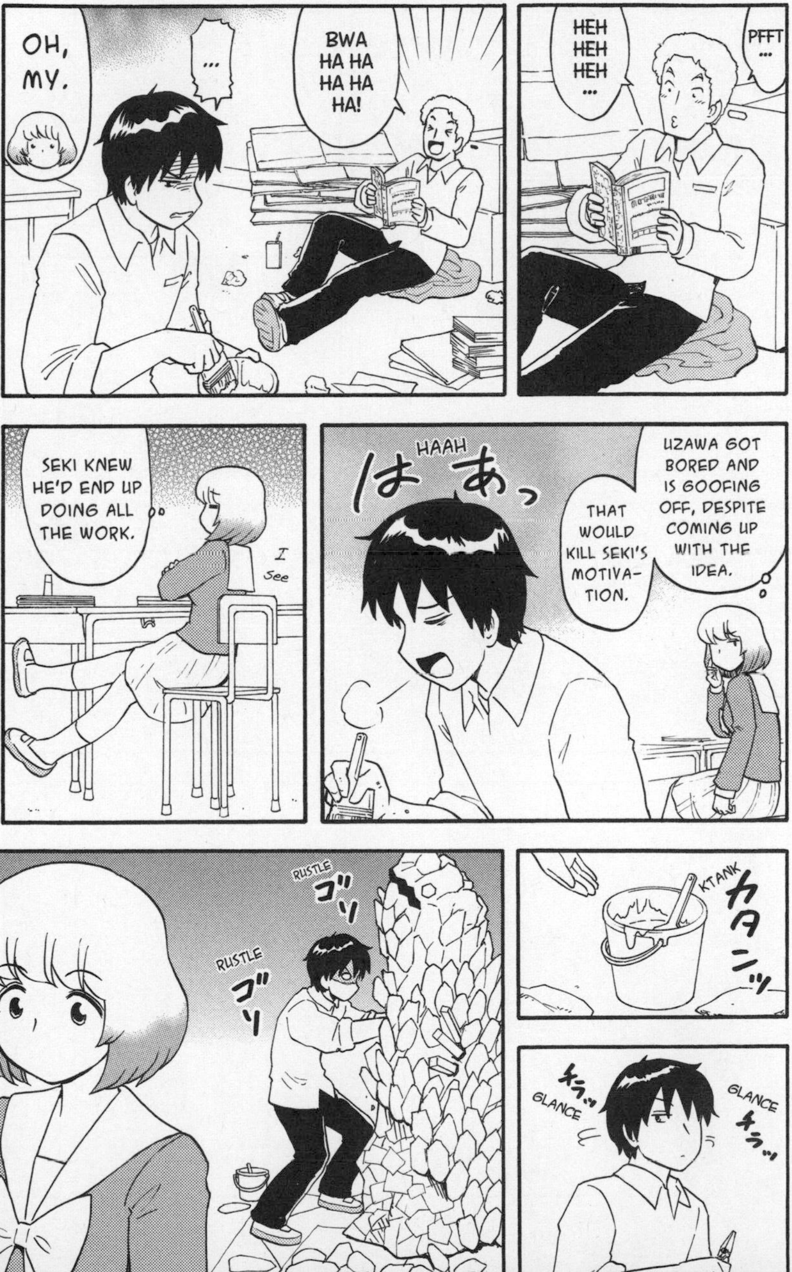
PFFT ...
HEH HEH HEH ...
BWA HA HA HA HA HA!
...
OH, MY.
HAAH
はあっ
UZAWA GOT BORED AND IS GOOFING OFF, DESPITE COMING UP WITH THE IDEA.
THAT WOULD KILL SEKI'S MOTIVATION.
SEKI KNEW HE'D END UP DOING ALL THE WORK.
I see
KTANK
カタンッ
GLANCE
チラッ
GLANCE
チラッ
RUSTLE
ゴソ
RUSTLE
ゴソ

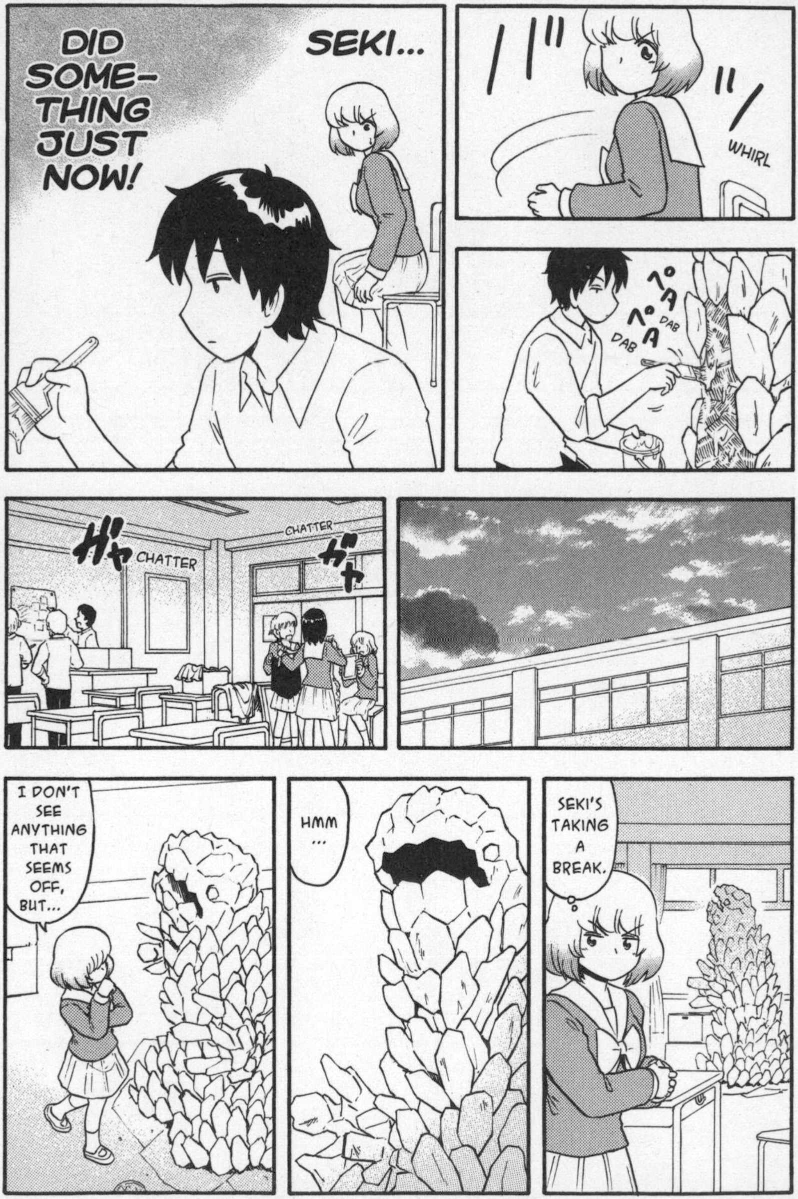
WHIRL
DAB
DAB
SEKI...
DID SOME-THING JUST NOW!
CHATTER
CHATTER
SEKI'S TAKING A BREAK.
HMM ...
I DON'T SEE ANYTHING THAT SEEMS OFF, BUT...

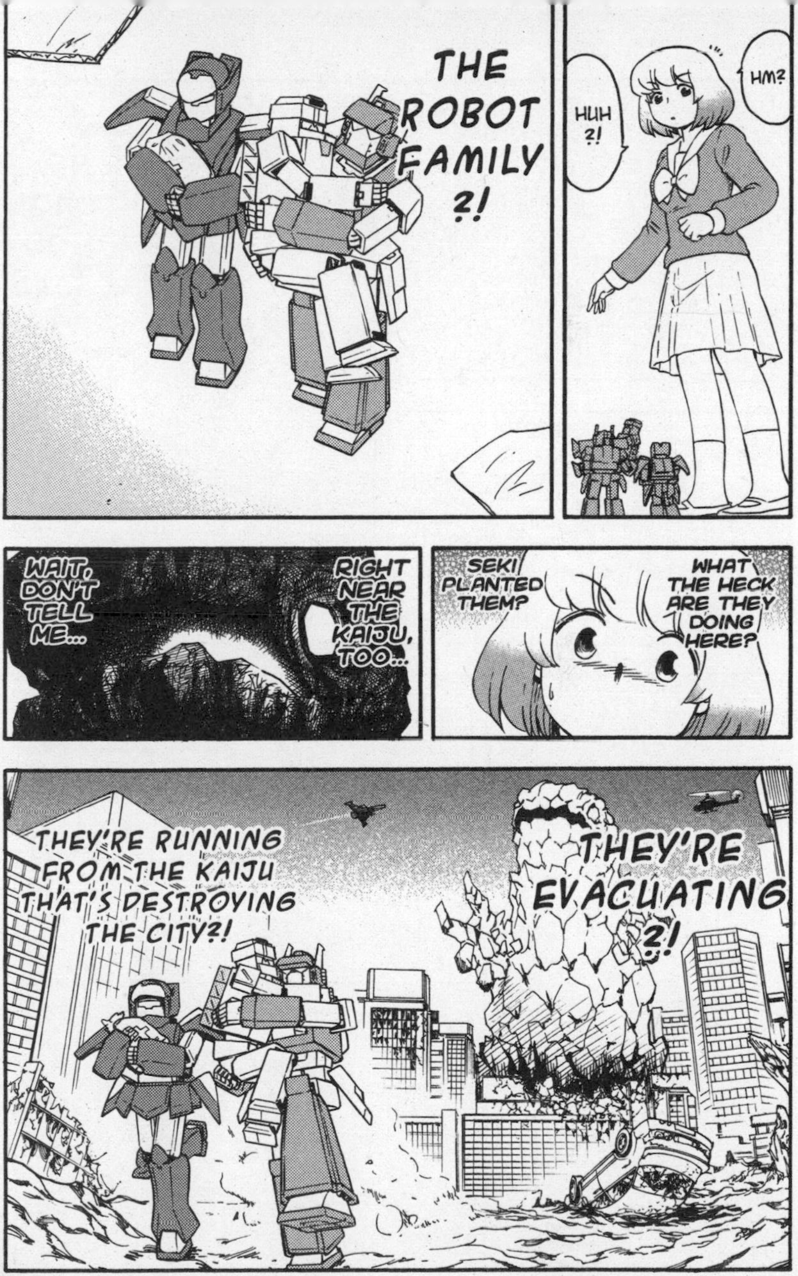
HM?
HUH ?!
THE ROBOT FAMILY ?!
WHAT THE HECK ARE THEY DOING HERE?
SEKI PLANTED THEM?
RIGHT NEAR THE KAIJU, TOO...
WAIT, DON'T TELL ME...
THEY'RE EVACUATING ?!
THEY'RE RUNNING FROM THE KAIJU THAT'S DESTROYING THE CITY?!

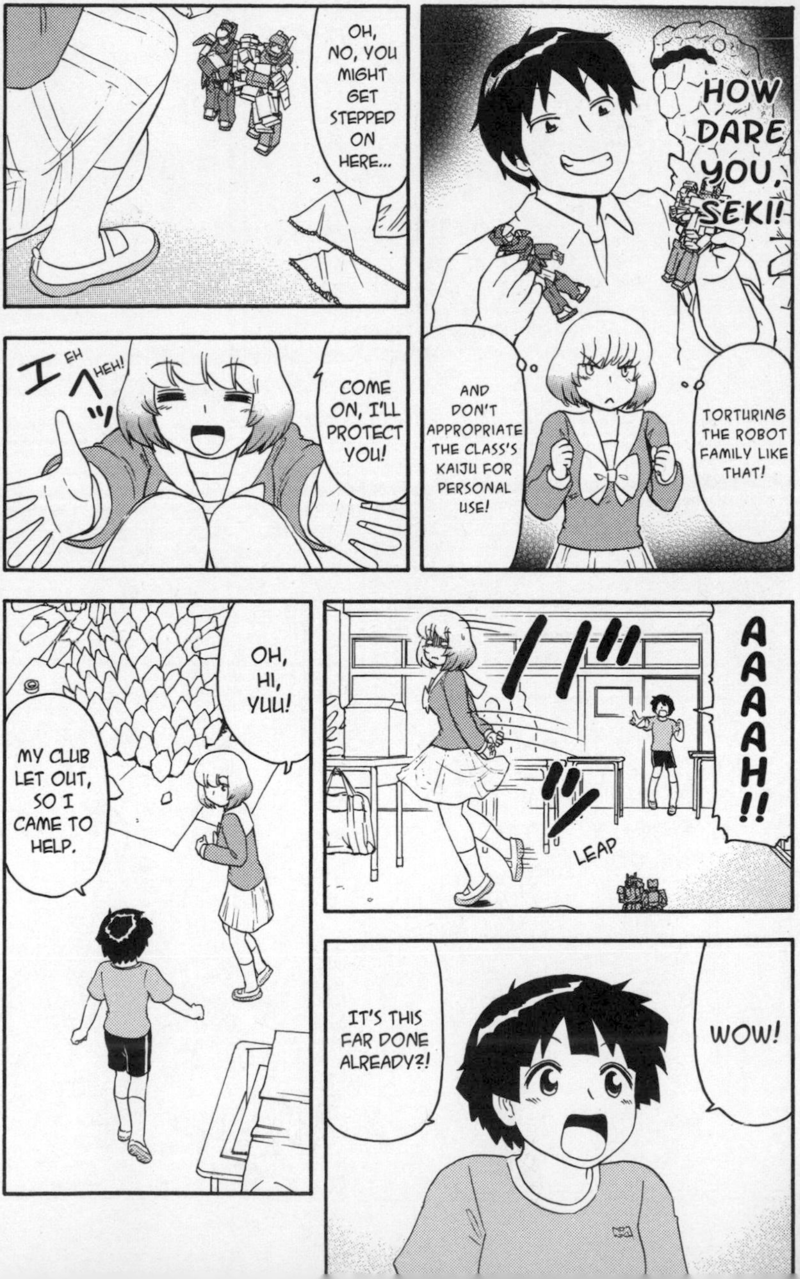
HOW DARE YOU, SEKI!
TORTURING THE ROBOT FAMILY LIKE THAT!
AND DON'T APPROPRIATE THE CLASS'S KAIJU FOR PERSONAL USE!
OH, NO, YOU MIGHT GET STEPPED ON HERE...
COME ON, I'LL PROTECT YOU!
EH HEH!
AAAAAH!!
LEAP
WOW!
IT'S THIS FAR DONE ALREADY?!
OH, HI, YUU!
MY CLUB LET OUT, SO I CAME TO HELP.

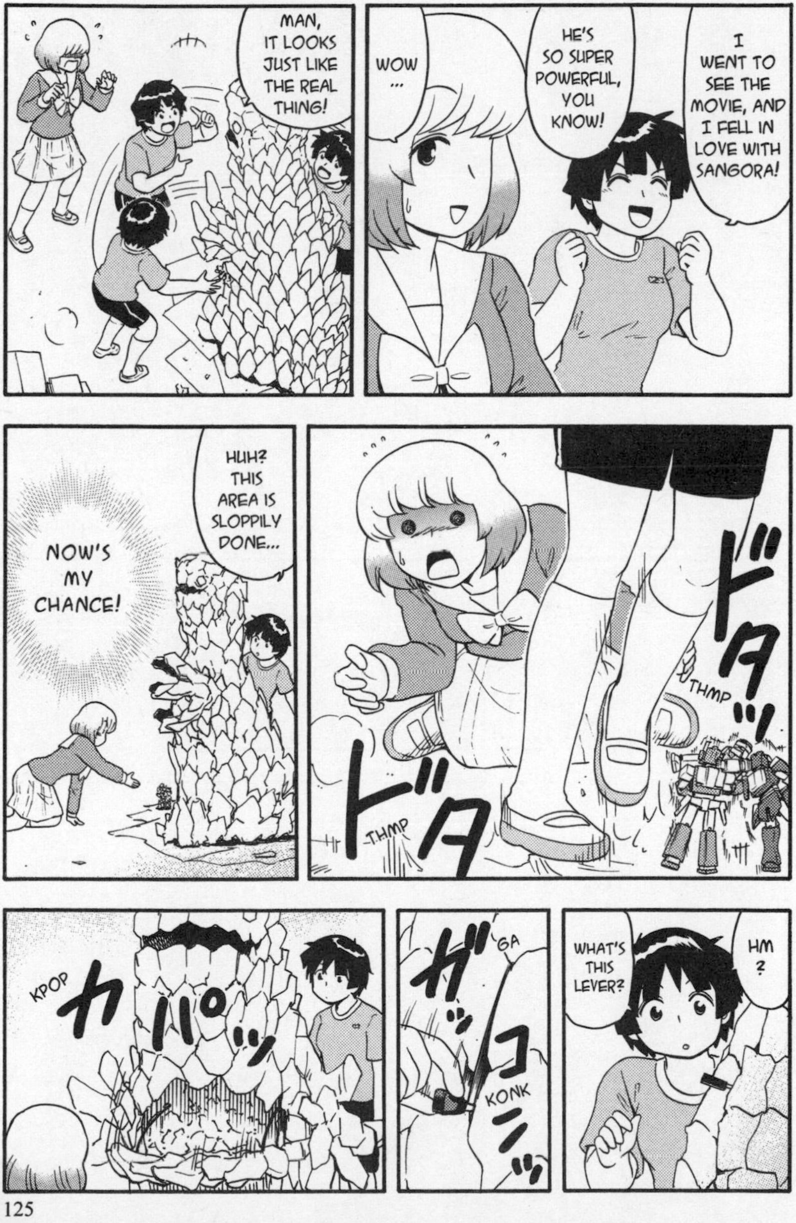
I WENT TO SEE THE MOVIE, AND I FELL IN LOVE WITH SANGORA!
HE'S SO SUPER POWERFUL, YOU KNOW!
WOW ...
MAN, IT LOOKS JUST LIKE THE REAL THING!
ドタッ!
THMP
ドタ
THMP
HUH? THIS AREA IS SLOPPILY DONE...
NOW'S MY CHANCE!
HM ?
WHAT'S THIS LEVER?
ガッ
GA
コンッ
KONK
カパッ
KPOP

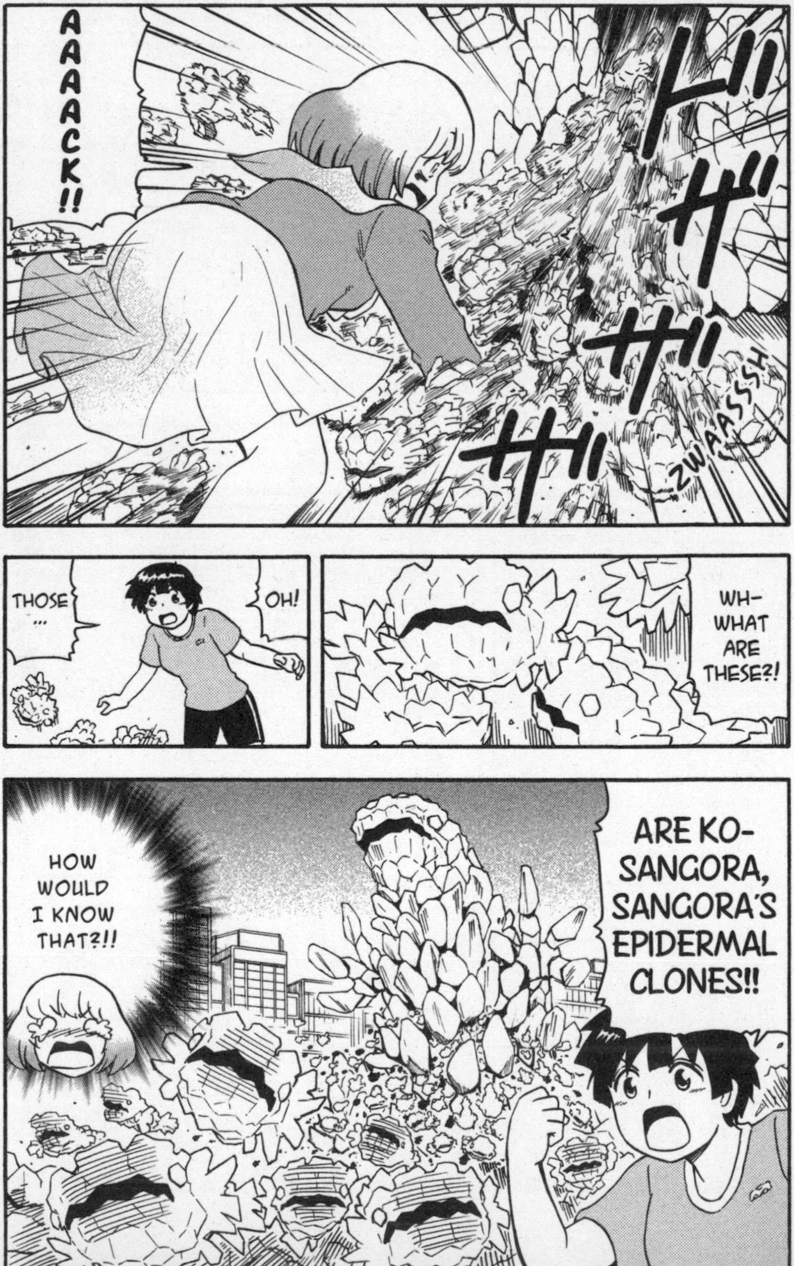

ドザザザ
ZWAASSSH
AAAAACK!!
WH-WHAT ARE THESE?!
OH!
THOSE…
ARE KO-SANGORA, SANGORA'S EPIDERMAL CLONES!!
HOW WOULD I KNOW THAT?!!

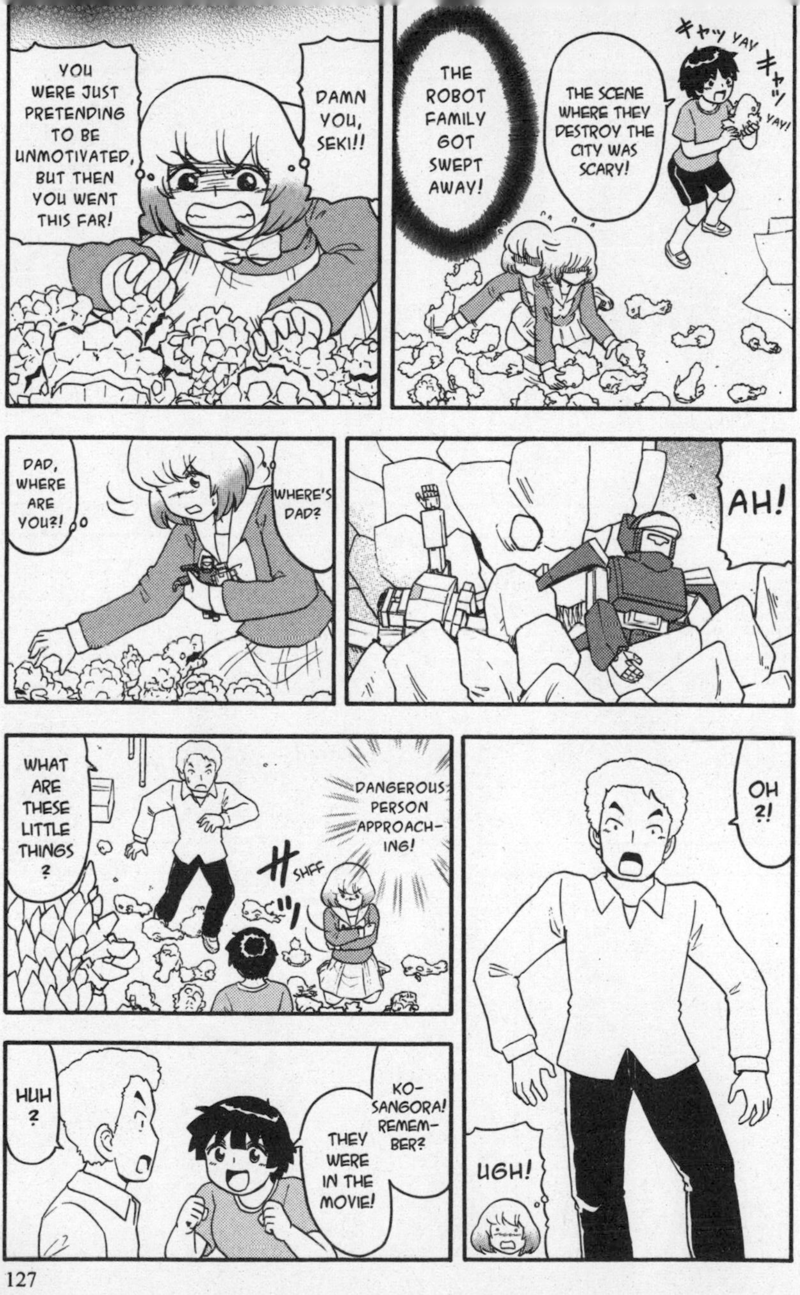
キャッ YAY
キャッ YAY!
THE SCENE WHERE THEY DESTROY THE CITY WAS SCARY!
THE ROBOT FAMILY GOT SWEPT AWAY!
DAMN YOU, SEKI!!
YOU WERE JUST PRETENDING TO BE UNMOTIVATED, BUT THEN YOU WENT THIS FAR!
AH!
WHERE'S DAD?
DAD, WHERE ARE YOU?!
OH?!
UGH!
DANGEROUS PERSON APPROACHING!
SHFF
WHAT ARE THESE LITTLE THINGS?
KO-SANGORA! REMEMBER?
THEY WERE IN THE MOVIE!
HUH?

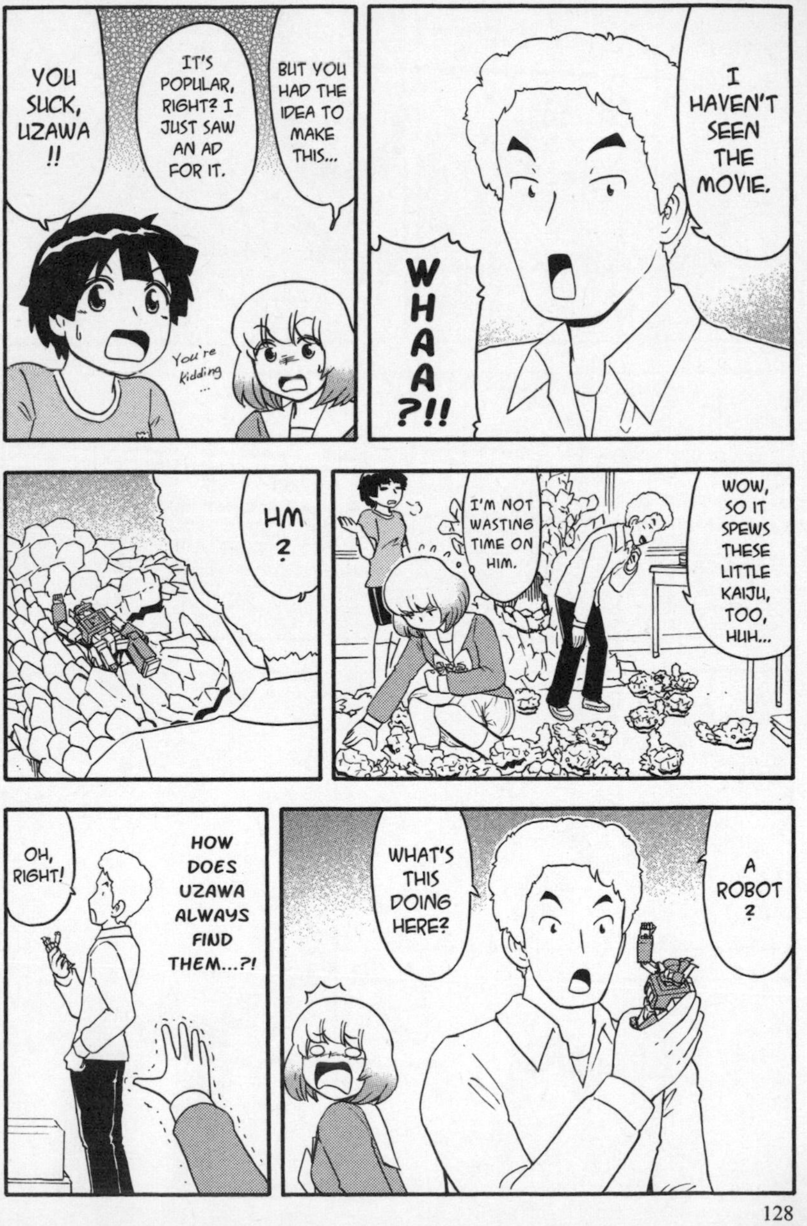
I HAVEN'T SEEN THE MOVIE.
WHAA?!!
BUT YOU HAD THE IDEA TO MAKE THIS...
IT'S POPULAR, RIGHT? I JUST SAW AN AD FOR IT.
YOU SUCK, UZAWA !!
You're kidding ...
WOW, SO IT SPEWS THESE LITTLE KAIJU, TOO, HUH...
I'M NOT WASTING TIME ON HIM.
HM ?
A ROBOT ?
WHAT'S THIS DOING HERE?
HOW DOES UZAWA ALWAYS FIND THEM...?!
OH, RIGHT!

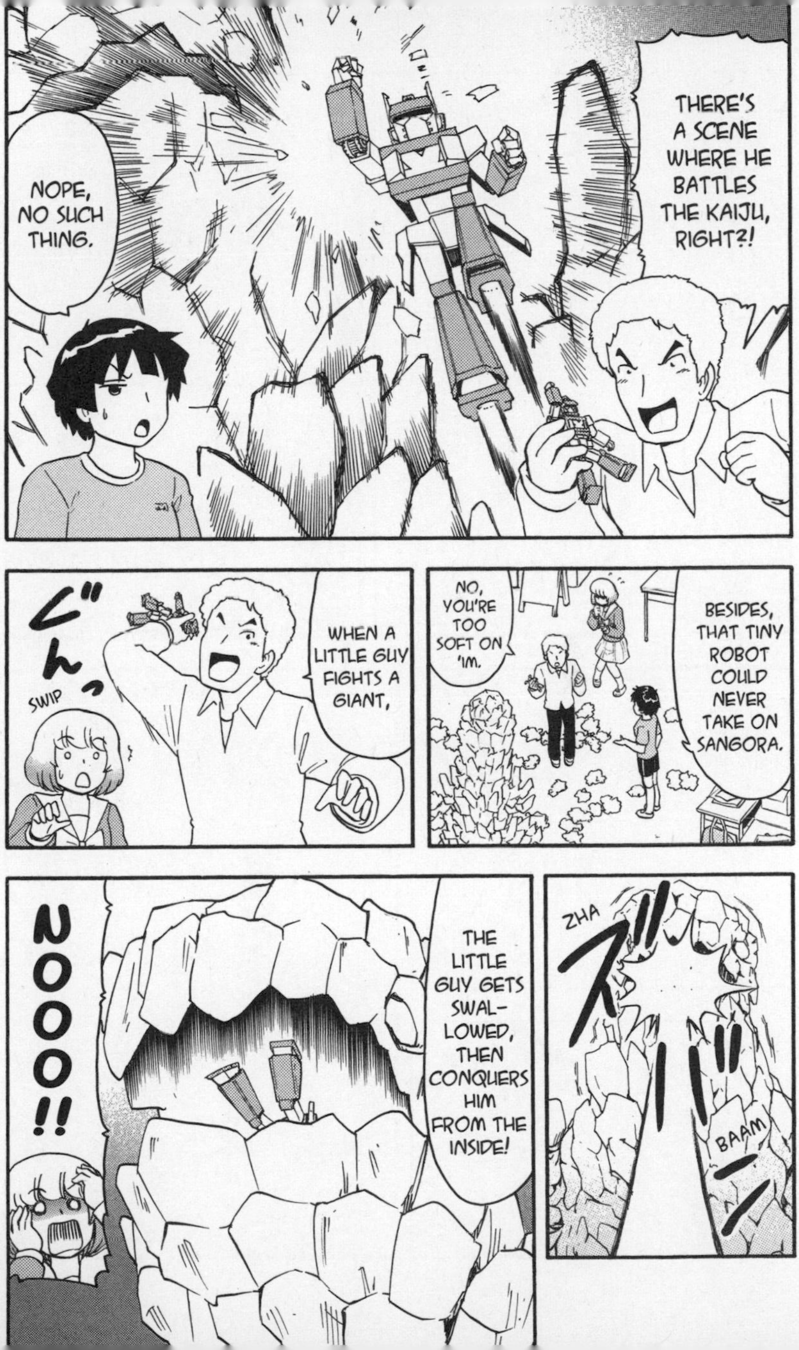
THERE'S A SCENE WHERE HE BATTLES THE KAIJU, RIGHT?!
NOPE, NO SUCH THING.
BESIDES, THAT TINY ROBOT COULD NEVER TAKE ON SANGORA.
NO, YOU'RE TOO SOFT ON 'IM.
WHEN A LITTLE GUY FIGHTS A GIANT,
ぐんっ
SWIP
ズバーン
ZHA
BAAM
THE LITTLE GUY GETS SWAL-LOWED, THEN CONQUERS HIM FROM THE INSIDE!
NOOOO!!

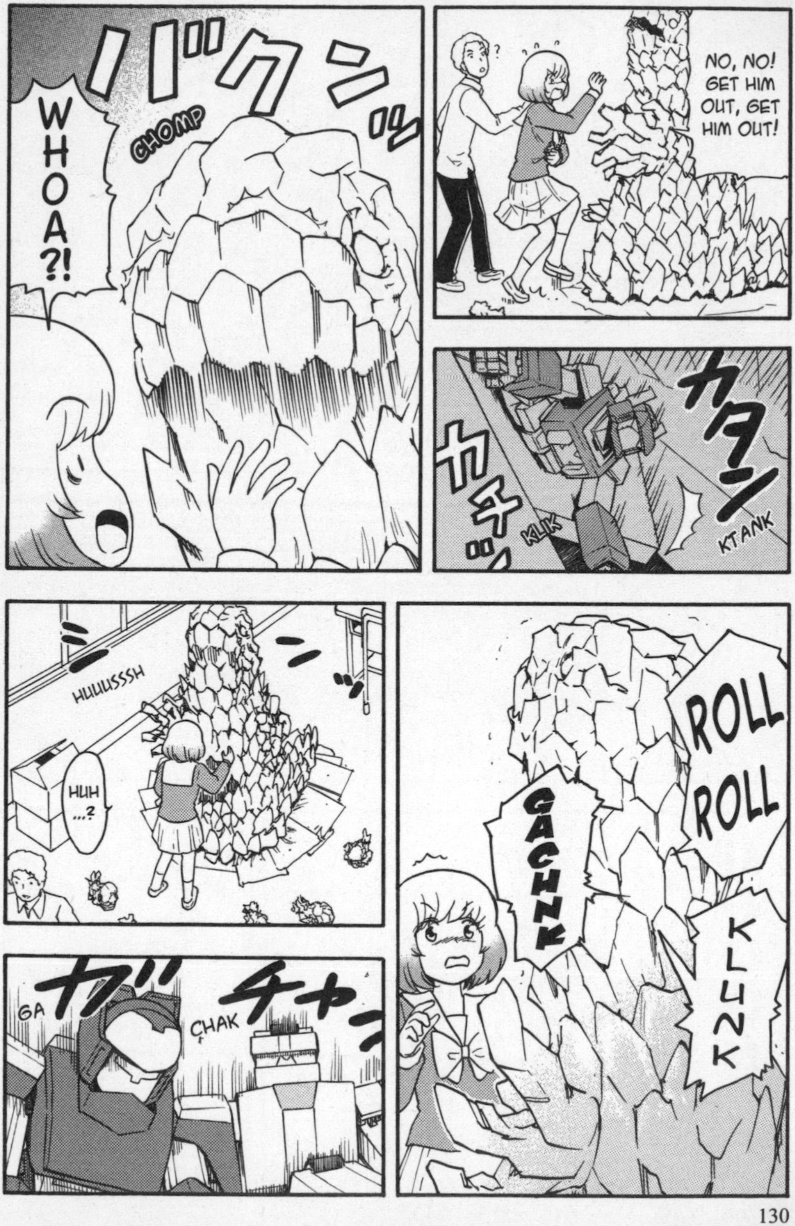
NO, NO! GET HIM OUT, GET HIM OUT!
カタン
KTANK
カチッ
KLIK
バクンッ
CHOMP
WHOA?!
ROLL ROLL
GACHNK
KLUNK
HUUUSSSH
HUH ...?
ガチャッ
GA CHAK

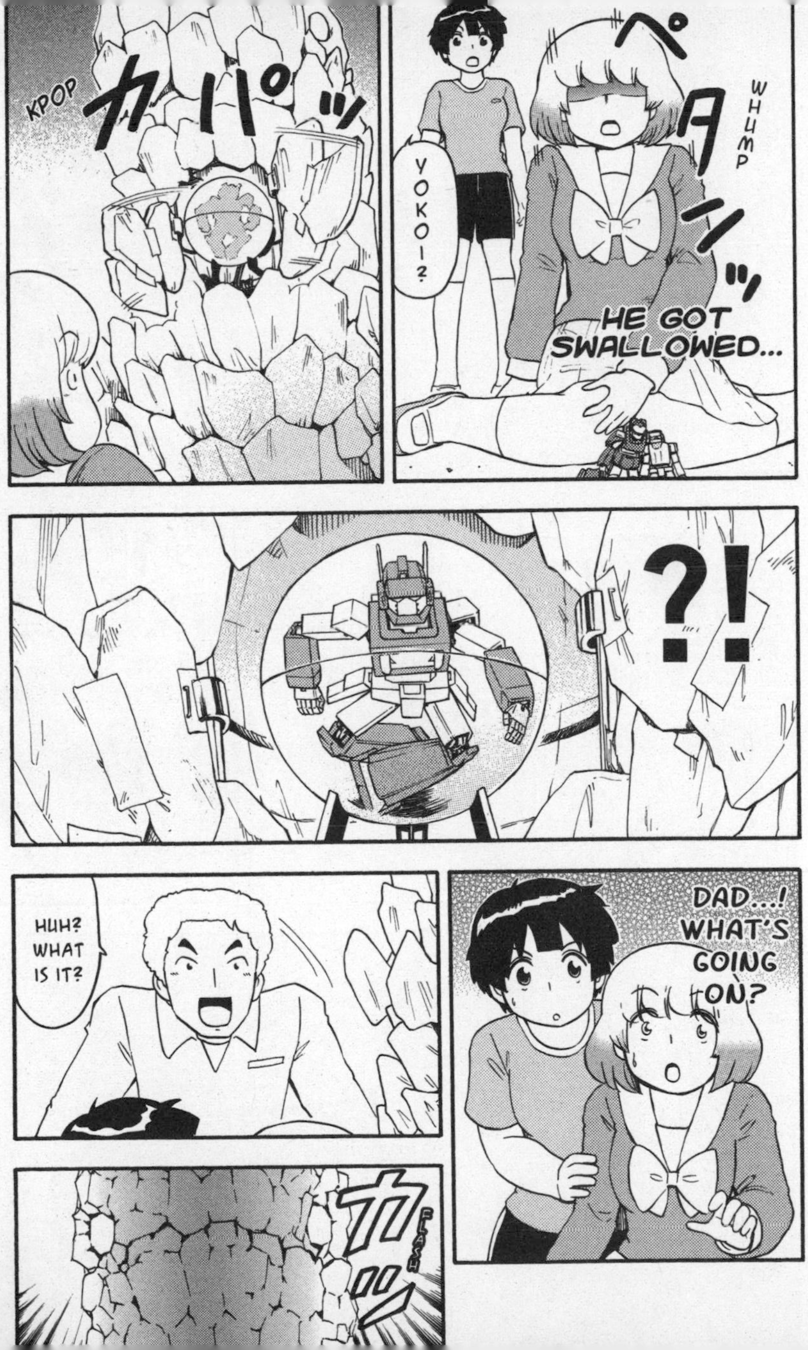
ペタンッ
WHUMP
YOKO-!?
HE GOT SWALLOWED...
KPOP
カパッ
?!
DAD...! WHAT'S GOING ON?
HUH? WHAT IS IT?
カッ
FLASH

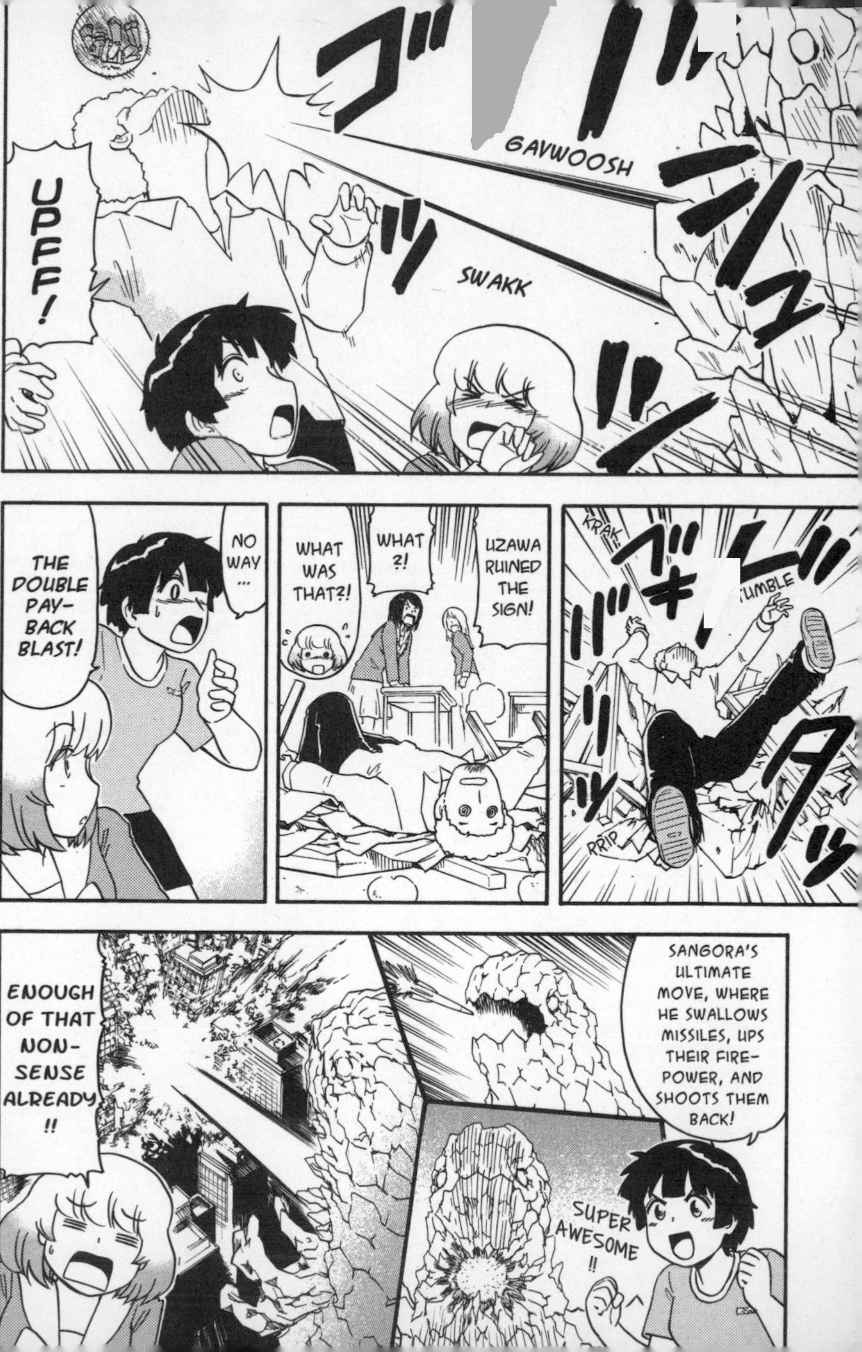
GAVWOOSH
SWAKK
UPFF!
KRAK
TUMBLE
RRIP
UZAWA RUINED THE SIGN!
WHAT?!
WHAT WAS THAT?!
NO WAY...
THE DOUBLE PAY-BACK BLAST!
SANGORA'S ULTIMATE MOVE, WHERE HE SWALLOWS MISSILES, UPS THEIR FIRE-POWER, AND SHOOTS THEM BACK!
SUPER AWESOME!!
ENOUGH OF THAT NON-SENSE ALREADY!!

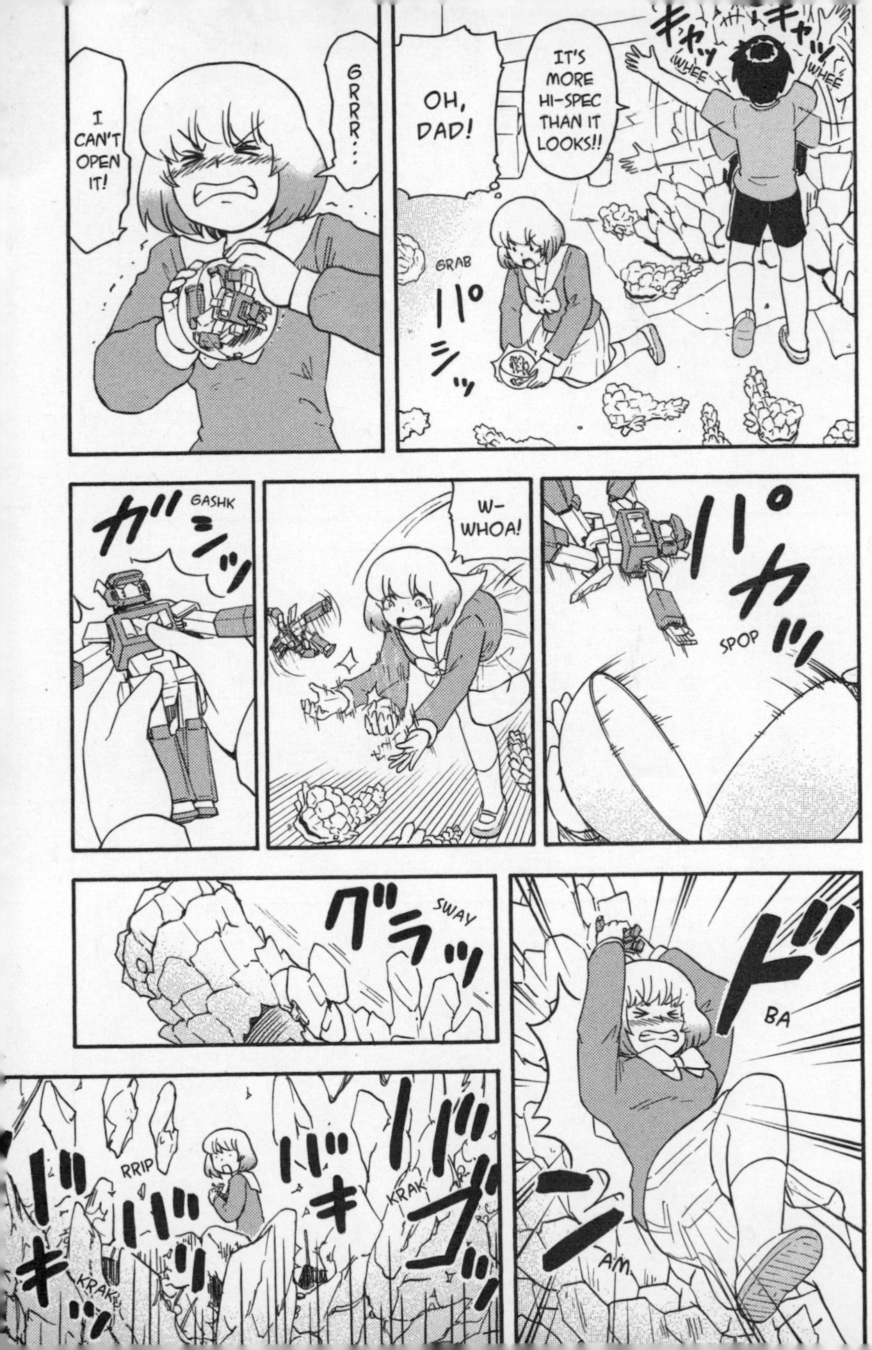
キャッ
WHEE
キャッ
WHEE
IT'S MORE HI-SPEC THAN IT LOOKS!!
OH, DAD!
GRAB
パシッ
GRRR...
I CAN'T OPEN IT!
パカッ
SPOP
W-WHOA!
ガシッ
GASHK
ドバーン
BA
AM
グラッ
SWAY
バキ
KRAK
RRIP
KRAK

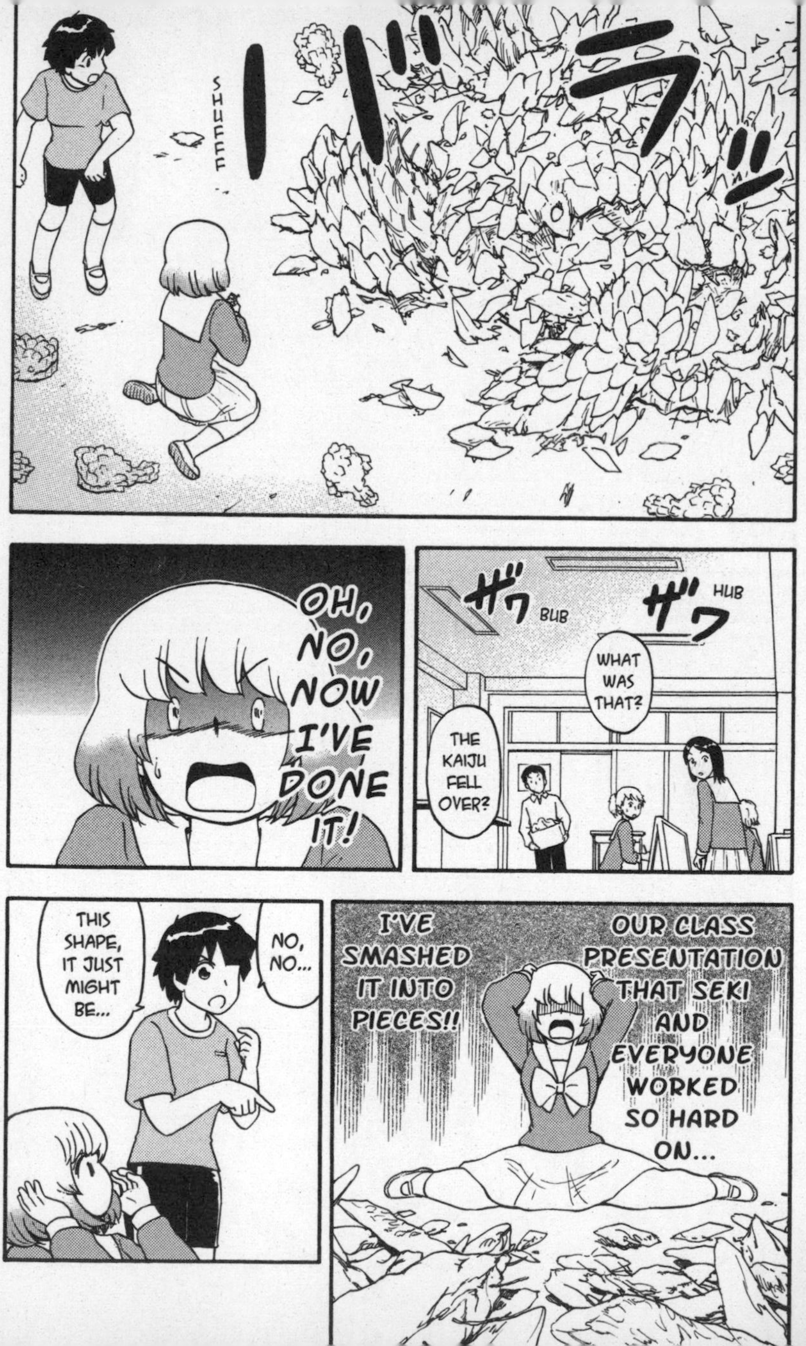
ードラッ
SHUFFF
ザワ BUB
ザワ HUB
WHAT WAS THAT?
THE KAIJU FELL OVER?
OH, NO, NOW I'VE DONE IT!
OUR CLASS PRESENTATION THAT SEKI AND EVERYONE WORKED SO HARD ON...
I'VE SMASHED IT INTO PIECES!!
NO, NO...
THIS SHAPE, IT JUST MIGHT BE...

WHAT?! FOR REAL?!

SANGORA'S FINAL FORM, WHERE HE LIQUEFIES AND ENGULFS ALL OF TOKYO!

HEH...

SHFF

SEKI!!

WHEW

SO IT'S NOT RUINED? I'M SO GLAD!

AH!

ZHFF

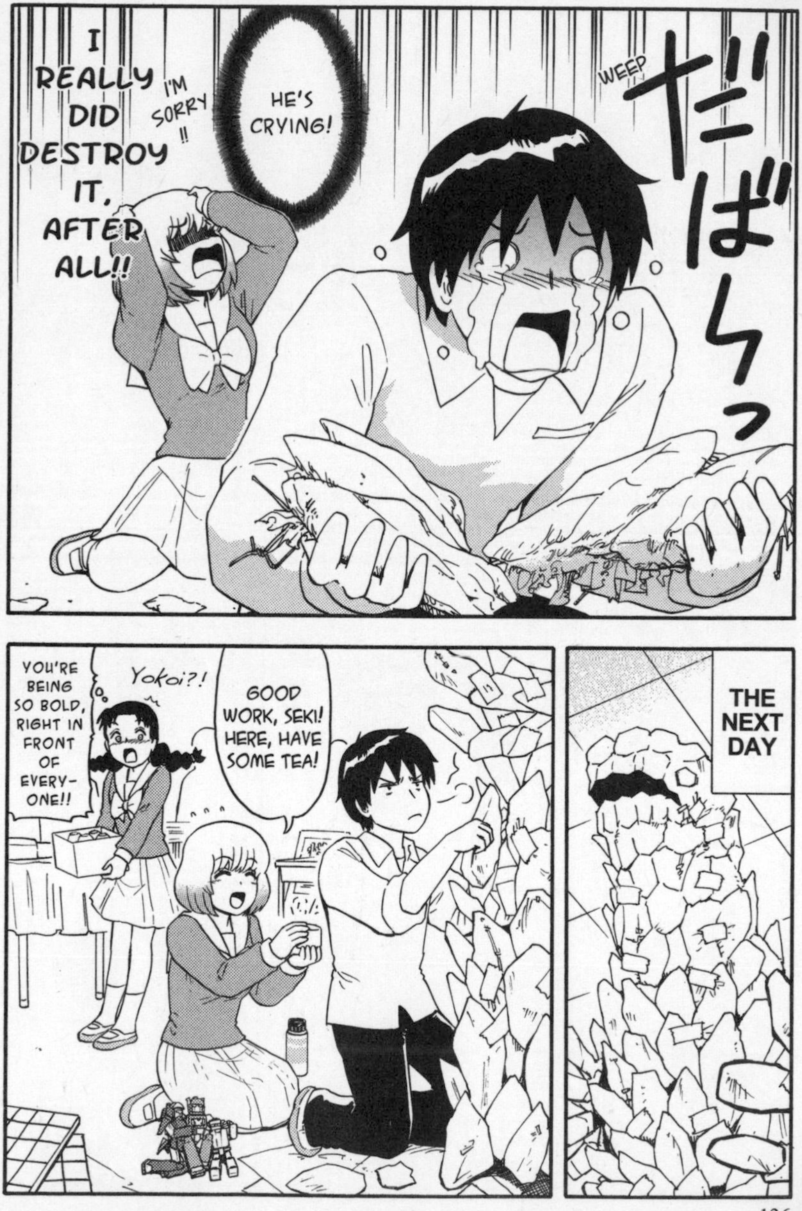
WEEP
だばらっ
HE'S CRYING!
I'M SORRY!!
I REALLY DID DESTROY IT, AFTER ALL!!
THE NEXT DAY
GOOD WORK, SEKI! HERE, HAVE SOME TEA!
Yokoi?!
YOU'RE BEING SO BOLD, RIGHT IN FRONT OF EVERY-ONE!!

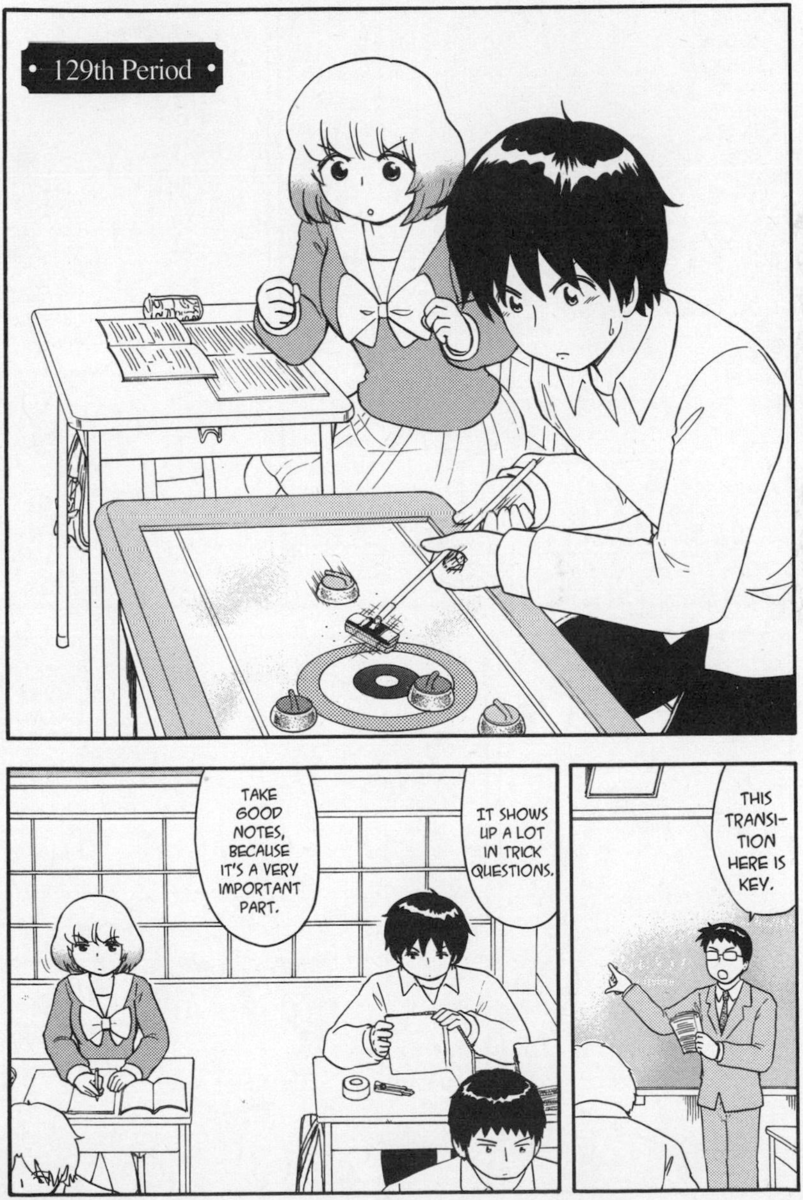
129th Period
THIS TRANSI-TION HERE IS KEY.
IT SHOWS UP A LOT IN TRICK QUESTIONS.
TAKE GOOD NOTES, BECAUSE IT'S A VERY IMPORTANT PART.

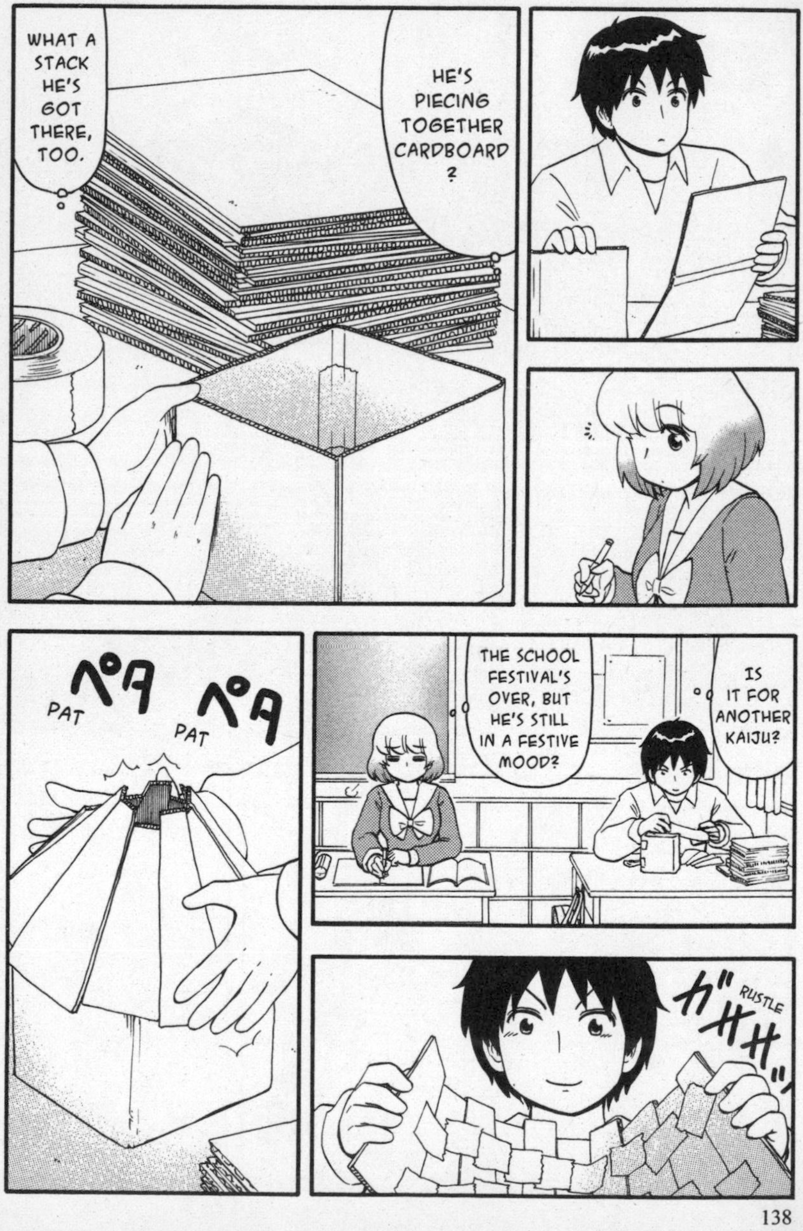
HE'S PIECING TOGETHER CARDBOARD?
WHAT A STACK HE'S GOT THERE, TOO.
IS IT FOR ANOTHER KAIJU?
THE SCHOOL FESTIVAL'S OVER, BUT HE'S STILL IN A FESTIVE MOOD?
ガサガサ
RUSTLE
ペタ
PAT
ペタ
PAT

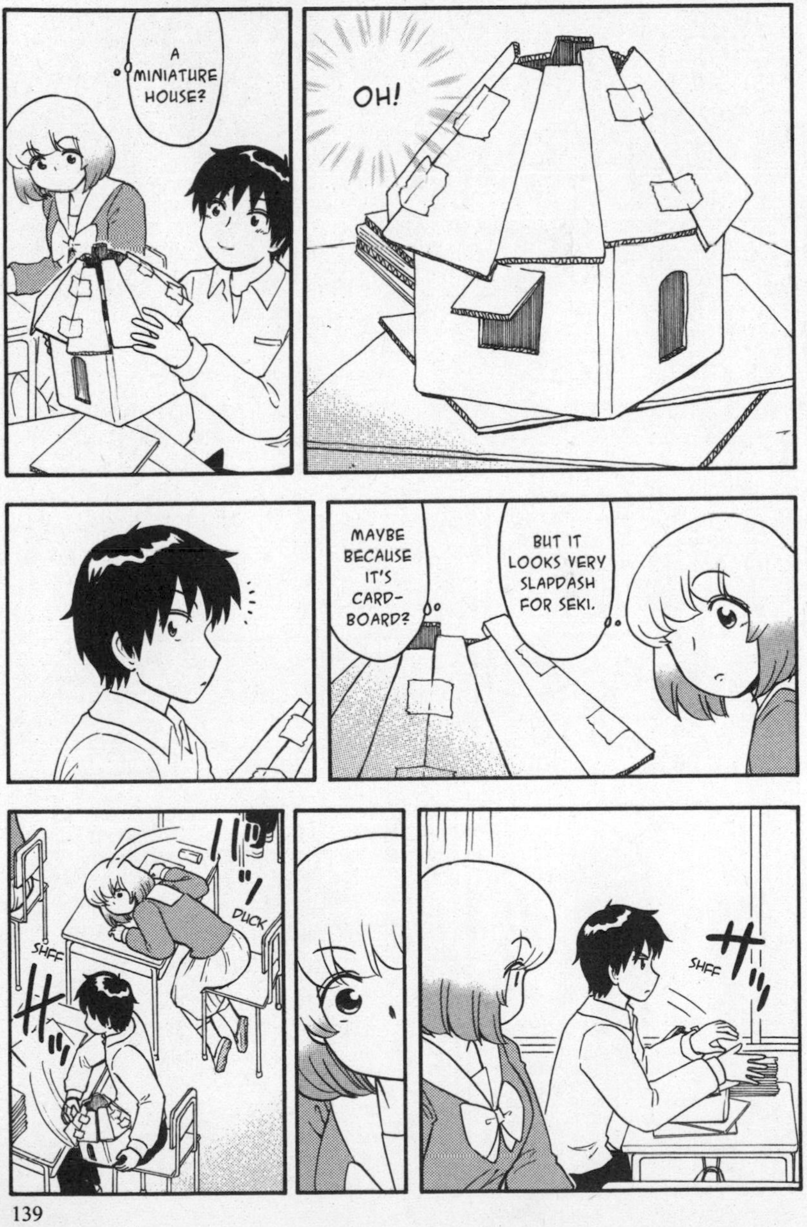
OH!
A MINIATURE HOUSE?
BUT IT LOOKS VERY SLAPDASH FOR SEKI.
MAYBE BECAUSE IT'S CARD-BOARD?
SHFF
DUCK
SHFF

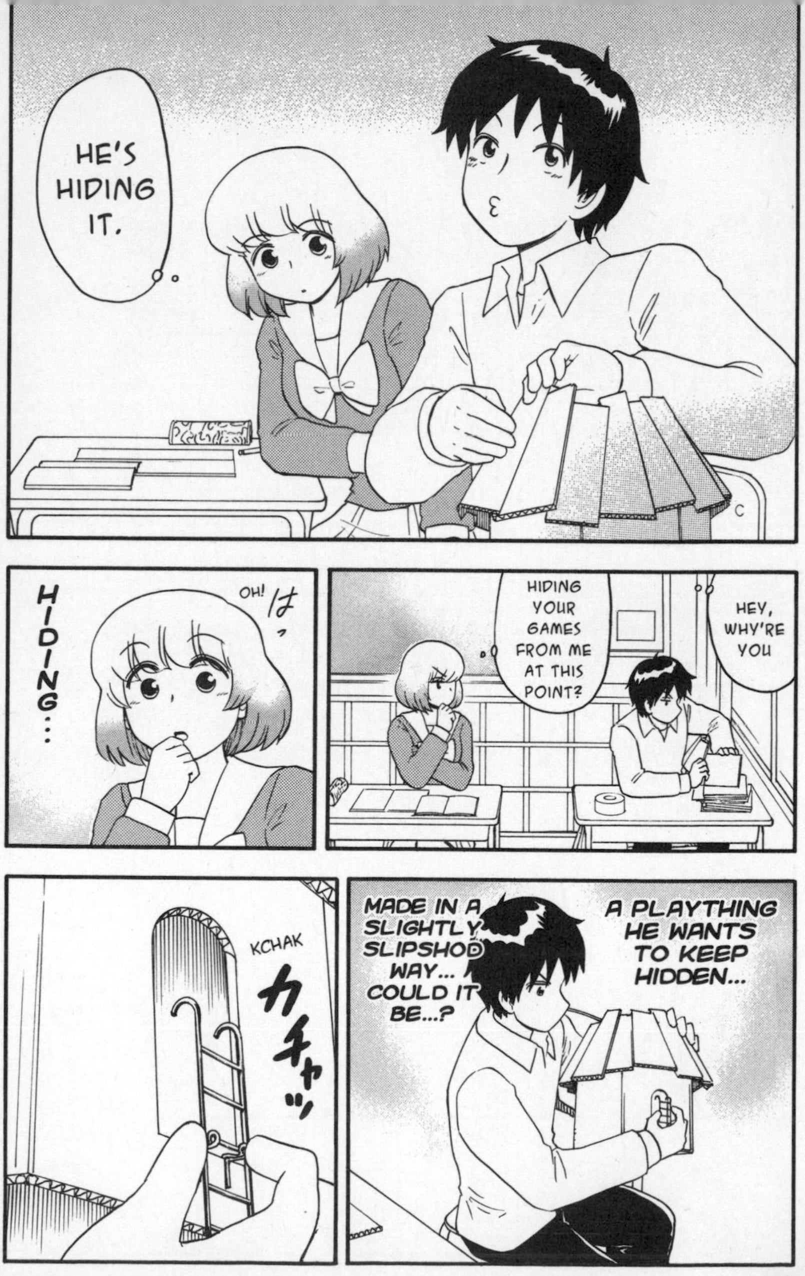
HE'S HIDING IT.
HEY, WHY'RE YOU
HIDING YOUR GAMES FROM ME AT THIS POINT?
OH! は
HIDING...
A PLAYTHING HE WANTS TO KEEP HIDDEN...
MADE IN A SLIGHTLY SLIPSHOD WAY... COULD IT BE...?
KCHAK
カチャッ

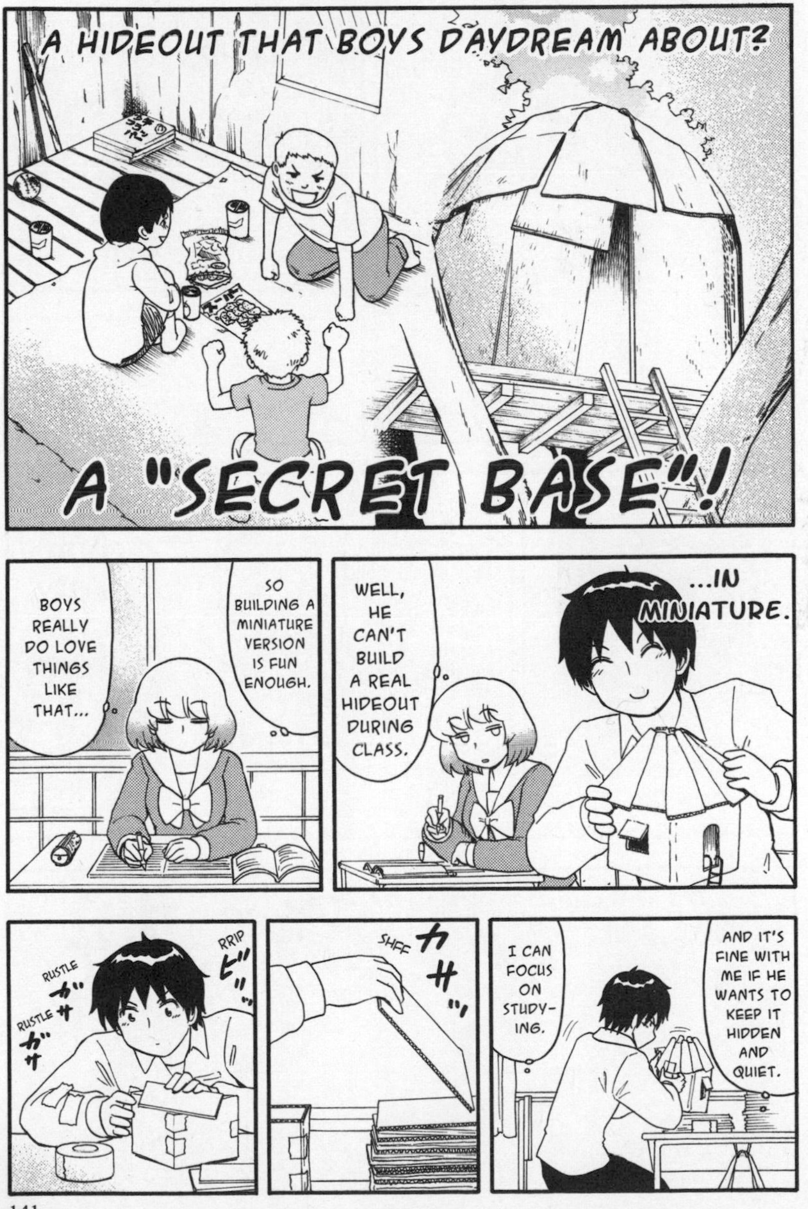
A HIDEOUT THAT BOYS DAYDREAM ABOUT?
A "SECRET BASE"!
...IN MINIATURE.
WELL, HE CAN'T BUILD A REAL HIDEOUT DURING CLASS.
SO BUILDING A MINIATURE VERSION IS FUN ENOUGH.
BOYS REALLY DO LOVE THINGS LIKE THAT...
AND IT'S FINE WITH ME IF HE WANTS TO KEEP IT HIDDEN AND QUIET.
I CAN FOCUS ON STUDY-ING.
SHFF
RRIP
RUSTLE
RUSTLE

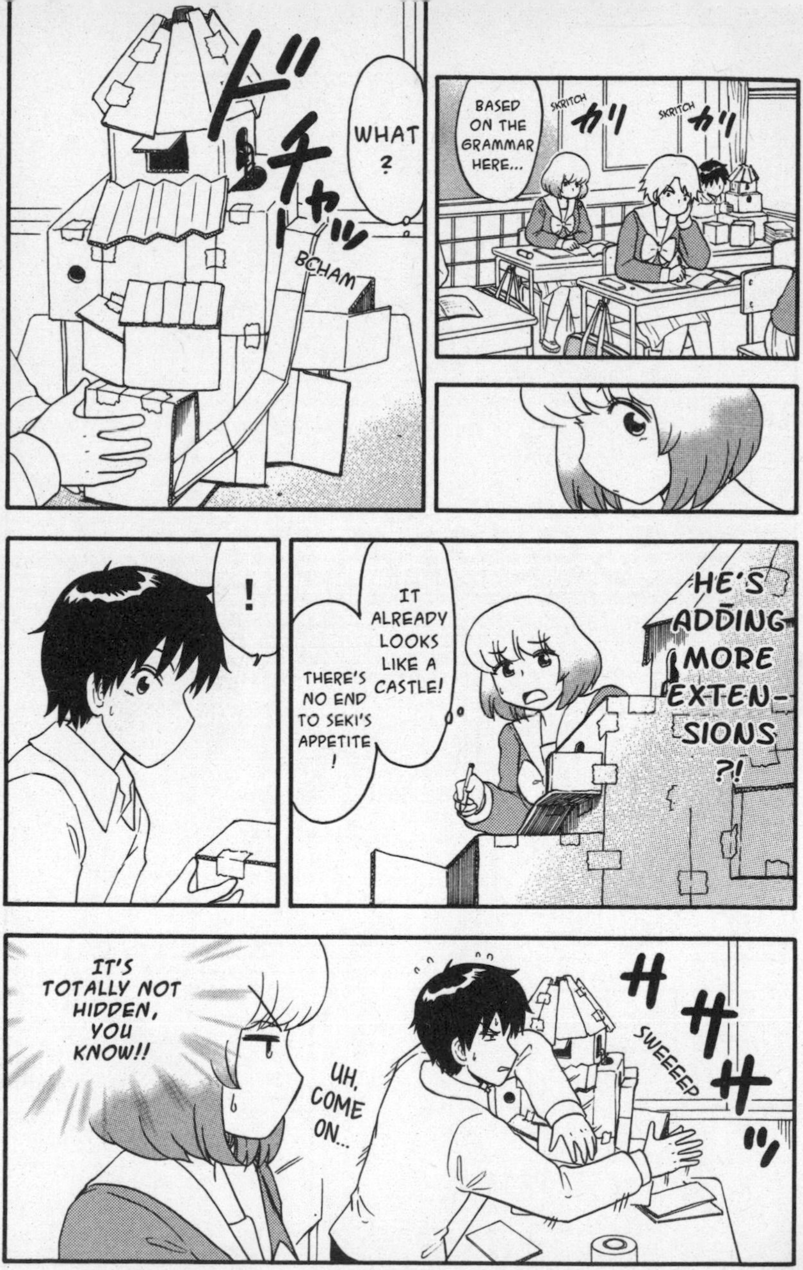
BASED ON THE GRAMMAR HERE...
SKRITCH
ガリ
SKRITCH
ガリ
ドチャッ
BCHAM
WHAT?
HE'S ADDING MORE EXTEN-SIONS?!
IT ALREADY LOOKS LIKE A CASTLE!
THERE'S NO END TO SEKI'S APPETITE!
!
ササササッ
SWEEEEP
UH, COME ON...
IT'S TOTALLY NOT HIDDEN, YOU KNOW!!

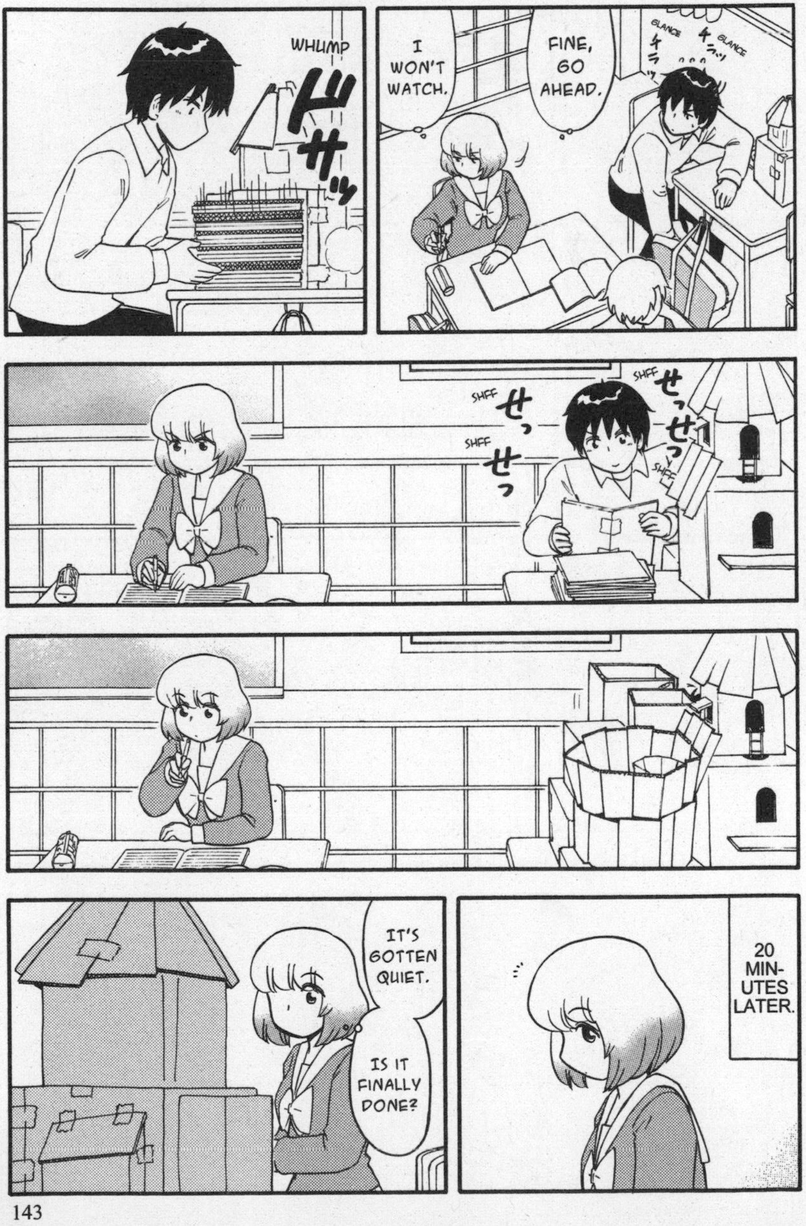
FINE, GO AHEAD.
I WON'T WATCH.
GLANCE
GLANCE
WHUMP
ドサッ
SHFF
せっ
SHFF
せっ
SHFF
せっ
SHFF
20 MINUTES LATER.
IT'S GOTTEN QUIET.
IS IT FINALLY DONE?

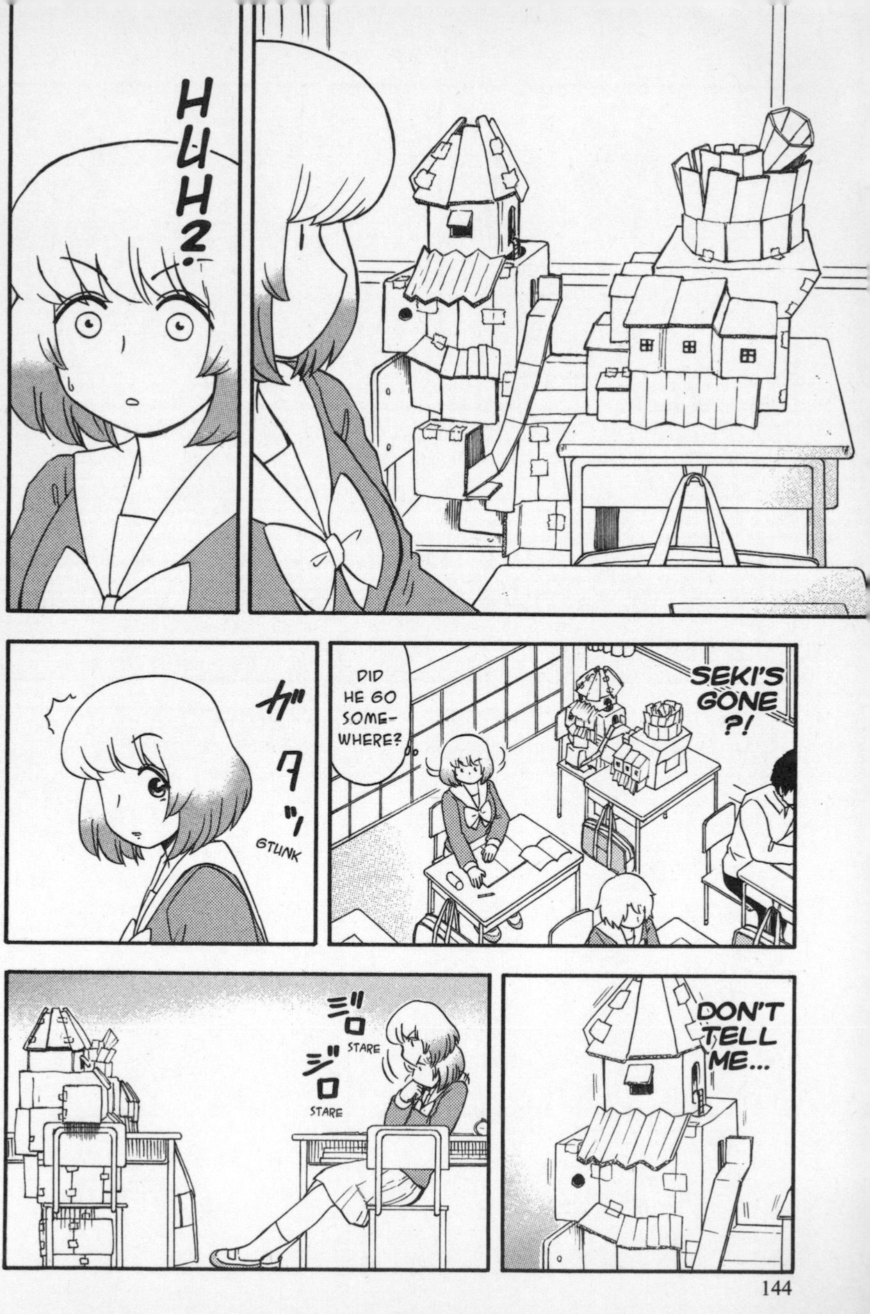
HUH?
SEKI'S GONE ?!
DID HE GO SOME-WHERE?
ガタッ
GTUNK
DON'T TELL ME...
ジロ
STARE
ジロ
STARE

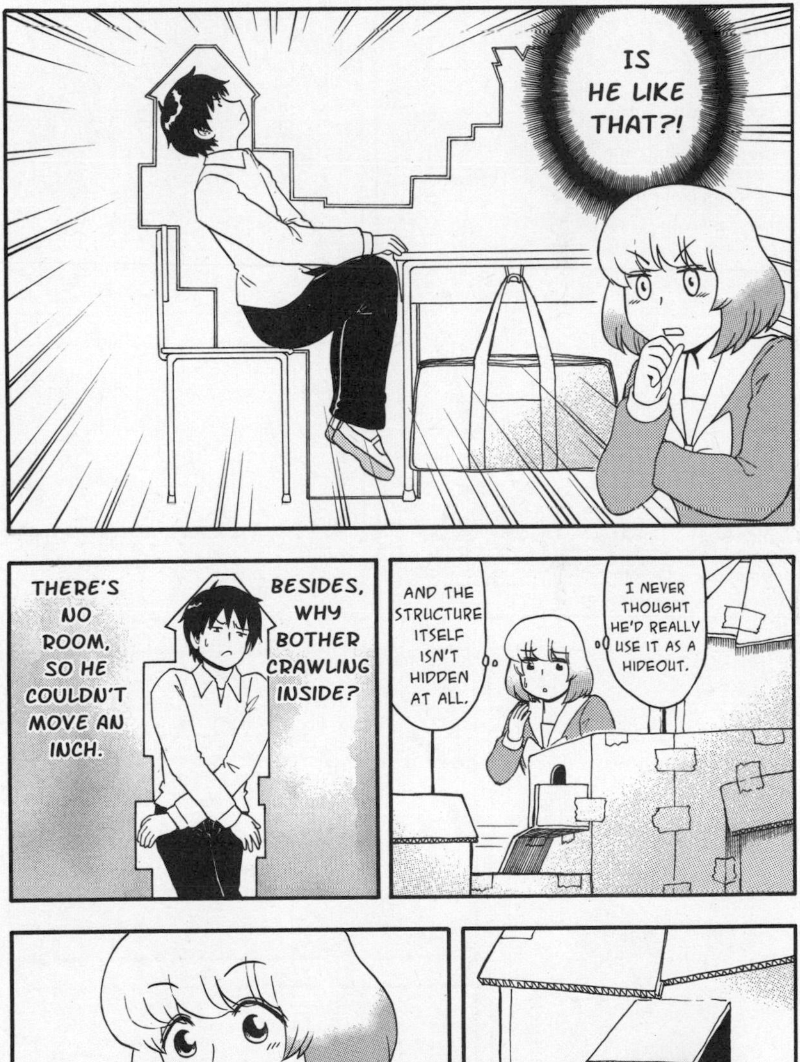
IS HE LIKE THAT?!
I NEVER THOUGHT HE'D REALLY USE IT AS A HIDEOUT.
AND THE STRUCTURE ITSELF ISN'T HIDDEN AT ALL.
BESIDES, WHY BOTHER CRAWLING INSIDE?
THERE'S NO ROOM, SO HE COULDN'T MOVE AN INCH.
OH, A WINDOW ...

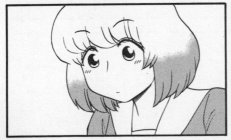

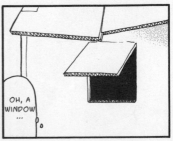

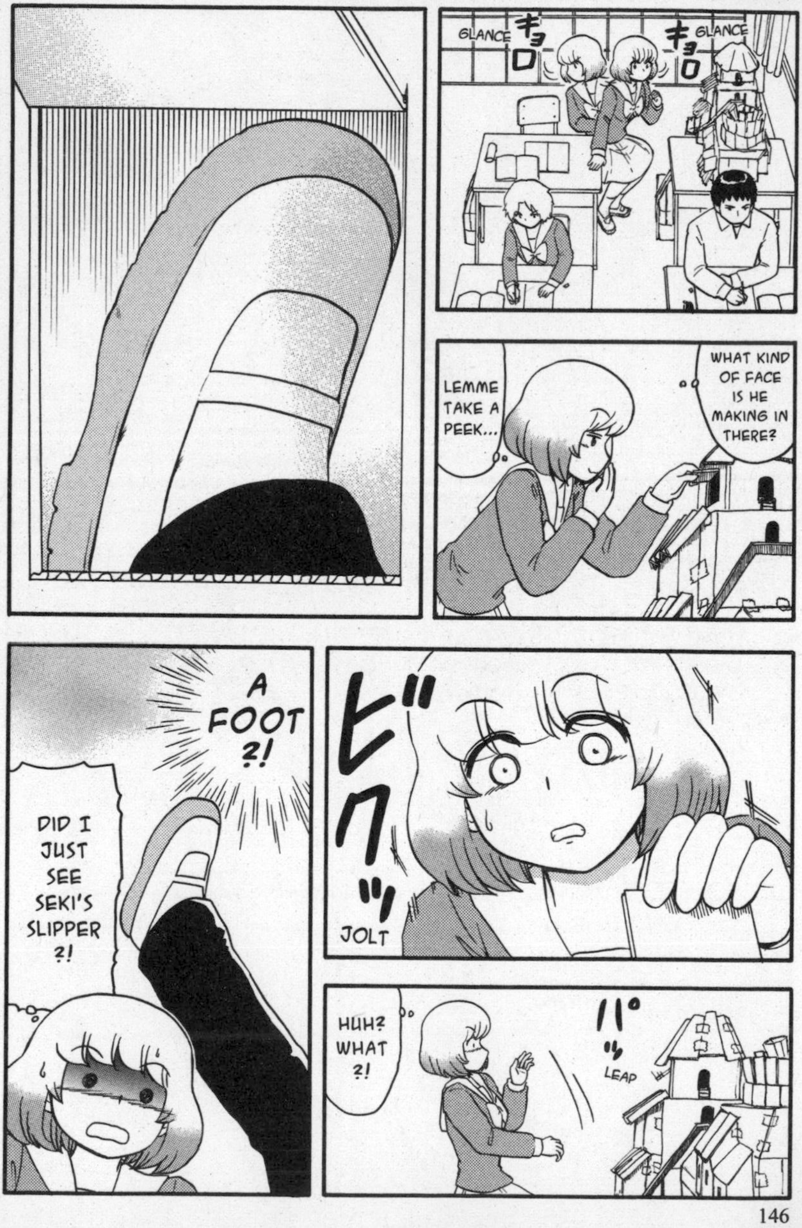
キョロ
GLANCE
キョロ
GLANCE
WHAT KIND OF FACE IS HE MAKING IN THERE?
LEMME TAKE A PEEK...
ビクッ
JOLT
パッ
LEAP
HUH? WHAT?!
A FOOT?!
DID I JUST SEE SEKI'S SLIPPER?!

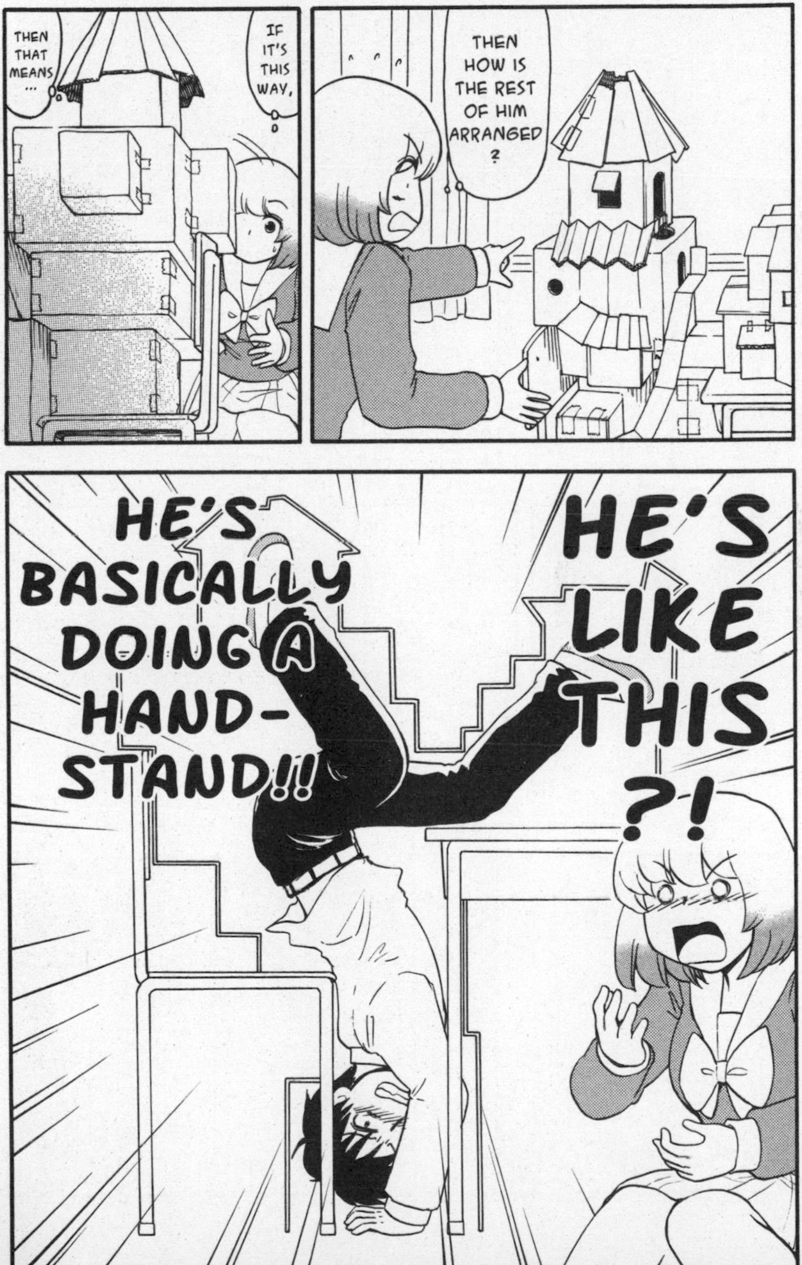
THEN HOW IS THE REST OF HIM ARRANGED?
IF IT'S THIS WAY,
THEN THAT MEANS...
HE'S LIKE THIS?!
HE'S BASICALLY DOING A HAND-STAND!!

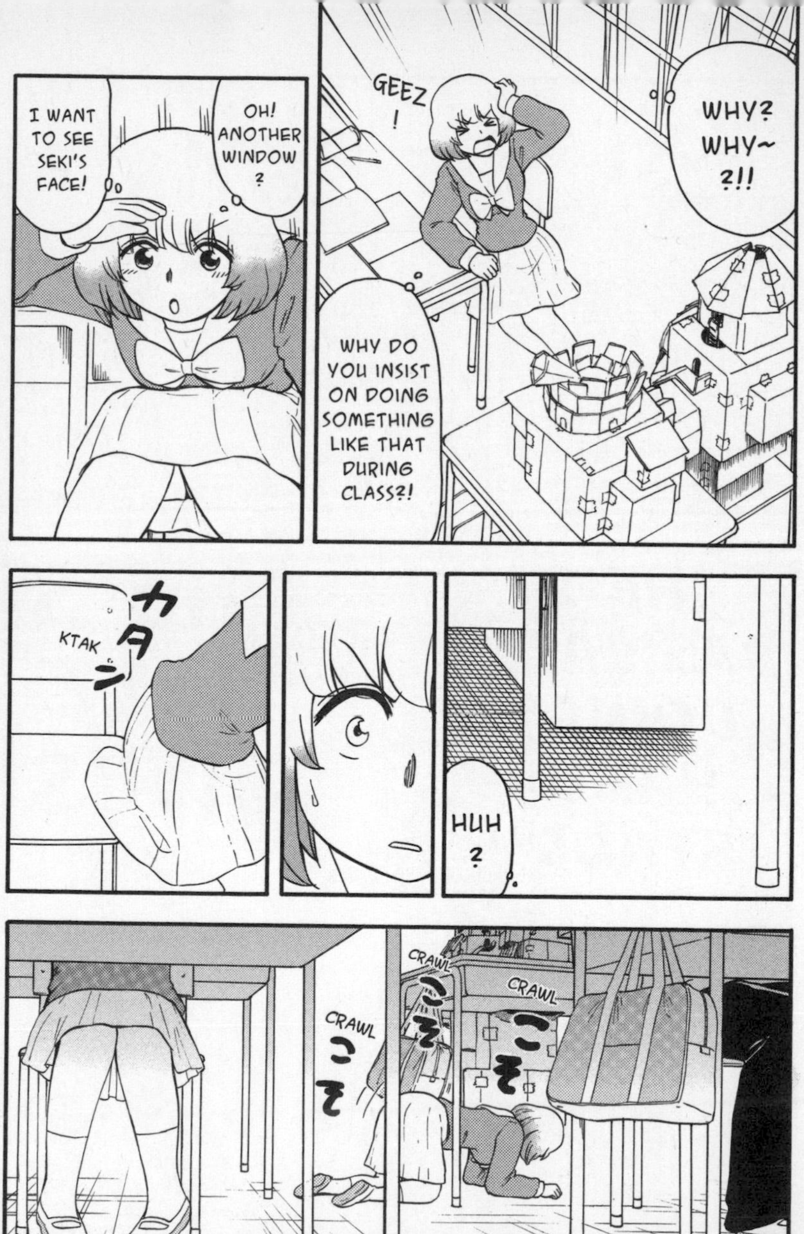
WHY? WHY~?!!
GEEZ!
WHY DO YOU INSIST ON DOING SOMETHING LIKE THAT DURING CLASS?!
OH! ANOTHER WINDOW?
I WANT TO SEE SEKI'S FACE!
HUH?
カタン
KTAK
こそ
CRAWL
こそ
CRAWL
こそ
CRAWL

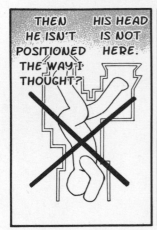

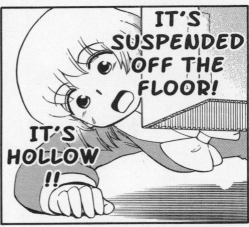

IT'S SUSPENDED OFF THE FLOOR!
IT'S HOLLOW !!
HIS HEAD IS NOT HERE.
THEN HE ISN'T POSITIONED THE WAY I THOUGHT?
I ONLY SAW ONE FOOT.
WHERE'S THE REST OF SEKI'S BODY?
HM ?
THERE'S A BULGE UNDER THE DESK.
THAT FABRIC... IT LOOKS KINDA LIKE HEAVY CANVAS...

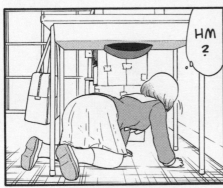

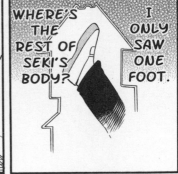

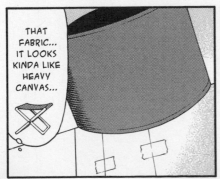

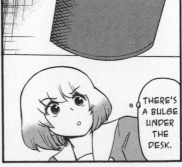

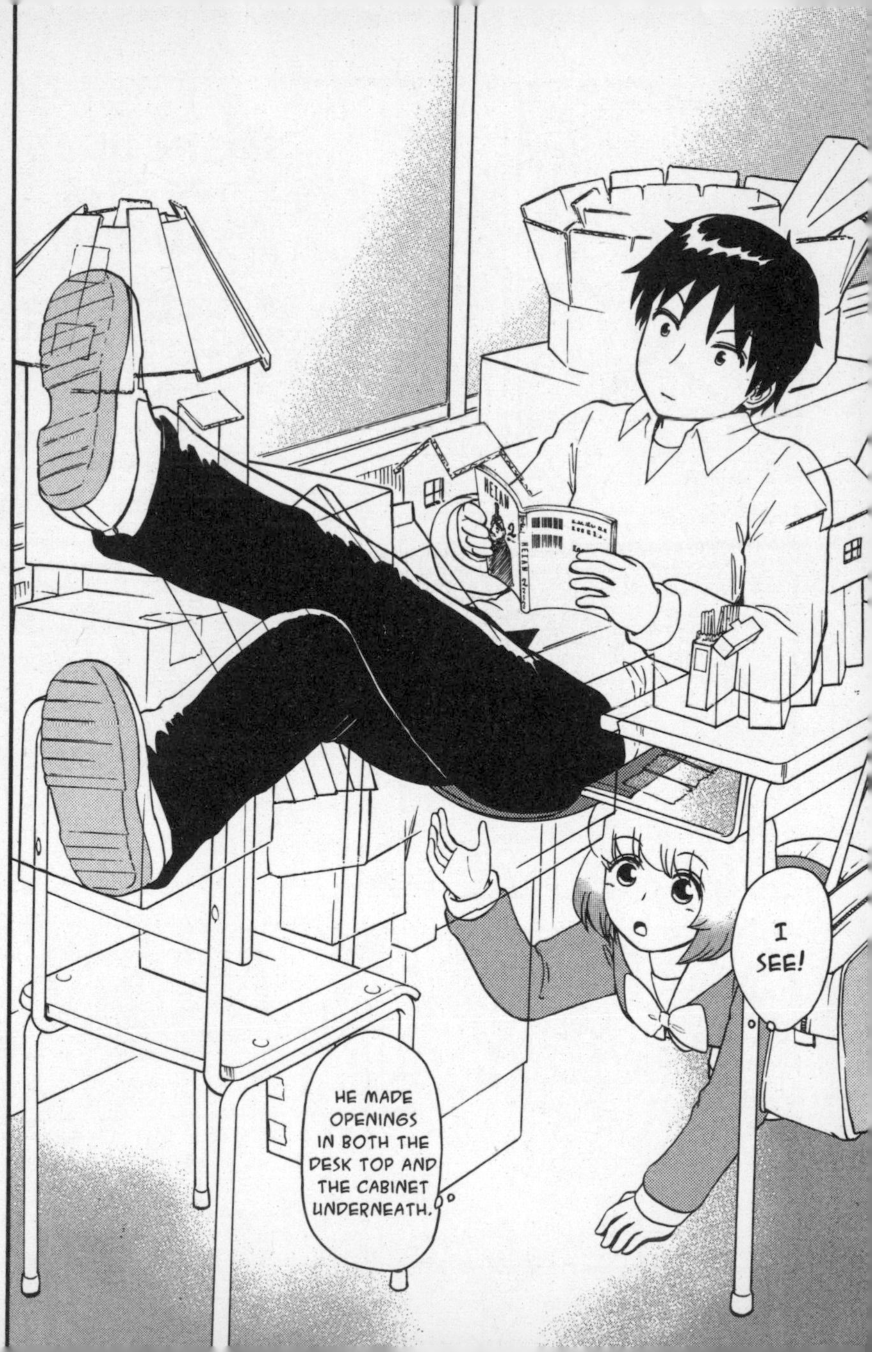
I SEE!
HE MADE OPENINGS IN BOTH THE DESK TOP AND THE CABINET UNDERNEATH.

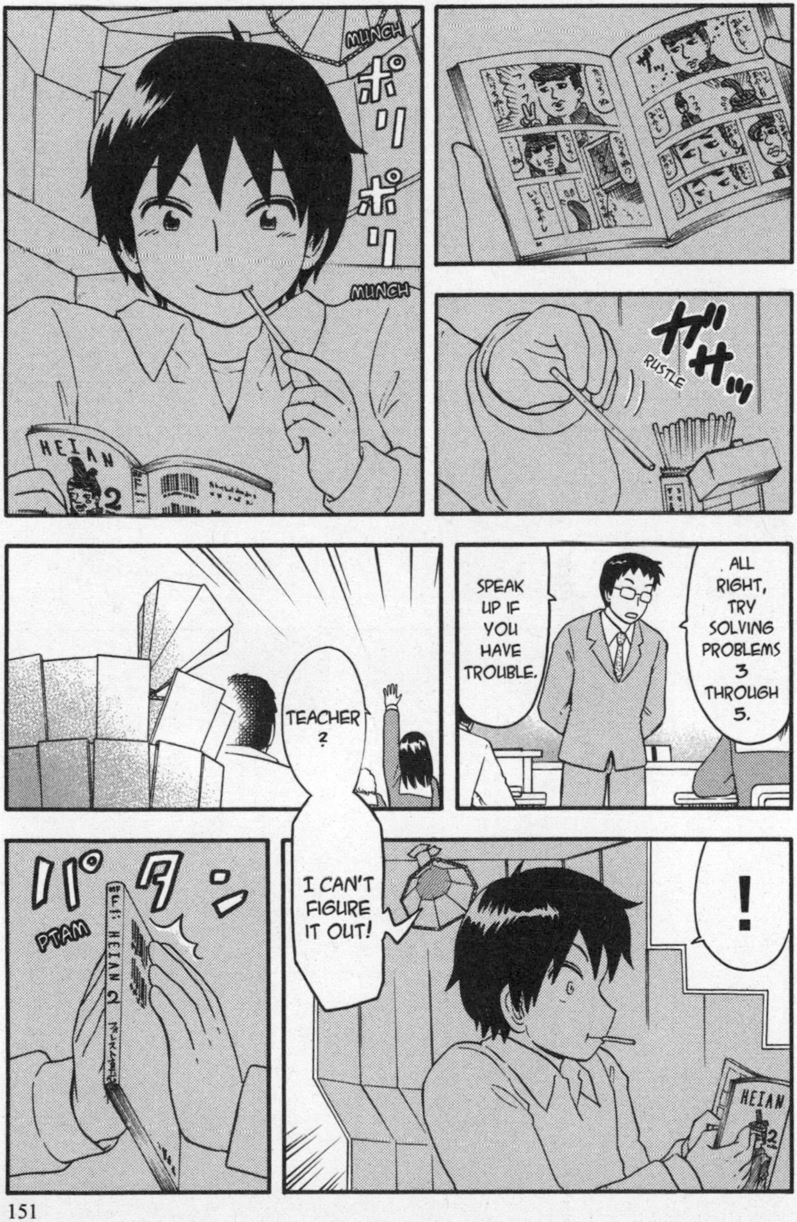
ガサッ
RUSTLE
ポリポリ
MUNCH
MUNCH
HEIAN 2
ALL RIGHT, TRY SOLVING PROBLEMS 3 THROUGH 5.
SPEAK UP IF YOU HAVE TROUBLE.
TEACHER?
I CAN'T FIGURE IT OUT!
!
HEIAN 2
パタン
PTAM
HEIAN 2

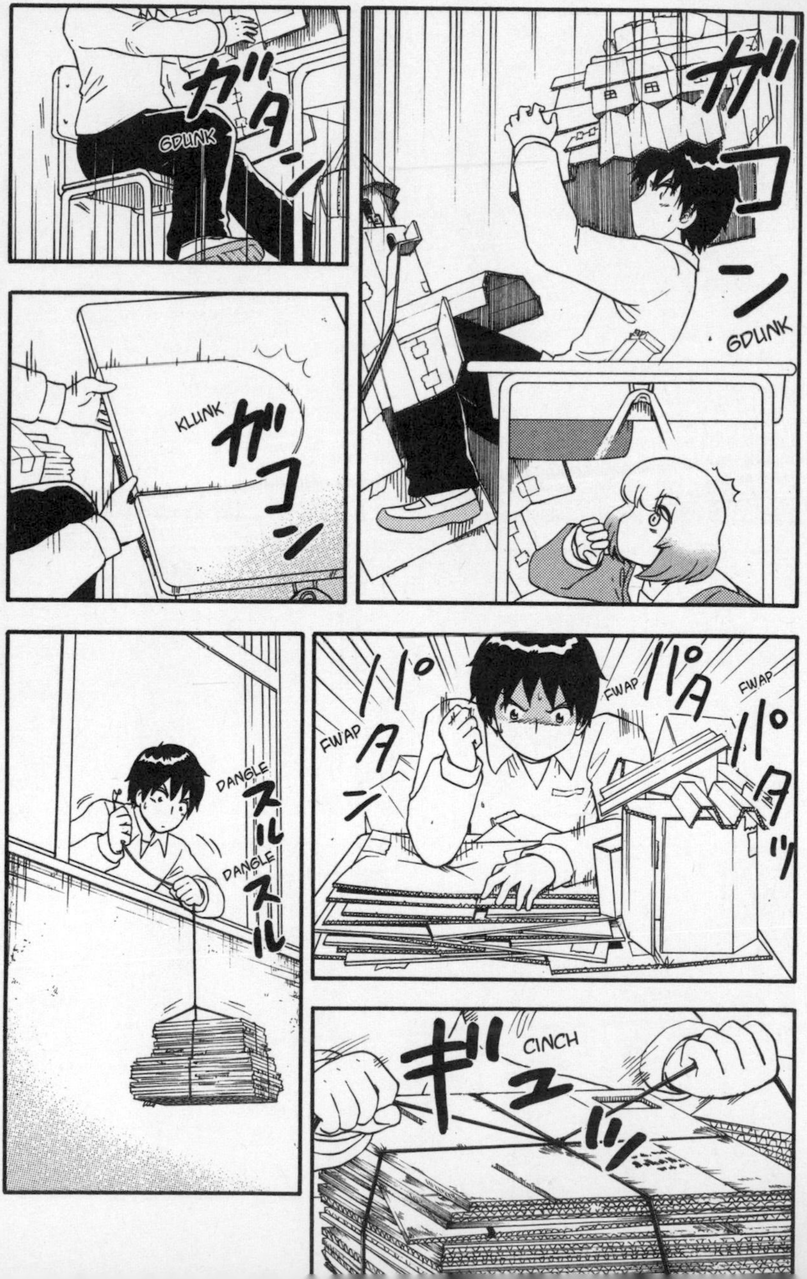
ガコーン
GDUNK
ガタン
GDUNK
KLUNK
ガコン
FWAP
パタッ
FWAP
パタ
FWAP
パタン
ギュッ
CINCH
DANGLE
スル
DANGLE
スル

WHEW...

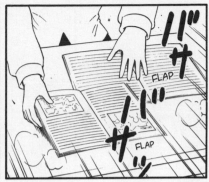

FLAP

FLAP

? ? ?

JUMP

HEY, SEKI!

153

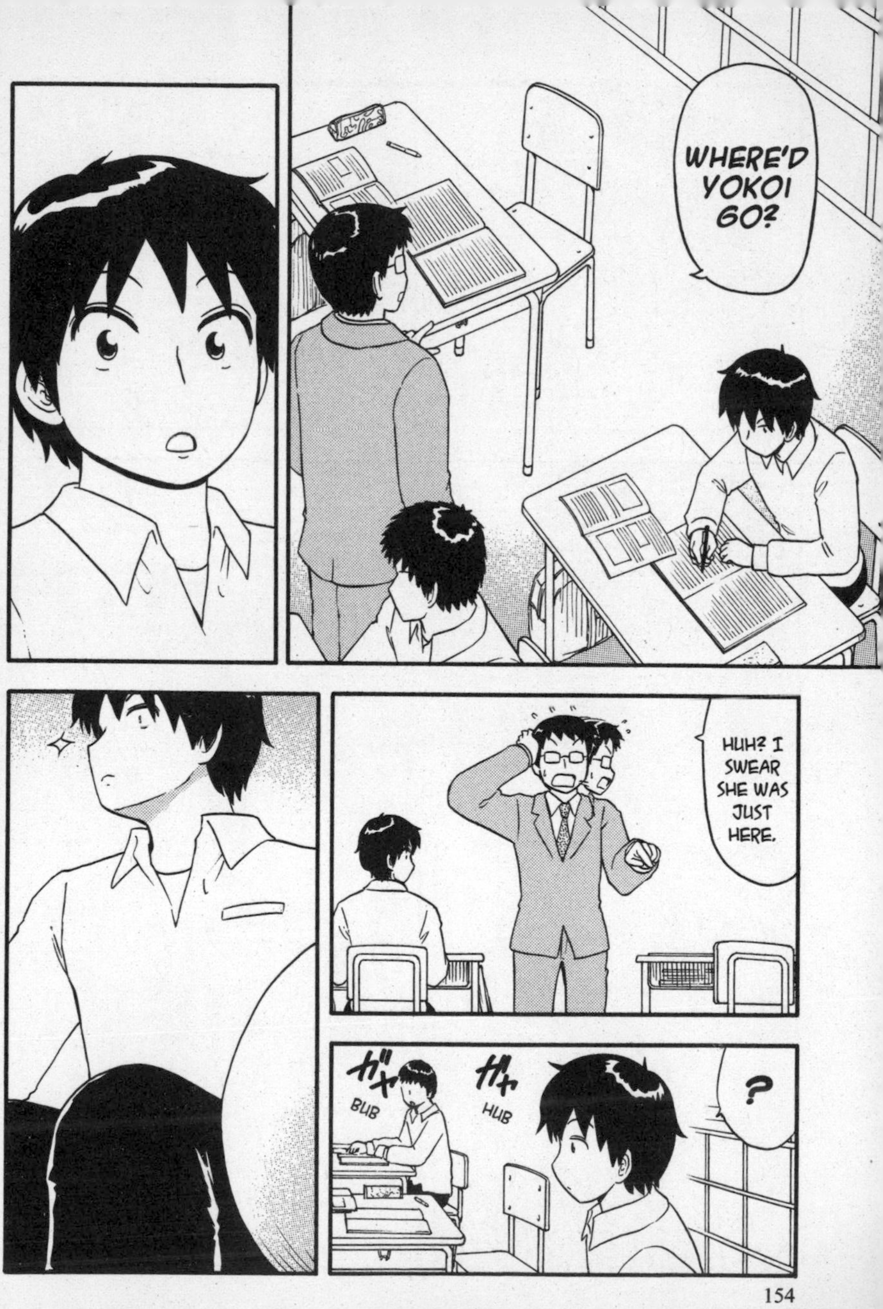
WHERE'D YOKOI GO?
HUH? I SWEAR SHE WAS JUST HERE.
?
ガヤ
HUB
ガヤ
BUB

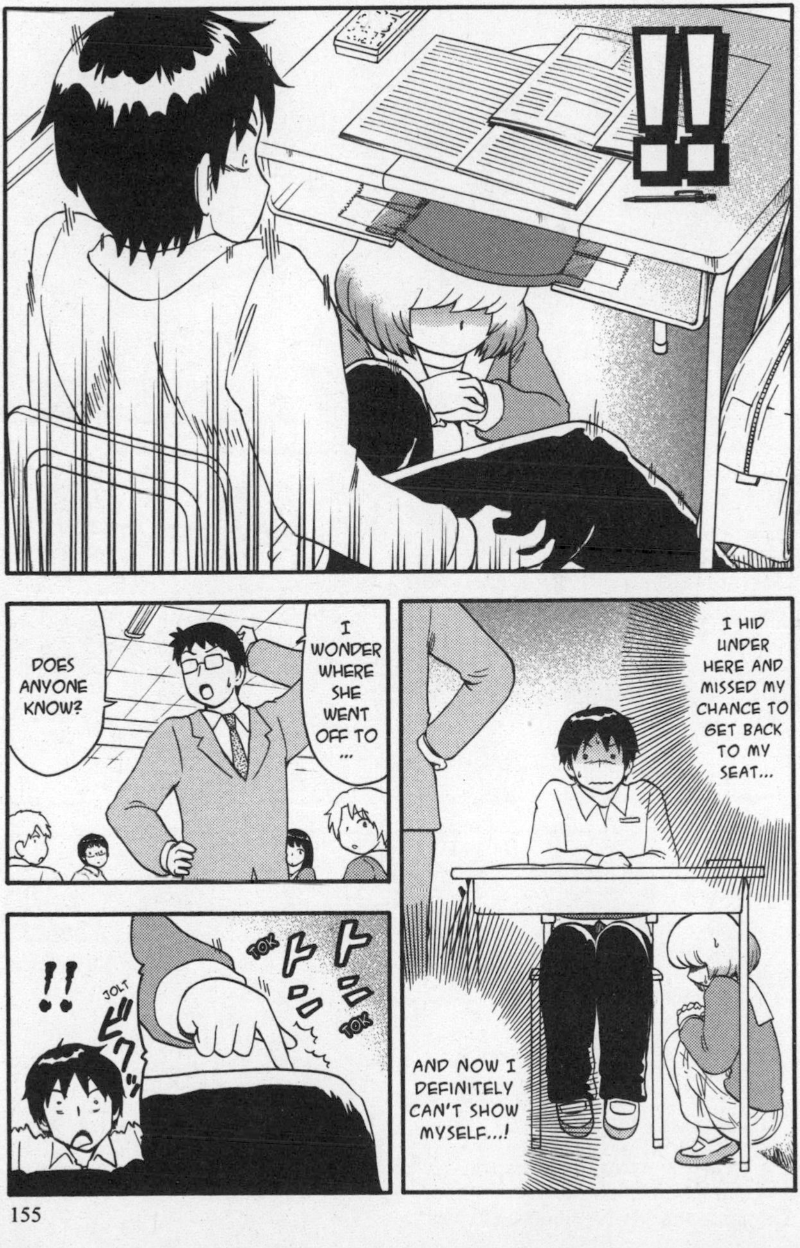
!!
I HID UNDER HERE AND MISSED MY CHANCE TO GET BACK TO MY SEAT...
AND NOW I DEFINITELY CAN'T SHOW MYSELF...!
I WONDER WHERE SHE WENT OFF TO ...
DOES ANYONE KNOW?
TOK
TOK
JOLT
!!

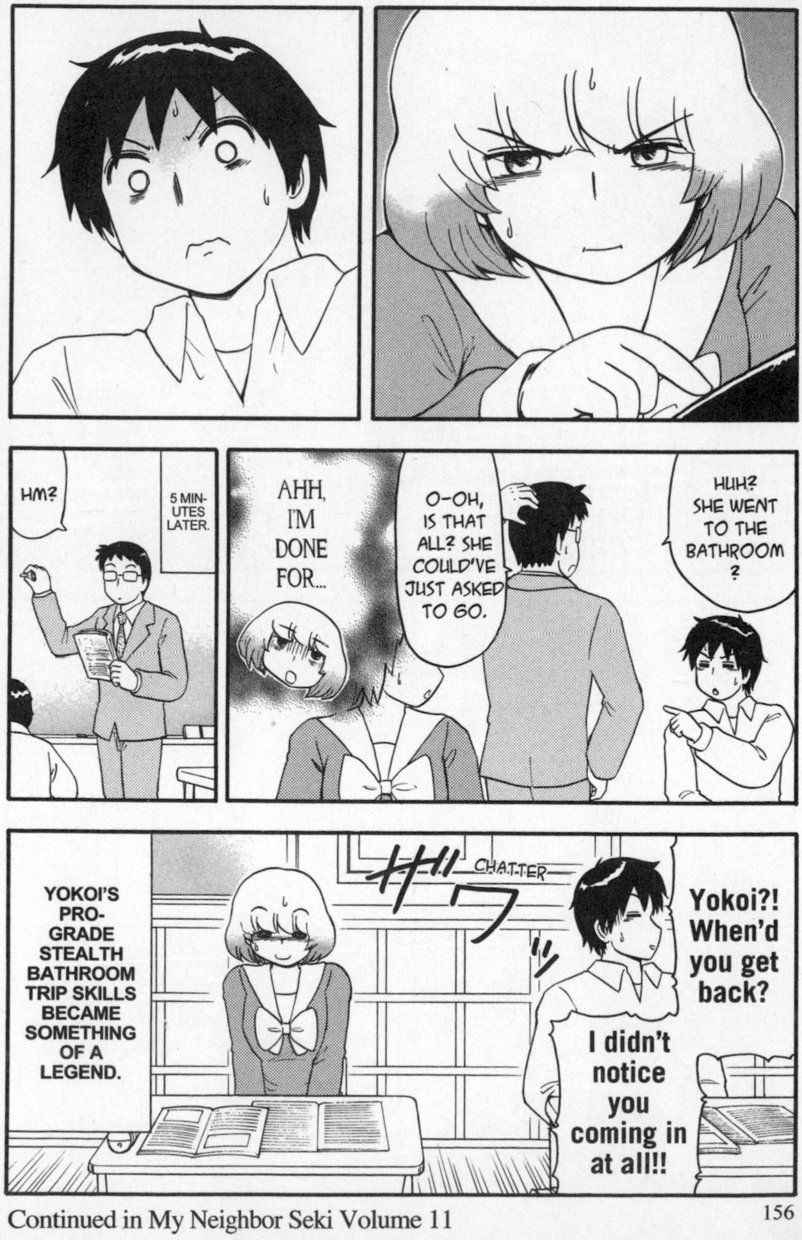
HUH? SHE WENT TO THE BATHROOM?
O-OH, IS THAT ALL? SHE COULD'VE JUST ASKED TO GO.
AHH, I'M DONE FOR...
5 MIN-UTES LATER.
HM?
Yokoi?! When'd you get back?
I didn't notice you coming in at all!!
CHATTER
YOKOI'S PRO-GRADE STEALTH BATHROOM TRIP SKILLS BECAME SOMETHING OF A LEGEND.

Continued in My Neighbor Seki Volume 11

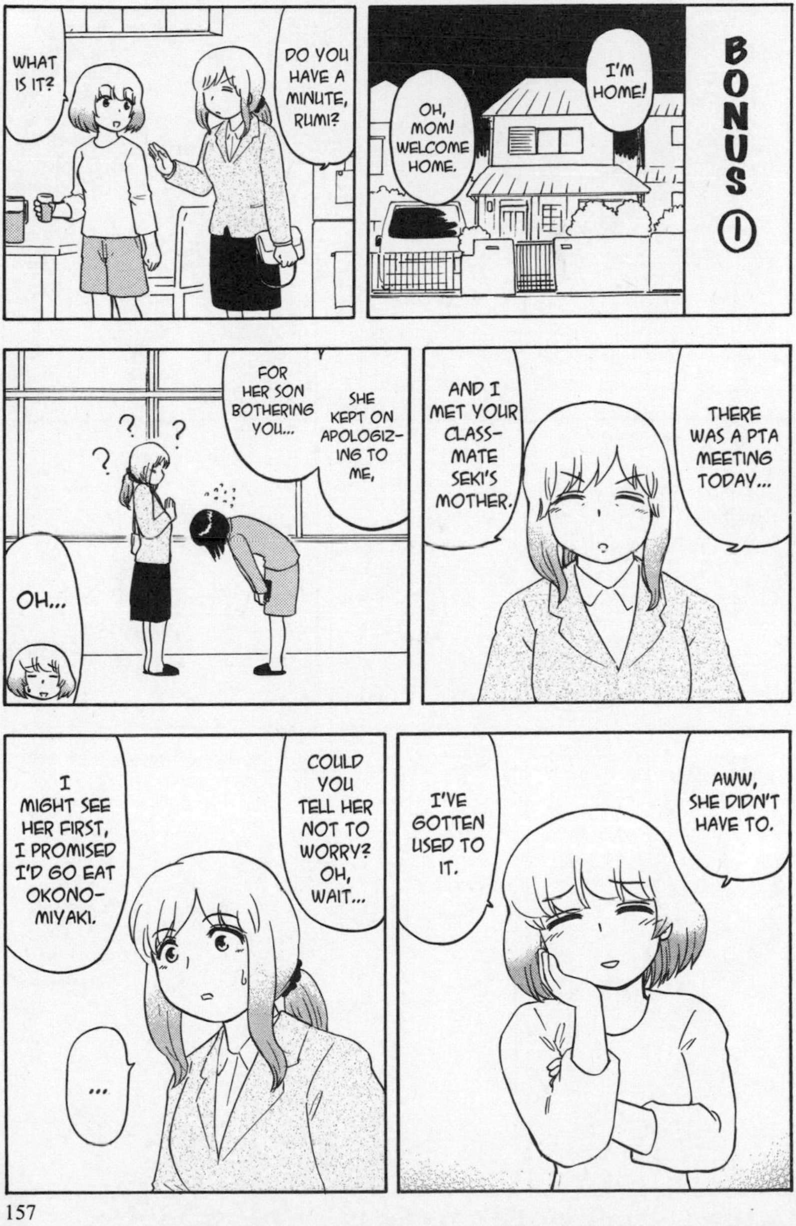
BONUS ①
I'M HOME!
OH, MOM! WELCOME HOME.
DO YOU HAVE A MINUTE, RUMI?
WHAT IS IT?
THERE WAS A PTA MEETING TODAY...
AND I MET YOUR CLASS-MATE SEKI'S MOTHER.
SHE KEPT ON APOLOGIZ-ING TO ME,
FOR HER SON BOTHERING YOU...
OH...
AWW, SHE DIDN'T HAVE TO.
I'VE GOTTEN USED TO IT.
COULD YOU TELL HER NOT TO WORRY? OH, WAIT...
I MIGHT SEE HER FIRST, I PROMISED I'D GO EAT OKONO-MIYAKI.
...

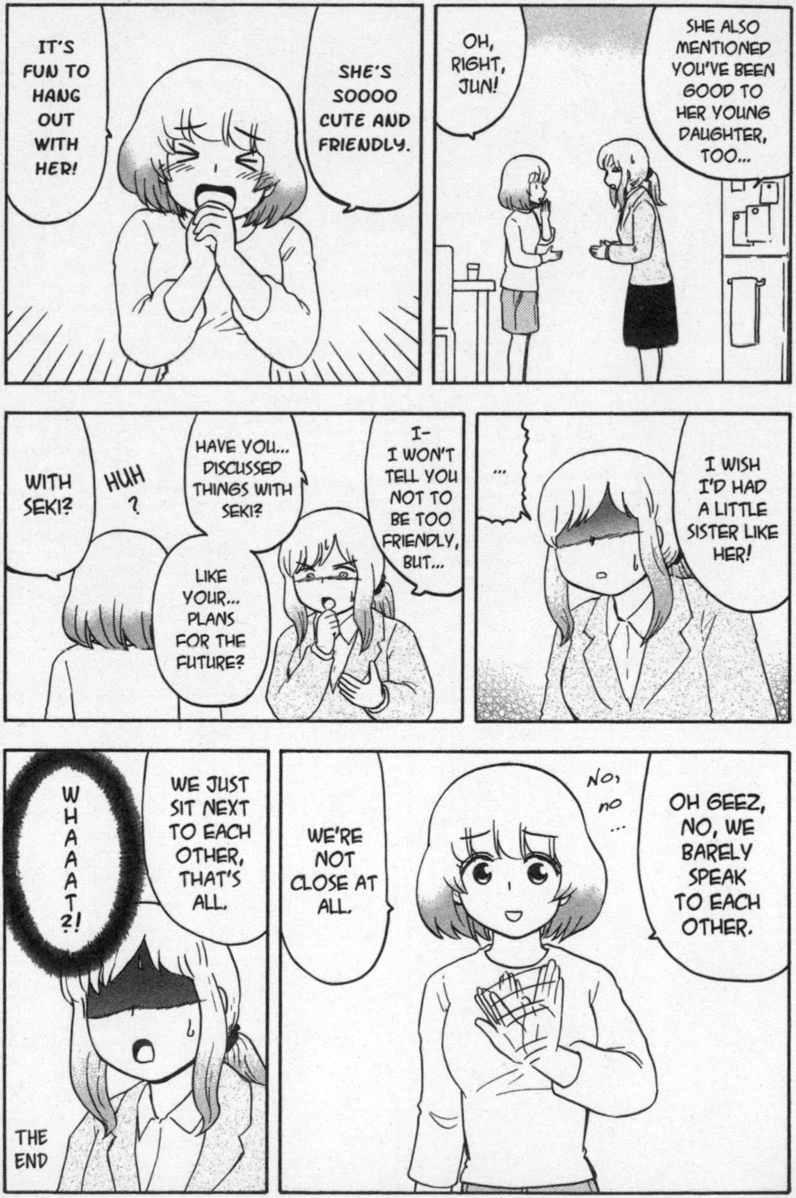
SHE ALSO MENTIONED YOU'VE BEEN GOOD TO HER YOUNG DAUGHTER, TOO...
OH, RIGHT, JUN!
SHE'S SOOOO CUTE AND FRIENDLY.
IT'S FUN TO HANG OUT WITH HER!
I WISH I'D HAD A LITTLE SISTER LIKE HER!
...
I- I WON'T TELL YOU NOT TO BE TOO FRIENDLY, BUT...
HAVE YOU... DISCUSSED THINGS WITH SEKI?
LIKE YOUR... PLANS FOR THE FUTURE?
HUH?
WITH SEKI?
OH GEEZ, NO, WE BARELY SPEAK TO EACH OTHER.
No, no ...
WE'RE NOT CLOSE AT ALL.
WE JUST SIT NEXT TO EACH OTHER, THAT'S ALL.
WHAAAAT?!
THE END

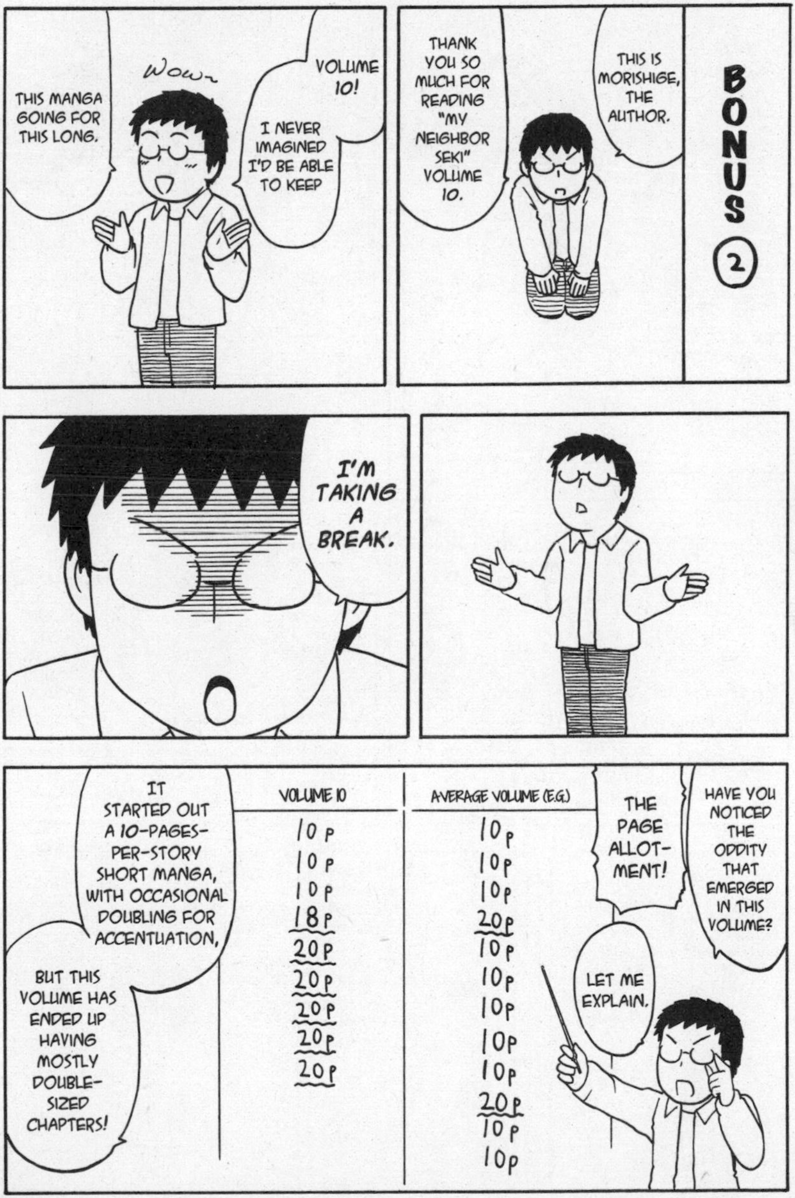
BONUS 2
THIS IS MORISHIGE, THE AUTHOR.
THANK YOU SO MUCH FOR READING "MY NEIGHBOR SEKI" VOLUME 10.
VOLUME 10!
I NEVER IMAGINED I'D BE ABLE TO KEEP
WOW~
THIS MANGA GOING FOR THIS LONG.
I'M TAKING A BREAK.
HAVE YOU NOTICED THE ODDITY THAT EMERGED IN THIS VOLUME?
THE PAGE ALLOTMENT!
LET ME EXPLAIN.
AVERAGE VOLUME (E.G.)
10p 10p 10p 20p 10p 10p 10p 10p 10p 20p 10p 10p
VOLUME 10
10p 10p 10p 18p 20p 20p 20p 20p 20p
IT STARTED OUT A 10-PAGES-PER-STORY SHORT MANGA, WITH OCCASIONAL DOUBLING FOR ACCENTUATION,
BUT THIS VOLUME HAS ENDED UP HAVING MOSTLY DOUBLE-SIZED CHAPTERS!

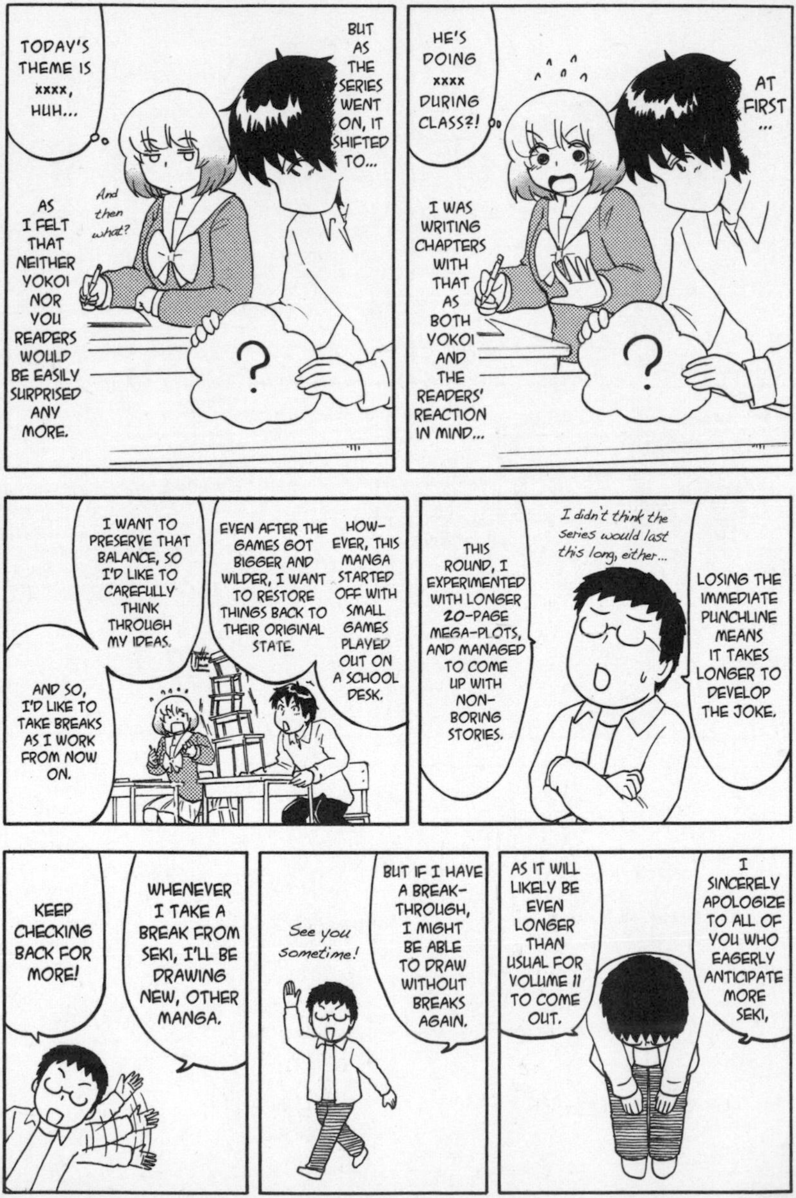
AT FIRST ...
HE'S DOING xxxx DURING CLASS?!
I WAS WRITING CHAPTERS WITH THAT AS BOTH YOKOI AND THE READERS' REACTION IN MIND...
BUT AS THE SERIES WENT ON, IT SHIFTED TO...
TODAY'S THEME IS xxxx, HUH...
And then what?
AS I FELT THAT NEITHER YOKOI NOR YOU READERS WOULD BE EASILY SURPRISED ANY MORE.
I didn't think the series would last this long, either...
LOSING THE IMMEDIATE PUNCHLINE MEANS IT TAKES LONGER TO DEVELOP THE JOKE.
THIS ROUND, I EXPERIMENTED WITH LONGER 20-PAGE MEGA-PLOTS, AND MANAGED TO COME UP WITH NON-BORING STORIES.
HOW-EVER, THIS MANGA STARTED OFF WITH SMALL GAMES PLAYED OUT ON A SCHOOL DESK.
EVEN AFTER THE GAMES GOT BIGGER AND WILDER, I WANT TO RESTORE THINGS BACK TO THEIR ORIGINAL STATE.
I WANT TO PRESERVE THAT BALANCE, SO I'D LIKE TO CAREFULLY THINK THROUGH MY IDEAS.
AND SO, I'D LIKE TO TAKE BREAKS AS I WORK FROM NOW ON.
I SINCERELY APOLOGIZE TO ALL OF YOU WHO EAGERLY ANTICIPATE MORE SEKI,
AS IT WILL LIKELY BE EVEN LONGER THAN USUAL FOR VOLUME 11 TO COME OUT.
BUT IF I HAVE A BREAK-THROUGH, I MIGHT BE ABLE TO DRAW WITHOUT BREAKS AGAIN.
See you sometime!
WHENEVER I TAKE A BREAK FROM SEKI, I'LL BE DRAWING NEW, OTHER MANGA.
KEEP CHECKING BACK FOR MORE!